DAVID HARE

Plays Three

Skylight
Amy's View
The Judas Kiss
My Zinc Bed

Introduced by the author

ff

faber and faber

This collection first published in 2008
by Faber & Faber Ltd
3 Queen Square, London WC1N 3AU

Typeset by Country Setting, Kingsdown, Kent CT14 8ES
Printed in England by CPI Bookmarque, Croydon, Surrey

Skylight first published in 1995
© David Hare, 1995, 1997

Amy's View first published in 1997
© David Hare, 1997, 2008

The Judas Kiss first published in 1998
© David Hare, 1998, 2008

My Zinc Bed first published in 2000
© David Hare, 2000, 2008

A CIP record for this book is available from the British Library

ISBN 978-0-571-24113-2

2 4 6 8 10 9 7 5 3 1

Contents

Introduction

*The editors at Faber & Faber
talk to the author about the plays in this collection*

How did you come to write Skylight?

Oh, the usual way – an image. A spluttering gas boiler on the wall, and a woman in a kind of voluntary exile, making life hard for herself. Very powerful, very evocative for me.

You'd spent your whole life as a writer avoiding plays set in rooms.

That's right. Perhaps I finally opted for a play with walls because I was exhausted by writing three huge plays for the Olivier Theatre – *Racing Demon, Murmuring Judges* and *The Absence of War* – and I was alive to the feeling that it's hard to characterise with density in an epic play. Yes, plainly, in *The Life of Galileo* or *Mother Courage* Brecht brings off great central characters – two of the greatest in literature – but he's careless, to say the least, in the way he flings minor characters on and off the stage. I was aware that my plays had become restless, always subject to the pressure of time, to the demands of narrative. Sometimes I was finding it easier to move on than to move in. In an epic play the scene you are writing is always waiting to be replaced by another. This creates a wonderful energy when properly done – the slate is wiped clean many times in the evening – but it can also mean that the people you create are not able to put down roots on the stage.

Skylight *is not quite a classic two-hander.*

I couldn't resist a little embellishment. Maybe it was shame at succumbing to the notion of writing a play in real time, so that's why I give the play a little kick of context at the beginning and at the end with the appearance of the son, Edward.

Do you think of it as a romantic play?

Most certainly.

A love story?

Not just a love story – I mean romantic in the proper sense, a play about people's limitless potential.

Do you think that accounts for its popularity?

I have no idea. Back in the 1980s, the critic of the *Daily Mail*, Jack Tinker, claimed I was not a proper playwright because my plays had prospered only in the hothouse of subsidy. Put them in the harsher climate of the commercial theatre and they would die. To my surprise, as much as to his, he turned out to be wrong. Three of the plays in this collection were profitable hits on Broadway. However, they were written to exactly the same criteria as my previous work. There was no element of calculation. There never is. When you're writing a play you have no sense of who it might appeal to. People certainly liked the spectacle of a big man flailing. And, again, three of these plays show big men flailing: Tom Sergeant, Oscar Wilde and Victor Quinn.

Let's take Sergeant first.

Obviously, the play is driven by the opposition between an entrepreneurial approach to life and an ethic founded in public service. Fortunately, this turned out to be an opposition which audiences understood. In *Pravda* Howard Brenton and I came up with a phrase, 'the melancholy of business'. Tom Sergeant embodies that melancholy. I always find that the more a businessman tells you everything's wonderful, the sadder you feel. Another phrase we might have come up with is 'the melancholy of maleness' – because Tom is a hopeless male, a man condemned to maleness, and all the ridiculous feelings that go with it. Also, I knew a little bit about restaurants, enough to know they represent capitalist endeavour at its most fleeting and heroic: every night you set out to prove yourself all over.

And Kyra?

Interestingly, when we went to America with the play, we had imagined that audiences would identify with Tom's get-up-and-go. To the contrary, we uncovered a massive well of anger to which the play spoke – the anger of those in public service who see themselves as overlooked and disregarded by all the callous priorities of the period. I had some modest feeling theatre was doing what it should.

Which is?

Giving heart to the broken-hearted.

Michael Gambon played Tom first, then Bill Nighy.

Yes. And there's a reprehensible snobbery among those who claim to prefer one or the other in the role. I'm sometimes buttonholed by people who tell me they saw Bill, or they saw Michael, and how superior either one was. In fact, Bill has played so many times in my work that his version of 'the big man' couldn't help but be fascinating. He was actually Gambon's suggestion when we didn't know how to replace him: 'Get the handsome fellow to do it.' But Gambon was also unforgettable. Lia Williams played Kyra, then Stella Gonet. Both superb.

And you wrote Amy's View *almost immediately after?*

I was inspired by the collapse of Lloyd's. It seemed so quintessentially English. Suddenly Squadron Leaders from Dorset, finding themselves swindled by the well-spoken crooks in the insurance business, were speaking the rhetoric of the most militant trade union leaders. Originally, people assumed the Thatcherite revolution was there to clear away the riff-raff, but now, like all revolutions, it was turning on its own supporters. A certain generation had believed itself entitled to money without having to work for it. There was an expectation that money was like yeast – it would just regenerate itself, and that the less you thought about it, the more morally worthy you were to receive it. And that particular sense of entitlement was deeply embedded in class – as was the kind of light comedy in which Esme Allen had made her name and prospered. I loved using the theatre as a metaphor for life.

But the play was sometimes misunderstood?

To a degree.

People thought it was an example of exactly the kind of old-fashioned theatre the play mocks.

I'd chosen a four-act structure, which is a demanding and interesting form, very rarely used nowadays, also devilishly difficult to bring off. What you don't show has to be as convincing as what you do – because what has happened between the acts is what gives the action on stage its undertow and power. Unfortunately a few critics couldn't see past Judi Dench's performance as Esme. One idiot even managed to suggest that she was writing her own lines – in one sense, you could say, a tribute to Judi's perfect mastery of the role, but in another, a rather revealing display of the critic's ignorance of the working practices of the modern theatre.

When the play was revived in 2006 with Felicity Kendal playing Esme, many critics re-evaluated their first reactions to the play.

This happens a lot.

Why do you think that is?

It seems to take critics ten years before they trust me.

Again, why do you think that is?

It's not for me to say. The weakest part of the play concerned the young man, Dominic. I often struggle with young men. I find them difficult, in life and on the stage. By the time we took the play from the West End to Broadway, then the Shavian ding-dong in the second act had been sharpened up and Dominic was better drawn. I hate all the clichés of theatre criticism: that a playwright has to love all his characters. Why? Does Shakespeare love Iago? Critics also like to claim that a good play is always even-handed. Is that really true? I can think of a series of belting plays, incendiary plays which are completely one-sided. Would *The Diary of Anne Frank* be more powerful if it gave the Nazis better arguments? I don't think so.

Amy's View also defends the medium of theatre itself.

Yes, I wrote it at a moment when the theatre-is-dead movement was at its most smug. Clearly, it's unfortunate that only a certain number of people can see and hear a single play at any one time. Does that make it elitist? Six billion are shut out and eight hundred admitted. What can you do?

Do you think the play itself suffered because of Judi Dench's performance?

Absolutely not. It glowed, because of her. When Judi read the play, she had no idea why the director Richard Eyre so wanted her to play the part. But as she herself says, it's in those very plays to which she doesn't immediately respond that she eventually does her greatest work. For her kind of talent, if things come too easily, they're not as good. Judi had a terrible struggle – often in tears, often in despair –

but the mark of the struggle was in the stature of the performance.

Then a very odd change of direction: you wrote a play about Oscar Wilde.

Yes. Actually, Mike Nichols had asked me to write a film. He thought the modern cinema was ready for a more honest account of the trial than had been possible in the days of Peter Finch or Robert Morley. By chance, I'd studied Wilde at Cambridge because I believed him to be a far more original thinker than was then credited. My tutor responded by telling me that if I made Wilde the subject of my special paper, I would be a laughing stock. Wilde was not a serious writer. I went ahead in the face of his advice. When that tutor himself wrote a play about Wilde which was produced at Hampstead Theatre some years later, I did allow myself a quiet smile. Anyway, I wrote the screenplay, but Mike didn't like it – not witty enough, he felt. Again, it was Nichols who said, 'I think it's a play. You should just do the bit where he's in exile.' I'm not a fan of the bio-pic generally, and the bio-play even less, so I chose to concentrate on two moments when Wilde does the inexplicable.

You love the mystery of Wilde.

Oh very much so. The self-knowledge. The agonising self-knowledge. And the dignity of his suffering. He protested, of course he did, and there were moments of terrible degradation and squalor. But there was also heroic resistance, stoicism at its finest. I regard the second act of *The Judas Kiss* as more or less the best thing I ever wrote.

Not the first?

The first's a bloody mess, we all knew that – pedalling uphill, so you can sail down. It was hell for the actors. They had to lay out the workings of the relationship in the

Cadogan Hotel, immediately before Wilde's arrest, in order that the audience could comprehend the poetry of Wilde's resignation at the moment in Naples when he is betrayed by the person for whom he has sacrificed everything. The actors had to work and work in that first act, pretty thanklessly – I was ashamed.

Did you have a sneaking sympathy for Bosie?

Oh yes, yes. Myself, I've spent my whole life floundering in situations I don't understand and for which I'm not morally prepared. Bosie was a young man, many fathoms out of his depth, searching for feelings he couldn't have been expected to have, and asked to make reciprocal sacrifices for which there was never any prospect of reward. Loved by Wilde, which of us could have done better? What is it Samuel Johnson says about Savage? 'No one who has not suffered the same misfortunes and persecution as Savage has the right to judge him, nor will any wise man presume to say, "Had I been in Savage's condition, I should have lived and written better than Savage." '

Do you think you took on too much with The Judas Kiss?

The first production did. It cast one of Ireland's most famous heterosexuals as Wilde, and then as Bosie it cast an actor who, however great his talent, did not embody the conventional gay dream of beauty. Both actors – Liam Neeson and Tom Hollander – were outstanding, but given that the author was meanwhile intent on entirely reinventing the myth of Wilde, then the boldness of the casting was bound to add a measure of resistance to what was already a venture against the grain. Merlin Holland, Wilde's grandson, was kind enough to say this was one of the more convincing representations of his grandfather. In Neil Armfield's production in Australia, with Bille Browne playing the part, it ran for eight months and became the play for which I'm best known.

Again, My Zinc Bed *is a very unexpected play.*

Yes. When I'm asked what my plays are about, it's usually impossible to answer. But of *My Zinc Bed*, it's easy – you can say, 'It's about alcoholism.'

But it isn't really, is it?

It's not a case study. I'm interested in the metaphor of addiction, not in portraying its daily rhythms. *Days of Wine and Roses* does that, unimprovably. You see, I knew so many people in AA who were telling me they could cure themselves by taking elements of danger and excitement out of their lives. If they weren't at risk, then they wouldn't fall. But if you remove those elements, are you really living? Some alcoholics end up living what Marion in *The Secret Rapture* calls 'a perfect imitation of life'.

There's an argument, isn't there, between those who believe you can control addiction, and those who believe you can only fight it by admitting its control over you?

Yes. Crudely, AA says it's a disease, a medical condition, and if you have the susceptible gene, you can never win. Will power alone is useless. But Rational Recovery argues that if you surrender will power as your primary instrument of control, then you surrender what makes you human. In the act of trying to save your life, you lose it.

Which side do you come down on?

Look, I went to a good many meetings to research the play and I had great respect for AA. I remember a meeting in a psychiatric ward, listening to people who had a forum to speak – and they were people at the very bottom of the pile, who would have been in trouble with alcohol or without it. AA gave them a valued place to address their problems. I'm not going to speak against it. On the other hand, I don't think you can deny that the nature of its cure raises fascinating questions. I understand that after its opening the play was much discussed at AA meetings, and typically the discussions were without rancour, more along the lines of 'You really ought to see this.'

It's also partly about new technology.

It was, in its original version. The play as it was presented at the Royal Court was two and a half hours long, with an interval. In 2007 I was asked to write a film adaptation for HBO, and I found a lot of the stuff about the internet and computers rather wearisome and dated. So after I had written the film, I then cut and slightly rewrote the play into a ninety-minute version – straight through – which is the one printed here. It's not yet been performed. The director of the TV film, Anthony Page, said a few times that he wanted the suggestiveness of a Maupassant short story – that's what the new version attempts. I don't normally go in for Audenesque tampering with my own work, but in this case I believe I've improved the play.

And at its centre another of your fluent lost souls? In a line from Lambert le Roux in Pravda, *through Tom in* Skylight, *to Oliver Lucas in* The Vertical Hour. *And a little like Saraffian, the rock manager in* Teeth 'n' Smiles.

I love Victor's character. The man who's lost his faith in communism and is now thrashing around.

Loss of faith is really the theme, isn't it, more than alcoholism?

I think so.

Why did you direct the stage production yourself?

I'd given up directing, and was enjoying a series of relationships with directors who were bringing nothing but good things to my work – Howard Davies, Richard Eyre, Jonathan Kent, Sam Mendes and Stephen Daldry.

But we had a couple of readings while I was writing it and the producer Robert Fox said to me, 'You plainly care about this play so much you should do it yourself.' So I did. I persuaded Tom Wilkinson to make one of his now rare appearances on the stage, with Stephen Macintosh as the young poet. Julia Ormond gave a dazzling performance as Elsa. I used to stand on the balcony above Sloane Square, watching hoards of young people arriving for the shows at the rebuilt Royal Court. It was the year 2000. A brand new audience in a great historic theatre. You can't beat it.

SKYLIGHT

For Nicole
à la folie

Skylight was first performed in the Cottesloe auditorium of the National Theatre, London, on 4 May 1995. The cast was as follows:

Kyra Hollis Lia Williams
Edward Sergeant Daniel Betts
Tom Sergeant Michael Gambon

Director Richard Eyre
Designer John Gunter
Lighting Mark Jonathan

The play transferred to Wyndham's Theatre, London, on 13 February 1996 with the same cast. It was then presented on Broadway on 10 September 1996 in the same production, with Christian Camargo playing Edward Sergeant and with lighting by Paul Gallo.

The play was subsequently revived at the Vaudeville Theatre, London, on 14 June 1997 in the original production, with the following cast:

Kyra Hollis Stella Gonet
Edward Sergeant Theo Fraser Steele
Tom Sergeant Bill Nighy

This is the definitive edition of *Skylight*, incorporating all the textual changes made during its West End and Broadway runs.

Characters

Kyra Hollis
Edward Sergeant
Tom Sergeant

We had fed the heart on fantasies,
The heart's grown brutal from the fare.

W. B. Yeats,
'The Stare's Nest by My Window',
Meditations in Time of Civil War

Act One

SCENE ONE

*A first-floor flat in north-west London. There is a
corniced plaster ceiling, and underneath the evidence of
a room well lived in: patterned carpets which have worn
to a thread and a long wall of books. The kitchen area
at the back of the room looks cluttered and much used.
There is a main entrance onto the landing outside. Off
to the other side, a bedroom and bathroom.*

*At once through the main door comes Kyra Hollis.
She is just past thirty. She is returning to her flat, blue
with cold. She is quite small, with short hair and a
practical manner. She has a heavy overcoat wrapped
round her, and is wearing thick woollen gloves. She is
carrying three large plastic bags. She puts two down at
once on her work table and takes the third into the kitchen
area. She takes out a packet of spaghetti and some tins
of tomatoes. Then she turns, not taking her coat off,
as she comes through the main room again. She goes
on through into the bedroom. The sound offstage of the
bath being turned on. In the kitchen, an Ascot flares.*

*At the main door, which is still open, a tall young man
appears. He is eighteen. He has blue jeans, leather gloves
and a denim jacket. He has turned the collar up against
the cold. He has a Walkman round his neck. He is also
carrying three plastic bags. His name is Edward Sergeant.
He comes in a pace or two, then stands, uncertain,
hearing the sound of the bath.*

*After a moment, Kyra reappears on her way back to
her shopping bag. She looks across the room, taken aback.*

Edward The door was open . . .

7

Kyra My goodness.

They stand a moment, both lost for what to say next. Then she gestures back offstage.

Just hold on a minute, I'd started running a bath.

She goes out. He stands, still not coming further into the room. Then she reappears.

Edward It's my fault.

Kyra No.

Edward I shouldn't have called in like this. I've grown. Yeah, I know. Everyone says that.

Kyra How tall are you?

But as he blushes, before he can answer, she moves towards him.

Well, will you give me a kiss?

She kisses his cheek. Then he raises his plastic bags.

Edward I brought these.

Kyra What's this?

Edward Some beer. It's a present.

Kyra Thank you.

Edward And some rap records. I don't know how much you know about this stuff.

Kyra Nothing.

Edward I just spent £30 in that shop round the corner. That's why I'm here. It's next to the Nepalese restaurant. There's this great specialist rap shop. All my friends go there. Then I realised you must live round here.

Kyra That's right. I do.

Edward waits, not knowing what to say.

Edward I had the spare time. I'm in my gap year. If you know what I mean.

Kyra Yes, of course.

Edward Out of school, not yet at university. I'm doing what everyone does.

Kyra You have a job?

Edward Yeah. I'm selling frankfurters outside football grounds. If you come close you can smell them.

Kyra It's all right, thanks, I'll stay over here.

She smiles, but she still has not asked him to sit down.

Edward It's freezing.

Kyra I know. Close the door. You gave me a shock standing there.

Edward (*as he closes the door*) I'm feeling embarrassed.

Kyra Why?

Edward I've never done this.

Kyra Hold on, I've got a small fire in here.

Edward looks round nervously, as she gets a small electric fire out and plugs it in.

Edward It's a very nice place.

Kyra My God! You are growing up. When did you start saying dumb things like that? 'It's a very nice place'! When I knew you, Edward, you always spoke your mind. You came to the point.

Edward Ah. OK. The point is my father.

Kyra has a glimmer of humour, as if she is about to reply. But instead she stands up and looks at the miserable one-bar fire.

Kyra I've plugged it in. I think you'll find it makes very little difference. The last few weeks it's been so damp I find you barely see it. Here, we even have indoor fog. You sit on that side of the room and peer, thinking, I'm sure it's on, I'm sure the fire is on. But you can't actually see. Do you want tea?

Edward No, thank you.

Kyra So why not tell me what you came here to say?

She rubs her mittens together, still on the opposite side of the room. It seems more like Russia than England.

Edward I'm not sure what you know. Did you know my mother had died?

Kyra I knew she had cancer. How long ago?

Edward It's about a year now.

Kyra A year?

Edward Dad hasn't told you?

Kyra I haven't seen him.

Edward That's why I came here today. I wasn't passing by . . .

Kyra No.

Edward I don't suppose anyone does. Pass by this area, I mean. Unless, I suppose, they're desperate to get from Willesden to South Finchley. Which I can't imagine most people are.

Kyra sits, not reacting to this familiar satire about her address.

Did you . . . I mean, you lost your parents . . .

Kyra I did. My father recently. My mother died young.
I barely knew her.

Edward Once they're dead, I find they keep changing.
You think you've got hold of them. And it's like you say,
'Oh I see. So that's what she was like.' But then they
change again in your memory. It drives you crazy. Now
I'd like to find out just who she was.

Kyra Alice?

Edward Yes. It's also . . . you see . . . I don't know . . .
it's had an effect on my father.

Kyra Why, surely.

Edward I mean if you see him . . . I'd love it. I mean, if
you did.

Kyra Why?

Edward Because he's changed.

Kyra And?

*She is giving nothing away. He becomes more nervous
again.*

Edward Now I'm really embarrassed. I'm guessing.
I think you can help him.

Kyra Help Tom? Tom needs help?

Edward Well, at least that's what I think.

Kyra is still so silent he is unnerved.

The tea actually . . . I would like the tea now. I'd like
some tea to help get me through.

*He laughs at this sudden admission of his own
nervousness and Kyra too seems to relax as she gets
up to put the kettle on.*

How am I doing? Am I doing all right?

Kyra You're doing fine.

Edward You don't think I'm being obnoxious? I mean, it's none of my business. If you want you can send me away.

Kyra You can say what you like. It's not going to bother me.

Edward I don't really know the whole history. I mean, between Dad and you.

Kyra Ah. So is that why you're here?

Edward No, I mean, yes, well, partly. But also Dad's got very peculiar. I am here for his sake as well. (*He has started to pace round the room.*) It can get pretty strange, I promise you. Silence at dinner, that kind of thing. We moved to Wimbledon.

Kyra My God!

Edward I know. Well, that doesn't help. The sense of all that sort of *nature*, trees and flowers, sort of flapping around. He did it for Mum, to give her some peace at the end. But now it just seems pointless and spooky. Me, I get on a bus and head for the street.

Kyra brings mugs and teabags.

I keep saying, Dad, you're not dead, you're fifty. It's too early for lupins. Jesus! What I liked about Dad, he was sort of ageless. I think that's why he was such a success. All ages, all types. He knew how to reach them. But now he's in this kind of hideous green fortress.

Kyra Does he talk to you? About what he feels?

Edward You know Dad. He's not what you might call 'emotionally available'. But also . . . let's face it . . . well, I can be quite a shit.

He faces Kyra directly.

Have you read Freud?

Kyra Some.

Edward I read some recently. I told Dad everything had to come out. That you pay a price. Is that true?

Kyra I don't know.

Edward For everything you repress there's a price to be paid.

Kyra You told him that?

Edward Yes.

Kyra And how did he take it?

But Edward is too preoccupied even to notice her question.

Edward It was the night before last. It was Sunday. We had the mother of all arguments. We had the most terrible row. I suppose I left home.

Kyra You did? Where did you go? Do you have a girlfriend?

Edward Sort of. There's a girl who's willing to take me in. She does the frankfurters with me.

Suddenly he starts defending himself from some unspoken attack.

So. I don't know. I'm only eighteen. I don't like the word 'girlfriend'. All that stuff's finished. Relationships. Permanence. It's out of date, I think. I stayed there last night. I'll stay there tonight.

Kyra Yes, but have you rung your father?

Edward looks at her resentfully, turning the question aside with a joke.

Edward She's the only girl who'll sleep with me. Because at least we both smell the same.

Kyra goes back to get the boiling kettle.

Dad is a fuckpig. I mean it. I don't think you see it. I talked to some people at work. He commands respect, yes, of course. People who have all that confidence do. But you scratch the surface, you talk to his employees, you find respect can be much more like fear.

Kyra returns with the kettle and starts pouring for both of them.

There's one woman, you know, I happened to talk to her, it was by chance, she's pretty high up, she's worked close to Dad for some time. She knows him well. And she said he is definitely sexist.

Kyra No!

Edward She said without question.

Kyra Thank God she spotted it. Milk?

Edward Oh, so, OK, what are you saying? You think it's me, it's just me being stupid . . .

Kyra No . . .

Edward Father–son. That sort of thing. There's a whole list of things I could tell you. Dad can be a real bastard, you know. (*He holds up a finger and thumb.*) The charm's that deep.

Kyra Are you keeping an inventory?

Edward All right, but you don't have to live with it, you don't have to deal with anyone at all . . . (*He waves airily* *round the flat.*) I do. There's always this doom. This heaviness. He comes home every night. Wham! He lands on the sofa. You feel the springs go. One night he actually destroyed a whole sofa. He cracked a sofa he landed so hard! Then –

Kyra Sugar?

Edward Guess his response? Guess his response to it! Next day he just bought a new sofa! A new sofa!

Kyra Well, that seems fair enough.

Edward No, you're wrong. It's an attitude, Kyra. It's all – *Yellow Pages*. Whatever. Leaves on the roof? *Yellow Pages*! The lavatory's blocked? *Yellow Pages*! That's how he lives. He even orders in meals. It's absurd! He flicks through. Pizza! Chinese! It's *Citizen Kane*! Only with *Yellow Pages*. I said to him, Dad, for God's sake get real. Not everything in life is in *Yellow Pages*.

Kyra is just drinking her tea.

Kyra Isn't it grief?

Edward Yes, of course.

Kyra He's grieving.

Edward He's sitting there alone in this bloody great house. Like some stupid animal. Licking his pain.

He turns towards her, more tentative as he talks of his mother.

Mum . . . of course, I mean, everyone said to me . . . Alice wasn't as clever as him. People assumed she was some sort of dumb ex-model. But she kept Dad moving. Now he just sits there.

He is vehement, trying to drive his pain away.

I say, for Christ's sake, it's been almost a year. We knew it was coming. It's been a long time. Let it out, for fuck's sake. Because, I tell you, otherwise . . . it's driving us both bloody mad.

Kyra Are you alone now?

Edward Yes. We're like a married couple. My sister's gone. She's at university. That's what I'm saying. We're both off. We're finished. Almost. Next year, I mean. They make you draw up this list, you know this? This absurd piece of paper . . .

Kyra Of course . . .

Edward Every student goes round: 'Look I've got my CV! . . .'

She grimaces at the mention of the word.

Edward I think I'll study CV when I get there. As my special subject. Why not? We never do anything because we might actually enjoy it. We do it so we can write it all down. You think, 'This is stupid! Doing things just so they'll look good on paper.' But then, I don't know, just tell me, what choice do I have?

Kyra You? You have none.

Edward What do your kids do?

Kyra Mine? Oh well, they're different.

Edward You're teaching in East Ham?

Kyra Uh-huh.

Edward How is that?

Kyra East Ham? Well, it has its drawbacks. I wouldn't say the kids are all great. But at least they're not on the ladder. So perhaps that means . . . they do things for their own sake.

Edward Yeah.

Kyra You don't need a CV to get a UB40.

At once Edward leans forward, intrigued.

Edward No, well, exactly, I mean *exactly*. As you say, it's different.

Kyra It is.

Edward The fact is . . . when I think about that kind of life . . . just ordinary kids . . . I know it sounds stupid, but I feel sort of envious.

Kyra Do you?

Edward I suppose you think I'm just spoilt.

Kyra No.

Edward I'm not saying . . . God knows . . . that my life is too easy, nobody could live alone with my bastard of a father and say that my life is easy at all . . . But I do look at the street, and think, shit! Shit! And here I am heading in the opposite direction.

Kyra just watches as he gestures rather randomly round the flat.

I mean, I think in a way you're so lucky, living like this . . .

Kyra Well, thank you.

Edward I'm not being rude. I mean it. In this kind of place. (*He pauses a second.*) Dad said . . .

Kyra What? What did Dad say?

Edward I suppose he hinted . . . he was implying . . . in a way he was saying that you made a choice.

Kyra looks at him a moment, then gets up to take the tea things out.

Look, whenever I mention it, he always says it's none of my business. He gets really angry. He says very little. I mean, I've been trying to get him to talk about you. Shit, that's what I mean, for fuck's sake. After all, it's my life as well. We saw you for years. Well, didn't we?

Kyra Yes. Yes, you did.

Edward Until just a few years ago. They were great times. Then you vanished. Why?

Kyra Think. Just think. It's probably the first thing you think of. And it's the reason.

She goes back into the kitchen area. Now Edward explodes, angry.

Edward And now are you saying I've no right to ask?

Kyra No.

Edward My mother died. She actually died. Not you. You did something else. You cut yourself off from us without saying anything. And in a way I'm coming to think that's much worse. Because you just left and said nothing. Alice had no choice. It wasn't her fault. But for you it's different. Because it's not necessary. Because yours is deliberate. And that makes it sort of more hurtful. I'm being hurt by someone for reasons they refuse to explain to me. And I'm left thinking . . . hang on, life is too short.

Kyra waits, still not answering, but he won't give up.

You know what it is? The thing that puzzles me, the thing I can't understand? It's odd, but it's true. Mum and Dad were much closer . . . they were always closer when you were there.

Kyra waits a moment, then answers quietly.

Kyra That's often true. Of a couple. They need a catalyst. A third person there, it helps them to talk.

Edward Is that all it was?

But this time it is Kyra who reacts as if it's at last too much.

Kyra Edward, come on, stop pushing me. This is a fight with your father. If you want to quarrel, then quarrel with him.

Edward is shocked by the reaction he has finally managed to provoke.

I'm glad you called round. I'm proud of you, Edward. You're a good boy. But you do seem to want to be judge and jury in some family court of your own making. And that's not the most attractive impulse to have.

Edward I'm sorry.

Kyra If you like judging, please: be a lawyer. Run a dog show. There's a whole lot of jobs if *judging* is your passion in life. But take my advice: if you want to be happy, keep your judging professional. And don't start putting in practice at home.

Both of them smile as she finishes her little speech. Now she goes to get one of her bags full of exercise books.

And now I'm afraid, I've a whole lot of homework . . .

Edward No, no, you're right. I've been really stupid.

Kyra No. Not at all.

Edward I was wondering . . .

Kyra What?

Edward At least . . . I've been wondering: what do you miss?

Kyra You mean, from your father's world?

Edward Yes.

Kyra stands in the middle of her shabby flat, mittens round her fingers, dreaming.

Kyra I miss a good breakfast. Toast wrapped in napkins. Croissants. And really hot coffee from a silver pot. Scrambled eggs. I never have those. And I do miss them more than I'd have thought possible.

Edward Nothing else?

Kyra Oh, maybe one thing.

There is the shadow of a blush on her face.

Edward You miss my father.

For a moment it looks as if she does not know how to respond. Now it is Edward's turn to blush.

And so saying, I think I shall go.

Kyra has picked up his plastic bag and is holding it out to him.

Kyra Edward, I enjoyed seeing you. Really. I mean it.

Edward Right. Then I'm off.

Kyra You've got all your stuff?

Edward Yes. Yes, thank you.

He still seems rooted to the spot, even with his bag in his hand. She reaches forward and kisses him on the cheek.

I expect I'll see you again.

Kyra Yes, well, I hope so.

Edward You didn't mind?

Kyra Edward, I've said so.

He has run out of ways to prolong his departure. So impulsively he blurts out his last instruction.

Edward Kyra, I wish you would bloody well help.

And he turns and leaves as fast as he can. Kyra is slightly shaken for a moment, then she goes to the open door and closes it. She thinks a moment, then she goes out to the bathroom. After a second, the Ascot flares again, and there is the sound of a running bath. The lights fade.

SCENE TWO

The lights come up again. In the kitchen the ingredients of the spaghetti sauce have been laid out – onions, garlic and chilli, none of them yet chopped. On the table the schoolbooks have been laid out for an evening's reading. After a moment there is a ringing at the door. Then a second ringing and the sound of Kyra getting out of the bath.

Kyra (*off*) Shit!

As she comes into the room, wrapped in a large towel and dripping wet, the ringing becomes more insistent.

Shit! Who is it?

She goes into the kitchen and looks down from the only window which gives on to the street. She responds instinctively, without thinking.

Jesus Christ! Shit! Go away.

The bell rings again. At once she opens the window and calls down.

Hold on a minute and I'll throw down a key.

She takes a key which hangs on a hook in the kitchen and throws it out of the window. She waits a moment to check it's been caught, then closes the window. She is panicking slightly. She goes into her bedroom, having collected jeans and a couple of sweaters. She goes across to the main door and opens it, then runs quickly back into the bathroom and closes the door.

After a moment, Tom Sergeant appears in the doorway. He is near fifty, a big man, still with a lot of grey hair. He wears beautiful casual clothes under a coat. He has an air of slightly tired distinction. He stands a moment, looking round the room, but very quickly Kyra reappears in her jeans and sweater, her hair wet and a towel still in her hand.

Kyra I wanted to say I'm not guilty.

Tom Not guilty? What do you mean?

Kyra You arrived like a fucking stormtrooper.

Tom Thank you.

Kyra Have you parked your tanks in the street?

Tom I was only ringing the bell.

She passes him to close the door, her tone dry.

Kyra You always were excessively manly.

Tom I brought you some whisky.

Kyra Thanks. Put it down over there.

Tom OK.

Kyra Beside the beer.

Tom frowns, seeing there is already a carrier bag full of beer on the table. Kyra passes back across the room, drying her hair.

Did somebody tell you? That if you called I'd be in?

Tom No. I was just guessing.

Kyra Oh really? Just passing?

Tom I wouldn't say that. I mean, does anyone . . .

Kyra Pass through this area? No. You've got a good point there. You mean this visit's deliberate?

Tom Yes. Sort of.

There is a moment's silence.

So.

Kyra Will you take off your coat?

Tom I won't. Just at this moment. Perhaps it's me. But it seems a bit parky.

Kyra It is.

Tom Well . . . I thought it was time. That's what I'm doing here. Time you and I saw each other again.

Kyra heads towards the kitchen. Tom starts wandering round the little flat.

Oh, I see you're making your supper. I'm sorry. Perhaps I should have phoned. I think I was scared you might hang up on me. I mean, I've had no idea. I mean, what you've been thinking. I suppose I thought perhaps you hated me.

Kyra Yes. If you'd rung, then you'd have found out.

Tom nods slightly, recognising and loving the old acerbity in her.

Tom It's not been easy. One way and another. It's been a hard time for me.

Kyra I heard about Alice.

Tom Did you? How?

Kyra I just heard.

Tom Yes. She died a year ago. It seems much longer. I mean, in a way it was fine. I'd already 'discounted' it. It's a term we use in business. Meaning . . .

Kyra I know what it means. You've already prepared yourself. So when it happens it isn't so awful.

Tom That's right. Yes. You're shocked?

Kyra Not at all. Should I be?

Tom No. Well, that's how it was.

He starts to move round the room correcting his apparent callousness.

And also Alice was so incredible. I can hardly tell you. I mean, she was so brave. Propped up in bed, wearing yellow. She spent the day watching birds, through this large square of light above her. The skylight over her bed. She was truly . . . truly fantastic.

Kyra Whisky?

She is standing with the bottle poised over the glass. He catches her tone which seems unimpressed by his eulogy.

Tom Yes.

Kyra pours in silence. He looks at the CDs on the table.

Kyra, I must say you always surprise me. I'd never have thought you'd have taken up rap.

Kyra Oh. No, well, I haven't. In fact only recently.

Tom You know that Edward's into this stuff?

Kyra Oh really?

Tom Who are your favourites?

Kyra Oh. You know. It varies.

Tom I suppose you picked it up from your kids.

Kyra Sure.

Tom You're still at that same place?

Kyra Yeah.

Tom How is it?

Kyra At the moment? It's doing fine. I mean, we had a not-bad head teacher, truly she really wasn't too bad, but then – it always happens – things started wearing her down.

   She has got a bottle of red wine and has begun to open it.

People started stealing her car. It was sort of a challenge or something. We think it must have been some of the kids. Then they broke into her flat. She lost her stereo. Also they got hold of her cat. She came back one night. The cat had been baked in the oven. She began to feel it was time to move on. She got a better job, you know, down in Dulwich.

Tom Dulwich is nicer.

Kyra Yes, I think she probably felt that as well.

   She looks at him witheringly, but he is imperturbable now.

Tom And what about you?

Kyra Me?

Tom Don't you get tired of it?

Kyra I talk to the police occasionally. They say it's a problem. Assaults on the police are growing all the time. Then they say, on the other hand, there's one thing they can't help noticing. It's the same coppers who get beaten up time and again.

Tom smiles, relaxed now with his whisky, as she goes to get herself a wine glass.

Tom So what does that mean?

Kyra Some people are victims. I walk in perfect peace to and from school. I'm not a mark, that's the difference.

Tom And what do you put that down to?

Instead of answering, Kyra suddenly looks him straight in the eye and raises her voice.

Kyra I wish you'd take off your fucking coat.

Her directness suddenly speaks of a whole past between them. Tom replies quietly.

Tom Well, I would. Of course. If you'd get central heating. Then of course I'd take off my coat. But since you've made a style choice to live in Outer Siberia, I think for the moment I'll keep my coat on.

They are like old friends now as she pours herself a glass of wine.

If you want central heating, look, it's no problem. I've got this really good bloke.

Kyra From *Yellow Pages*?

Tom I'm sorry?

Kyra No, nothing.

Tom If you like, he'd come round. It wouldn't take long.
This bloke does all of my restaurants. I'm pretty sure
I can spare him next week. Unless of course you say,
no thank you. I mean, no doubt you'd prefer to be cold.

Kyra No, I'd prefer to be warm.

Tom Well then.

Kyra Warm, but not indebted. If it's all right, I'm going
to cook.

Tom Oh really? I was going to ask if you'd like proper
dinner.

Kyra Meaning mine isn't proper? Spaghetti!

Tom Oh Lord, so touchy! No, I meant, would you like
to go out?

Kyra looks at him as if the question were absurd.

I'm just asking if you'd like to go out.

Kyra What for?

Tom An evening.

Kyra Tom, don't you think I've got enough memories?
Why should I want any more?

She goes back to the cooking.

So tell me, how is the business?

Tom (*refusing to be downhearted*) Business? Business
has generally recovered. Yes, I'd even say it was thriving.
Of course I'm not my own boss any more. In theory.
Like everyone, I now have a chairman. The chairman of

course has a bloody great board. That's the price I paid for going public. I report to this sort of management guru.

Kyra (*grimacing as she comes out opening a tin of tomatoes*) My God!

Tom I know, but, like all really top-class management gurus, he only comes in for four hours a week. He wanders in. Makes a few gnomic statements. Mutters the words 'core competence'. Or whatever trendy management mantra happens to be in fashion this week. Then he wanders out. For that the banks just love him. They adore him. Why? Because he once was a banker himself. So for this insider's sinecure he is paid more or less twice what I am paid as full-time chief executive. The person who created the company. The person who knows the business of hotels and restaurants. But that is the way that things are now done . . . (*He swirls the scotch in his glass.*)

Kyra What's he like?

Tom He's one of those people who's been told he's good with people. That means he smiles all the time and is terribly interested. He keeps saying, 'No, tell me, what do *you* think?'

Kyra In other words . . .

Tom Yes, he's completely insufferable.

Kyra is beginning to enjoy him now.

It was how I was always told you could get women into bed. By doing something called 'listening to their problems'. It's a contemptible tactic.

Kyra You wouldn't do it?

Tom No. Of course not. You know me, Kyra. I wouldn't stoop to it. Either they want you or else they don't. Listening's halfway to begging.

28

Kyra smiles as she goes to get a chopping board, with which she comes back.

But this bloke . . . he does it all the time in the business. 'How interesting. Really? Is that what you think?' Then he does what he'd planned in the first place. It's called consultation. Buttering you up and then ignoring you.

Kyra (*setting down the board*) I can imagine.

Tom Oh yes, that's how things go nowadays . . .

Kyra Is there no way you can get rid of him?

Tom No. It's the price I paid for floating the company. It made me millions, I can hardly complain. I offered you shares, remember? I never knew why you refused.

Kyra flashes a look at him to suggest he knows perfectly well why she refused.

When we went public they jumped thirty-fold. You could have had the house in the West Indies. Like me.

Kyra Oh, really?

Tom Well, maybe not quite. But at least you could have moved up in the world.

Kyra ignores this, choosing to go on chopping the onions.

Banks and lawyers! That's all I see. So perhaps you did well. Perhaps it wasn't so stupid. Coming here.

Kyra It wasn't stupid.

Tom No.

She has spoken with such quiet firmness that he looks up. Then he moves away, implicitly accepting what she's just said, but happy to resume his stories.

Me, I'm with shits and shafters all day. I went in to one guy, the other day, I said to this fellow – he's lending me money at eleven per cent – I said: 'You want it? Well you can have it. You want the shirt off my back? I will hand you my shirt. Here it is! And still, as God is my witness, you will not stop me, you will not stop me from trying to build a business out there.'

He stands now, re-creating the moment.

I said, 'I'm an entrepreneur, I'm a doer. I actually go out, I make things happen. I give people jobs which did not previously exist. And you . . . you sit here with your little piles of money. Doing fuck all.'

Kyra How did he take it?

Tom Oh, no problem! The odd thing was, he agreed.

He is in his stride, the raconteur happy with his favourite audience.

He said, 'Yes of course, you're right, that's right. It's true. You take the risks and I never do. I hate risk!' he said. 'But also,' he said, 'has it occurred to you that this may be the reason finally why it's *you* who always has to come grovelling to *me*?'

Kyra He didn't say 'grovelling'?

Tom (*suddenly exasperated*) Kyra, there's nothing more irritating . . .

Kyra All right, I'm sorry . . .

Tom No, Alice . . . Alice would do this. I would say, I'm telling a story. For God's sake I'm telling a story. If I say it, it's true.

Kyra I know.

Tom 'Oh, I don't believe it,' Alice would say . . .

He is more emphatic than ever, as if mystified why anyone would doubt him.

I wouldn't say it if it wasn't what happened. *I wouldn't say it!*

Kyra I know.

Tom That's what he said to me!

Kyra He used the word 'grovelling'?

Tom Those exact words! 'And that is why you come grovelling to me . . .'

Kyra laughs again, now Tom is back on track, his humour restored.

Kyra Well I must say . . . who was he?

Tom Some fucking graduate in business studies. Twenty-five. Thirty. Knows nothing. The Rolex! The fucking lemon-yellow Gaultier tie!

Kyra Goodness, the banks have got trendy.

Tom They're beyond trendy. The banks are running the world. You think – oh fuck! – you think, I'll run a business, I'll build a business. You remember, Kyra, we started out, my God it was great! Actually counting the money, you counted it with me . . .

Kyra Of course.

Tom Actually handling the money each morning, after you'd joined us, totting it up each Saturday night . . .

Kyra I remember.

Tom Then – oh Christ! – there's this fatal moment. Expansion!

Kyra Sure.

Tom And then you borrow. And then you're no longer in business, you're no longer in what I'd call business, because it's nothing to do with the customer. It's you and the bank. And it's war! (*He stops, incisive.*) There was a moment, I tell you, in the middle eighties . . .

Kyra Oh yeah . . .

Tom Yeah, just for a moment, I tell you, there was a time. I think, through that little window – what was it? Four years? Five years? Just through that little opening in history you could feel the current. For once you could feel the current running your way. You walked into a bank, you went in there, you had an idea. In. Money. Thank you. Out. Bang! They gave you the money! It was like for a moment we all had a vision, it was a kind of a heavenly vision, the idea of how damn fast and fun it could be . . . (*He turns, whisky in hand.*) And then of course everything slipped back to normal. The old 'Are you sure that's what you really want to do?' The 'Wouldn't it be easier if we all did nothing at all?' They always have new ways of punishing initiative. Whatever you do, they think up new ways.

Kyra looks up a moment, but Tom is already going on to tell her more.

You know, you read all this stuff in the papers – this stuff about banks – you read it, you know what I mean . . .

Kyra No. I'm afraid I've stopped reading the papers.

Tom What are you saying? Not altogether?

Tom is taken aback, but Kyra is going on, amused at her own story.

Kyra It's funny, I remember my father. Dad used to say, 'I don't watch the news. I don't approve of it.' I used to say, 'Dad, it's the news. It's the *news*, for God's sake. How can you not *approve* of it?' But I must say, now . . . perhaps I'm my father's daughter . . . I tend to think that he had a point. I don't have a television either.

Tom But that is just crazy. You're . . .

Kyra What?

Tom Well, you're missing what's happening. You're missing reality.

Kyra Oh, do you think?

Even Tom is only half serious, knowing his argument doesn't sound too good. And Kyra is completely unfazed.

I just noticed the papers were full of . . . sort of unlikeable people. People I couldn't relate to. People who weren't like the decent people, the regular people I meet every day at the school. So I thought, I start reading this stuff and half an hour later, I wind up angry. So perhaps it's better I give it up.

Tom So what do you read?

Kyra On the bus I read classic novels. Computer manuals. It's like that game. Name a politician you actually admire. So what is the point of sitting there raging at all the insanity?

Tom That's not the point.

Kyra It's the same with new films. I just won't go to them. Old films I like.

Tom Ah. Those you like because they're romantic.

Kyra You can hardly deny it. They have something we don't.

Suddenly her words hang in the air between them. Almost to cover the embarrassment, she resumes.

And Edward?

Tom What?

Kyra How is Edward?

Tom looks at her blankly as if not knowing who she's talking about.

Kyra Edward. Edward, your son?

Tom Oh, bloody Edward, that's who you mean. He's fine. I mean, he's living. He's alive. I mean, he gives the external signs. He eats. He tries to spend all my money. What can you say except he's eighteen?

Before Kyra can react, Tom is off again, on a half-serious complaint.

I saw that old film. *Invasion of the Body Snatchers.* You know, where they look the same. They look like humans, but it turns out they're creatures from Mars. They're pods. Well, another way of putting it, they're male adolescents. It's like they get taken over. Someone comes and surgically removes all the good qualities they have, and turns them into selfish hoodlums . . .

Kyra I don't really think it's that bad.

Kyra picks up the board and takes it out to the kitchen. Tom has already moved away to pour himself a second scotch.

Tom I mean, you spend all this money on education. A generation builds something up. And the children learn nothing but how to stand back from it . . .

Kyra Tom, that is nonsense.

Tom And all they want is to knock everything down.

*Kyra reaches now for a frying pan, not thinking he's
serious. But he shakes his head, bitter, his indignation
now real.*

He called me a brainless animal.

Kyra No? Really? That's unspeakable.

Tom That's what he called me. Buying and selling. That's
what he said. Without ever questioning. He called me a
zombie . . .

Kyra No!

Tom Just doing business without asking why . . .

*He doesn't see her quiet amusement at this story as
he reaches past her to pour water into his scotch from
the tap.*

I said, perhaps it's true, perhaps I'm not brilliantly
contemplative, perhaps I do not stop like some Oxford
smartarse philosopher to ask myself the purpose of it all.
But the rough effect of all my endeavour – my putting
my house, my mortgage, my car, the whole of my bloody
life on the line – as I reminded him *I have done in my
time* – has been to embody this unspeakably crude
assumption that it's still worth human beings trying to
get something done . . .

*He has landed on this last phrase, getting pleasure
now from his own rhetoric.*

Kyra And what did he say?

Tom Say? *Say?* You mean, like 'say' as in the concept of
actually replying? Kyra, you don't understand. This is
the modern game. This is men's tennis. People don't
bother with rallies. You put in your big serve and you

hope to hell it never comes back. (*He turns, expansive, bitter.*) He's not like what you'd call rational-articulate. He doesn't want argument. For Christ's sake, Kyra, you teach. Language belongs to the past. This is the world of Super Mario. Bang! Splat! Spit out your venom and go. (*He looks at her, his tone softening now.*) It's not like, you know . . . when we were together. You and me talking. Talking down the stars from the sky. This is . . . oh, you know . . . it's instinct. This is a young man wanting to hurt.

Kyra And does he hurt?

Tom No, of course not. For God's sake, look, I've fought bigger than him. He can't get a glove on me. That's why he's angry.

He is aware that Kyra thinks his bravado sounds a little unconvincing. So he moves away a few paces.

There's no problem. It's all in hand.

Kyra nods. It has gone quiet. Both of them know he is not telling the truth. He has gone to the kitchen door and now watches as she pours the olive oil into the frying pan. She looks at him as she works because he is standing so close.

Kyra What? No, really. What are you thinking?

Tom Are you putting the chilli in first?

Kyra looks at him uncharitably. He is at his most boyish, hesitant.

No, it's just I usually . . . I fry the chilli, so it infuses the oil.

Kyra Uh-huh. I see. I don't do that. I'm doing it the way I prefer.

Tom Yeah. (*He shifts a moment, uneasy.*) I haven't quite asked you. I mean, if I'm going to stay. I mean . . . I just mean for supper. I'm actually asking. I mean, are you laying two plates?

In reply she takes plates from the rack and goes to the table at which she has been meaning to work. She clears the books to one side. Then she puts two plates down at opposite ends of the table. Then she goes back to the kitchen and resumes. All in silence. He makes a little bow.

Thank you. Believe me, I'm really grateful.

Kyra Think nothing of it.

Tom Oh, and put the chilli in first.

Kyra gives him a filthy look, but he is already out of range, relaxing again.

You never cooked.

Kyra No, I didn't.

Tom I remember in those early days once you asking if you could try it some time . . .

Kyra I never did. I was a happy waitress.

Tom You weren't a waitress for long.

Kyra I was a waitress for forty-five minutes. Alice made me the boss on the spot.

Tom is happily shaking his head at the memory, as Kyra now cooks.

Tom That was a night.

Kyra It was.

Tom Hilary's accident!

37

Kyra It was my first trip to London, I just walked in off the street.

Tom You were eighteen.

Kyra Incredible!

Tom You were the same age Edward is now.

Kyra I was so thrilled, I remember. At last I'd escaped. I was walking down London's famous King's Road. I saw the sign 'Waitress Wanted'. I walked in. Alice told me I could start right away. Then after an hour of it, she came running over. She said her daughter was in hospital, she'd fallen off her bike. She said she'd looked round and she'd decided. Could I run the place for the night?

Tom laughs at the ridiculousness of it. Kyra has stopped at the frying pan.

I said, 'I've only just started, I only started an hour ago.' She said, 'I know. I've watched you. I trust you. Now you must trust me, you're going to be fine . . .'

Tom What time was that? Do you remember?

Kyra Oh, it can't have been later than eight o'clock.

Tom Before the rush?

Kyra I mean, oh yes. I handled it. I know I did the whole thing. Then I closed up. All the waiters were great, they were great, considering I'd only just arrived yet I was in charge. They all said, 'Look, we promise, there's really no need for you to hang on here. Just lock up the door and we're all going home . . .'

She has left the cooking, and is now standing at the kitchen door.

But I don't know . . . I just had this instinct. Somehow I didn't think it was right. I can't quite explain it. I wanted

to be there when Alice got back. It's funny. Of course,
I would have met you anyway. Surely I would have met
you next day. Who knows? But there was something about
that evening. Something to do with the evening itself . . .

*She looks away absently. Tom has sat down and is
rapt.*

I sat alone. Drank espresso. Smoked cigarettes. I'm not
sure I'd ever sat through a night. This deserted restaurant
all to myself. But filled with inexpressible happiness.
This crazy feeling. 'I don't know why but this is where
I belong.'

Tom And then?

Kyra And then . . . Need I continue? Then towards
morning she came back with you.

*Kyra turns and goes back to work. For the first time
Tom is at peace.*

Tom Earlier she'd rung. I'd driven like a madman from
some meeting. In those days I had the Jag. Praying.
Weeping. You know, feeling not like myself, because I
thought . . . I was thinking, I'm not a person who cries.
Crying with relief, too, at the sight of Hilary. Fast asleep
in the little bed. Her leg in plaster. Some fucking nurse.
What terrible parents! How could you let your daughter
play in the road?

*Kyra has stirred her pan and now is listening to him
at the kitchen door.*

Then, when we came back, you brought us brandy and
coffee. In our own restaurant. At four o'clock. It was
completely natural. I thought, this is the strangest night
of my life. This girl I'd never met before, bringing brandy
and coffee. It's as if she's been with us the whole of
our lives.

Kyra looks down, moved by this.

Yeah, that was something.

Kyra It was.

Tom Didn't you stay with us?

Kyra I did. I stayed at your place. On the floor. Well, I have to say that was my moment. From that moment on . . . I'd have done anything, just to stay with you, just to stay in that house.

She goes back to the cooking.

Tom I remember I got really angry soon after, after a few weeks or so, you saying you weren't going to give up a place at university. You weren't going to make your life in the catering trade.

Kyra I didn't say 'catering'! I never used the words 'catering trade'! Honestly, you make me sound like a prig.

Tom No? A prig? Impossible! You're a seaside solicitor's daughter! Are you saying that some of that hadn't rubbed off?

Kyra has picked up her glass of red wine, laughing at his account. At last, she is unguarded.

Kyra It's just . . . for goodness' sake . . . I loved mathematics. I did. I loved it. I wasn't going to give up halfway. And what's more, it meant finally escaping my father. I was hardly going to pass up that chance.

Tom shrugs, unimpressed.

It wasn't easy. You started to lecture me. I was quite shocked. 'Don't waste your time on higher education, it's only a way of postponing real life . . .'

Tom So it is.

Kyra I was so worried, I went to Alice. I said, 'Does he mean it?' She said, 'Never take any notice of Tom . . .'

Tom Thank you, Alice . . .

Kyra 'And even if you go, he knows you'll always want to come back . . .'

She looks at him, serious now, the words etched out, sincere.

You gave me a place. It was there. I could count on your welcome.

There is a slight pause, Tom moved by Kyra's acknowledgement of how much their home had meant to her.

And I never doubted, not for a moment, that when I came back to London, there'd be a job waiting.

She stops a second. Then a real mischievousness comes into her manner.

In spite of – my God! – whatever else I was doing. Far more, let me tell you, far more than you ever knew . . .

Tom Yes, well, I have to say I assumed, I hardly thought – you were young enough, for God's sake – I hardly thought you lived the life of a nun.

Kyra You wish!

Tom You thought I was jealous?

Kyra You did tear that painting from the wall.

Tom I did not tear it. As God is my witness, I did not remove it. It fell.

Kyra Oh yes, I see, pure coincidence, this picture painted by a man of whom you happened not to approve . . .

Tom Colin! The original art-school wanker . . . the greasy beard and the clogs.

Kyra Who had painted me at college, as I felt rather beautifully.

Tom Rather beautifully, but wearing no clothes.

Kyra That was the point. You could not stand it. You saw me there on the wall.

Tom It's true. I looked at it. I just looked at it. I sent beams of hatred from across the room. And without my touching it, I admit it fell down.

Kyra Oh, sure.

She turns and goes back into the kitchen to put the spaghetti into boiling water.

Tom (*defending himself, half serious, half not*) It wasn't – be fair! – it wasn't the sight of you, it wasn't just the image of you, it was my disbelief . . . my horror that this young woman who seemed so capable . . . so smart –

Kyra Thank you . . .

Tom – should have had the clothes ripped off her as if they were tissue as soon as some phoney used the word 'art'.

He sums up his charges as she cooks on.

I thought you were gullible!

Kyra No, I was open-minded. And what's more, twenty years younger than you. And living a life. You actually tried to give me a lecture . . .

Tom is about to deny it.

You did! You said, 'In a way you're part of the family, in a way, Kyra, you're like a daughter of mine . . .'

Tom I didn't say 'daughter'!

Kyra Oh, but you did.

Tom Where was this?

Kyra That ghastly hamburger restaurant you had. You were in your chargrilled hamburger phase.

Tom Oh God, I'm ashamed! I mean, I'm ashamed of the lecture, I'm ashamed of those burgers as well.

Kyra (*suddenly shouting as if there is no end to the awfulness of it all*) The burgers! The lecture!

Tom I must say, it begins to come back . . .

Kyra And I thought, yes, oh I see. I realised then: here we go.

Tom What?

Kyra I thought, hold on. This is it. This is only going to be a matter of time.

She has come back into the room and finds herself standing right by his chair, close enough to touch. The contact is now so intimate between them that it suddenly feels as if either of them might say anything. Then Tom speaks as if the next thought were completely logical.

Tom Pressing on. You know, that's the thing in business. My chairman keeps telling me: never look back. In business, he says, the world was created this morning. No such thing as the past . . .

Kyra turns to go and look after her pasta.

He says that modern management asks you to look at your assets, *really* look at them – this is a fierce, competitive world, all that crap! – how you got here's not part of the story, the only story is what you do now . . .

Kyra And what do you do?

Tom Oh, expand, inevitably. I mean, expand, I hardly need say that. Defend market share. Build another stainless steel restaurant, this one larger, more fashionable than ever, turning over hundreds of covers in a day. It need never end.

Kyra Nor will it. You love it.

Tom Oh yes. I must admit that I do.

He looks at her, on safe ground, the feeling once more easy and warm.

All that time, I must say, I can't deny it, while Alice was . . . you know . . . while she was lying in that bloody room . . . well, it was true for me, I saw no alternative but to redouble my efforts. It was like some lunatic board game. Not helped of course by your having quit.

He looks at her a little sheepishly.

It's true, though, I must say I missed you professionally.

Kyra Thank you.

They both know this thought is incomplete and how it will be, in a moment, completed.

Tom I kind of missed you in person as well.

Kyra looks at him a moment, just non-committal, as she works. Tom is serious.

I really did, Kyra. I never . . . I've never got used to it. Ever.

Kyra What, missed me so badly it's taken you three years to get back in touch?

It is said lightly, Kyra not wanting the atmosphere to darken, but he at once starts to protest strongly.

Tom Now look . . .

Kyra I mean, come on, let's be serious.

Tom You think I haven't wanted to? My God, you think I haven't wanted to call? To pick up the telephone? You think I haven't wanted to jump in the car and bust my way through that bloody door?

Kyra But then why didn't you?

Tom Kyra, why do you think?

They both know a bridge is about to be crossed even before it happens.

Because I knew once I saw you, then I'd be finished. I knew I'd never be able to leave.

He is so clearly speaking from the heart that Kyra cannot say anything. So instead she turns and goes back to her pasta.

Kyra OK, well, I must say, that's an answer . . .

Tom You see.

Kyra What?

Tom I'm getting better. Well, aren't I?

Kyra Getting better at what?

Tom Talking about my feelings. You always told me I had no gift for that stuff.

She frowns, puzzled at this.

Kyra As far as I remember we had no need for it. We had no need to discuss our feelings at all. Or rather, I didn't. I could always tell what you were feeling. It never had to be said. You'd wander about the office in Chelsea. Later we'd go home to work. We'd sit in the kitchen with Alice. I'd spend the evening reading to your kids.

There is a moment's silence. Tom is serious, low, when he speaks.

Tom I could never understand it. I still don't. You never felt the slightest sense of betrayal.

Kyra There we are. I always felt profoundly at peace. (*She waits a moment, wanting to be precise.*) I don't know why, it still seems true to me: if you have a love, which for any reason you can't talk about, your heart is with someone you can't admit – not to a single soul except for the person involved – then for me, well, I have to say, that's love at its purest. For as long as it lasts, it's this astonishing achievement. Because it's always a relationship founded in trust.

Tom It seems mad to me.

Kyra I know. You didn't feel that. I knew you never understood it. Why I was able to go on seeing Alice. Why we were always at ease. Why I loved her so much. But I did. It's a fact. There it is. The three of us. It gave me a feeling of calm.

She has got a small lump of cheese in greaseproof paper out of the fridge, and a cheese grater, and is coming back into the room.

You were the person I fell in love with. And as it happened you arrived with a wife.

Tom stands unimpressed by her argument, and rather hurt by her cheerfulness about it all. Kyra holds the cheese out to him.

Do you mind?

Tom Do I mind what?

Kyra No, I'm just asking . . .

Tom What?

Kyra I'm asking. Will you grate the cheese?

Tom takes the sweaty piece of greaseproof paper from her and holds it in his hand.

Tom Do you mean this?

Kyra I do.

Tom Are you serious? Is this what you're calling the cheese?

Nonchalant, she smiles and goes back to the kitchen as he moves, genuinely affronted by the cheese in his hand.

Kyra Yeah, I haven't had time to go shopping.

Tom I wouldn't give this greasy lump of crud to my cat.

Tom is holding out this piece of cheese somehow to represent the final insanity of her way of life. He raises his voice as if everything has become too much for him.

I do not believe it. Kyra, what's happening? Are you really *living* like this? Why didn't you say? For God's sake, I have this supplier . . .

Kyra I'm sure!

Tom For cheese – all types of cheese – I have this really great bloke.

Kyra Of course! Your whole life is great blokes!

Tom I mean, I can get you a weekly delivery – no problem – he'll send you fresh parmesan whenever you need.

Kyra Nevertheless.

She nods at the cheese in his hand to say he has no choice. But Tom already has another plan.

Tom I'm going to get Frank.

Kyra I'm sorry?

Tom I'm going to call down to Frank, this is ridiculous, to send out, just to go to a deli and get us something for now . . .

Kyra Hold on a moment, what are you saying? Are you saying that Frank is sitting out there?

Tom Sure.

Kyra Waiting out in the car all the time we've been talking?

Tom Yes. I mean, yes! For Christ's sake, what's wrong with that?

He is bemused but she has her hands on her hips, as if Tom will never learn.

Kyra You leave him down there? You really are quite extraordinary.

Tom Why?

Kyra You used to tell me you had this great gift! I remember, you prided yourself on what you called your man-management skills. And yet you still treat people as if they were no better than objects . . .

But Tom is already moving in to her, refusing to accept any of this.

Tom For God's sake, Kyra, the man is a driver. That's what he does. You know full well that drivers don't drive. The greater part of their lives they spend waiting . . .

Kyra Tom, there is some sort of limit!

Tom And furthermore, that is what they expect. Frank, I may tell you . . . Frank, as it happens, is perfectly happy. Frank for a start is bloody well paid. He is sitting

48

in a spacious limousine listening to Kiss 100 and reading what is politely called a 'men's interest' magazine . . .

But Kyra is already pointing to the window in the kitchen area.

Kyra Have you looked out the window? Have you seen the weather? Have you seen there's snow about to come down?

Tom Don't give me that tosh! Frank is a bloody sight better off sitting in a warm Mercedes than he would be in this fucking fur-store which you call your home.

Kyra Well . . .

Tom (*suddenly exploding with rage*) I mean, here we are! This is the problem! That's what it was. That was the problem. This ridiculous self-righteousness! I mean, to be fair, you always had it. But also, I knew, I *knew* it wasn't going to get better. And, let's face it, it was only going to get worse once you decided you wanted to teach.

Kyra It's nothing to do with my teaching, it isn't to do with the work that I do, it's just a way of respecting people.

Tom Frank isn't people! Frank is a man who is doing a job!

He moves away, all his worst suspicions confirmed.

You were always salving your own bloody conscience . . . these stupid gestures, nothing to do with what people might want. They want to be treated . . . respected like adults for the job they are paid for, and not looked down on as if they were chronically disabled, as if they somehow need *help* all the time. I mean, yes, this was the craziness! This was the whole trouble with business and you! You looked down – always! – on the way we did things. The

49

way things are done. You could never accept the nature of business. I mean, finally that's why you had to leave.

He has no sooner said this than he realises how absurd it is, and at once tries to retract.

Kyra Well, I must say . . .

Tom I mean . . .

Kyra I never knew that was the reason!

Tom All right, I'm sorry . . .

Kyra I never knew that was why I had to leave.

Tom is desperately trying to backtrack but Kyra won't let him off the hook.

Tom I put it badly.

Kyra Badly? You did. I thought I left because your wife discovered I'd been sleeping with you for over six years!

Unable to resist it, she has said this so forcefully that he can only look at her, admitting his own absurdity.

Tom I mean, well, yes. That as well, that played a part in it.

Kyra I should say it fucking well did.

Tom That was part of the problem.

Kyra Part of? *Part* of?

Tom But you did have a problem of attitude. Your attitude to business you never got straight!

Kyra Well . . .

She gestures as if this was hardly the worst of her problems and goes back into the kitchen to carry on laying the table.

Tom (*trying to retrieve what ground he can*) What I'm saying is, you'd have left anyway. I could sense it. You were feeling it was time for a change.

Kyra Tom, I left because I'd always warned you: 'If Alice finds out, then I shall go.'

She has said this quite simply as if re-creating the moment. Tom shifts, uncomfortable, more like a little boy than ever.

Tom All right . . .

Kyra I told you, I told you a thousand times . . .

Tom Yes. I know you did.

Kyra I can only do this for as long as she doesn't find out. When she found out, then it changed things. Instantly.

Tom 'Instantly' says it. You were gone in an hour. Wham! Out the door! With me left explaining to all the other employees . . .

Kyra Oh, really?

Tom I don't think anyone was very convinced.

Kyra I had no choice. I know it sounds stupid. You have something worked out in your own mind. Then something changes. The balance is gone. You no longer believe your own story. And that, I'm afraid, is the moment to leave.

She turns and goes out into the kitchen. Tom moves away, thinking, by himself. He picks up the cheese and the grater and, as if conceding defeat, starts to grate it into a little bowl. Kyra speaks quietly from the kitchen.

Kyra I heard you moved.

Tom Yes. We did that quite quickly. We moved when Alice was starting to get ill.

Kyra How long was her illness?

Tom She was . . . well, let's see . . . She was in the bed, in the bad bit, I suppose, it was getting on for a year. I mean we'd known, I mean soon after you left us . . . then she began to experience dizziness. She'd taken no notice at first.

Kyra has stopped cooking, and is just watching him now.

We were in such total confusion, at that time things were already so tough, so that news of the illness . . . to be honest, at first, when it was first diagnosed, it seemed like kind of a joke. How much misfortune? and so on. Where are the gods?

Kyra just watches, not reacting. The cheese and grater are idle in his hands.

She needed a place where she could be peaceful. I built this extraordinary bedroom – this builder, the one I mentioned, you know – with this wonderful sloping glass roof. The Common outside. Fantastic! We gave her the picture she wanted, exactly what she wanted to see.

Then he frowns, knowing what he will say next is difficult.

She became quite . . . well, she became quite mystic. I don't mean to sound cruel, but it was kind of difficult for me.

Kyra In what way?

Tom You know Alice. She got hold of this bloody word 'spiritual'. It's one of those words I've never quite understood. I mean, I've always hated the way people use it. They use it to try and bump themselves up. 'Oh I've had a spiritual experience,' they say . . .

Kyra Yes.

Tom As if that's the end of the argument. 'Spiritual', meaning: 'It's mine and shove off.' People use it to prove they're sensitive. They want it to dignify quite ordinary things.

Tom has started by half sending himself up but now he gets firmer as he goes.

Religion. Now, that is something different. I like religion. Because religion has rules. It's based on something which actually occurred. There are things to believe in. And what's more, what makes it worth following – not that I do, mind you – there's some expectation of how you're meant to behave. But 'spiritual' . . . well, it's all wishy-washy. It means, 'Well, for me, for *me* this is terribly important, but I'm fucked if I can really say why . . .'

Kyra is smiling at this characteristic talk, but Tom is genuinely aggravated.

Kyra Is that how Alice was?

Tom Oh look, I don't mean to downgrade it. Alice was dying. Let's face it, in my view she grabbed at whatever she could. She was always faddish. But that's what it was. Grabbing. It wasn't solid. It wasn't like she really believed. If you'd said, 'Oh look, what do you believe in? What is there? What's happening? What's real?', she couldn't say. It was all sensation.

Kyra is looking askance now, a little shocked by Tom's dismissiveness.

Kyra Yes, but Tom, surely, that's not so unusual . . .

Tom I know!

Kyra That's how most people die. They die in that state. Not knowing. Half knowing. Surely that's what you'd expect?

Tom (*turning round, determined again to confront his own unease*) I don't know. I could see the room was beautiful. I mean, it was a beautiful room. And so it should be. I'm not being wholly facetious, but the fact is I had spent a great deal. I mean, I'm not kidding. I spent a great deal of money. All that glass, the sandalwood floor. The sky! The greenery! The light! I gave her everything.

Kyra So what are you saying?

Tom I don't know. I just felt frustrated. I felt out of contact.

Kyra What you're saying is the two of you never got straight.

Tom No.

It is suddenly quiet. Kyra is standing with the cooking spoon still in her hand. Tom is just staring out. There is a feeling of shame and complicity. Briefly, they're like two criminals.

Kyra What you mean is, you never got over your guilt.

She goes back towards the kitchen.

Tom (*quietly, a little hoarsely*) Guilt. I don't know. I mean, guilt's another word. It's one of those words people use. I mean, sure. In a way. I mean, yes, I can hardly deny it. Both of us knew. Both Alice and me. We knew our time together was wrecked. But Alice was far too proud to reproach me. And then of course, being Alice, she began to withdraw. Gardening! Sewing! Reading! All those feminine things! The effect? To make me feel much worse than if she'd stood up and fought.

Kyra is standing listening again now, recognising his description of Alice.

54

She kept saying, 'No, you go on with your life, Tom. We're such different people,' that's what she said. 'Don't mind me. Forget me. I'm happy reading and gardening.' Christ! Fucking gardening! If I could make it illegal I would!

Kyra smiles.

She'd say quietly, 'Well, you know, Tom, I think we were always mismatched. For a man like you, Kyra is much more intelligent.' She'd praise you. Always. 'Kyra's attractive. She's clever. She's smart.' I mean, she'd actually say that. 'I'm much too docile, I know.' Jesus! I look back on that time in our lives, my own wife telling me in tones of absolute sweetness how right I was to love someone else. And what's more, what a good choice! (*He turns back, despairing.*) Then when she got ill . . . you think, 'I see, is this some sort of punishment? Do You always punish the meek?' Alice's peace of mind taken from her. Her friendship with you. She's just beginning to absorb this. And then she's told that she's going to die.

He starts to cry.

Kyra And now?

Tom Now?

Kyra What are you feeling?

Tom looks at her blankly for a moment, then characteristically covers up again, at once trying to hide his distress.

Tom Oh, not too bad. I think I'm all right. No, really. I've found ways of coping. In the way that you do. I mean, I've got the business. No problem. I've got the house.

Then he grins, relieved to be able to get back to an anecdote.

55

A woman came – I didn't tell you this – a woman came
to the door. She said she was from a local support group.
I couldn't believe it. She told me she'd come to help me
to grieve. I said, 'I beg your pardon?' She said, don't
worry, it's not going to cost you. It's on the rates.' Or the
Poll Tax, whatever it's called. I said, 'I'm meant to feel
better? You mean that's meant to make it all right?
That's meant to make all the difference?' Oh good, this
is great, I think I'll do this, I'll mourn my wife in the
company of this total stranger, after all it's going to be
free . . .

*Now he is becoming disproportionately angry, his
scorn for his visitor complete.*

I said, 'Look, lady, I'll tell you one thing. When I choose
to grieve for this woman . . . this woman with whom
I spent such a . . . *large* part of my life, it will not be in
the presence of a representative of Wimbledon Council.'
She said, 'Oh, we're in Merton now.'

*He stands, genuinely furious, lost, all his anger
displaced on to this story.*

I mean, please tell me, what is it? Don't they know
anything? You suffer. That's what you do. There are no
short cuts. There are no easy ways. And I have been doing
my share of suffering.

Kyra Yes. I know that. That's what I've heard.

*Tom frowns, brought up short, suddenly hearing her
say this.*

Tom What do you mean? What do you mean by that?

Kyra I talked to Edward.

Tom Edward?

Kyra That's right.

Tom When? You've talked to Edward?

Kyra Oh shit, the pasta is going to be done . . .

She moves quickly to reach into the oven for the plates.

Tom (*infuriated*) For Christ's sake, forget the pasta.

Kyra Oh God, I think it's going to be spoilt.

Tom What are you saying? Have you kept on seeing Edward?

Kyra No. He's only been over here once.

Tom When?

Kyra As it happened, this evening. He came, he told me that you'd been impossible. He says you still can't live with yourself. He said you spend the whole day in a fury.

Tom Fury? What fury?

Kyra He says you're totally lost.

Tom How dare he? How dare he come here and talk about me?

But Kyra, pouring the water off the pasta, is catching some of Tom's anger.

Kyra He came out of kindness. He came because he's concerned for his father.

Tom Concerned? Concerned for his father? Like fuck! He came because he's a little shit-stirrer. Because he likes making other people's business his own.

Suddenly Kyra's patience goes. She picks up a tray of cutlery and throws it violently across the room. The crash is spectacular. Tom stands dazed.

Kyra This is it. I mean, *shit*! I've heard you, Tom . . .

I mean, you've done this, you've done this your whole bloody life . . .

Tom Done what?

Kyra Pretended not to understand anything. Pretended, when you understand perfectly well.

Tom Understand what?

Kyra You've taken this boy . . .

Tom I've *taken* him?

Kyra You've taken this son of yours. Edward. You've made his life miserable. He told me. You had a row. For God's sake, earlier this week, he left home.

Tom *So?*

Kyra You're making his life unendurable. And only because you happen to be so bloody guilty . . .

Tom Me?

Kyra And so you take your guilt out on him.

Tom Is that what I do?

Kyra It is.

Tom Oh, really?

Kyra Yes.

Tom I see. Is that his opinion?

Kyra I think so.

Tom Is that his *version*? Is that what he says?

Kyra He didn't need to say it. I lived with your family, remember? Do you think I don't know what the hell's going on?

Tom moves away again, happier now, hoping he's off the hook.

Tom Ah, now I see, Kyra, you're actually inventing. I see. This is guesswork. The truth is, you're making this up. From your knowledge of the family you once walked out on . . .

Kyra All right.

Tom Edward didn't actually say any of this . . .

But she won't give way. She is still standing resolute, determined to take him on.

Kyra I think he saw your behaviour.

Tom My behaviour?

Kyra The way you behaved at the end.

She stops, knowing she has hit home.

He was there. He knew your real feelings. And I think that's why you're punishing him now.

Tom just looks at her. Knowing it's true, she goes further on to the attack.

Do you think, please, Tom, do you think I've believed this stuff you've been telling me?

Tom Stuff?

Kyra 'I'm enjoying the business, it's wonderful. I get on great with my son. Alice dying was hard, but of course I survived it. No problem. I just dropped round to see you . . . Oh, no reason, I just thought it was time . . .' (*She is bitter at the absurdity of it.*) And me, I'm standing here, nodding, smiling, agreeing like some ape . . . and thinking, is this man lying to me deliberately? Or does he not even notice? Or is he so used to lying to himself? It's all right for me. I'm fine. You can tell me anything. Any old story. I'm lucky because I've moved on. But Edward is young. He needs his father. He deserves honesty. He deserves not to be treated like dirt.

59

Tom looks guiltily at her a moment, not wanting to give way completely.

Tom That isn't fair.

Kyra Oh, isn't it?

Tom It isn't one-sided. Sometimes, I know, I can be hard on the boy.

Kyra And why?

Tom He's such a jerk. That's the reason.

Kyra Oh come on, Tom.

He looks at her reproachfully a moment, then suddenly admits the truth.

Tom All right, it's true. I couldn't face Alice. I couldn't. Not at the end. Any excuse. I went travelling. I opened hotels abroad. New York. Los Angeles. The further the better. I couldn't – I know it was wrong of me – do you really think I don't know it? – but, Jesus . . . I could not stay in that room. All right, I'm not proud. We both knew what was happening. I kept thinking, 'It's not like a test. What's happening is chance. It's pure chance. It's simply bad luck.' But I couldn't fight it. I felt . . . oh, everyone's watching. Her friends. I know what they think. This is some sort of trial of my character. And no doubt the bastards are saying I fail. (*He is suddenly vehement.*) But Edward was as bad. Don't ever think otherwise. He failed just as badly. In a different way. I came home, six friends of his lying on the floor, drinking Heineken. Drugs. Shit, I don't know . . . I remember screaming, 'What the hell are you doing? Don't you know your mother is lying up there?' I was so angry. I felt this anger, I never got over it. Every day this fury that you had walked out. Walked out and left me to handle this thing. I did try to use it. I used your memory.

60

I kept saying, 'Look, I must behave well. I must try. Because who knows? If I behave well, I still have a chance here.'

Kyra A chance?

Tom Yes.

Kyra What sort of chance?

Tom I think you know what I mean. I kept on saying, 'If I behave well, if I get through this, then maybe Kyra is going to come back.'

Kyra stands stunned, understanding how deep his feeling is. He goes on haltingly.

Sitting by the bed. Just awful. Looking at Alice, propped up on the pillows, her eyes liquid, cut off . . . I'd think, 'Oh shit, if Kyra were with us, if Kyra were here . . .'

He stops a moment and shakes his head.

Jesus, why weren't you? 'If Kyra were here, she'd know what to do.'

Kyra stands absolutely taken aback, as if not knowing what to think about his shocking devotion to her. He knows how much this has affected her.

But you ran and left us.

Kyra Yes. I had to.

Tom You did what you said people never should do.

Kyra I had no alternative. I had to get out of Alice's way. I had to make a new life of my own.

Tom And this is it, Kyra? This is the life that you made? Will you tell me, will you tell me, please, Kyra, what exactly are you doing here?

Suddenly there are two shocked people in the room. She is holding the edge of the table. When she speaks she is very quiet.

Kyra Are you going to go down? Will you speak to Frank then?

Tom What shall I say to him?

Kyra Send him away.

Without looking at her Tom walks across the room and opens the door and goes out. Kyra is alone, dazed now, white, like a shadow. She goes into the kitchen and pours the sauce into a bowl. She puts the bowl on the table, mechanically, not really thinking. She puts a second wine glass on the table. Then she gets a loaf of bread, takes a knife and cuts slices. The room seems dark, like a painting, the little red fire burning and the shadows falling across her face. Then Tom appears at the door. He closes it but does not yet move towards her.

Tom He's gone.

He moves across the room. They take each other in their arms and she holds him tightly, hugging him desperately, and beginning to cry, shaking with grief in his arms. He puts his hand through her hair.

Kyra, Kyra I'm back.

He runs his hand over and over through her hair. The lights fade to darkness.

Act Two

The door to the bedroom is slightly ajar. A white light, reflected off snow, comes from outside the kitchen window. The bar heater Kyra lit hours ago is still on, and glowing. It's around 2.30 a.m.

Kyra appears in the doorway. She is wearing a white flannel nightdress, over which she has put a sweater and a cardigan. She has clearly just woken up. She moves across the room trying to make as little noise as possible. The tray of cutlery she threw earlier is still scattered all over the floor. The abandoned meal is still on the table, uneaten. She looks at it a moment, then takes the spaghetti sauce she made earlier, picks up a piece of bread and carries them both across the room. Kyra puts them down by the big armchair, then looks for the school exercise books which she had put on the floor for the meal. She picks them up, then turns on a low side-light. She pulls the little heater nearer the chair, then sits down with it at her feet. She puts the books on her knee, then dips her bread in the cold sauce and starts to eat.

This is how Tom finds her as he now appears in the doorway of the bedroom. He has put on his shirt and trousers, but his feet are bare. He stands a moment, trying to make sense of the scene in front of him: the teacher sitting with books on her knee, the glow of the heater on her face.

Tom What are you doing?

Kyra Eating the sauce. I'm starving. Remember? We never had supper.

63

Tom God, I'm sorry. I fell asleep. What time is it?

Kyra I think it's two-thirty.

Tom I must say . . .

Kyra It's no worry. I must have fallen asleep as well.

She looks at him, genuinely affectionate. He moves towards her, an easy warmth between them, and kisses the top of her head in the chair.

Tom Why don't Baptists like to fuck standing up? Because they're frightened God will think they're dancing. Is it me? Or has something happened to make it warmer in here?

Kyra looks up, amused. He wanders away, more skittish, definitely pleased with events.

Kyra It may be you. But also it's snowing finally. Everything's covered in snow.

Tom My God, you're right. It's beautiful. I'm beginning to like it. I think I've decided I'm going to move in.

Kyra just sits back, as he looks round, comfortably at home.

I was lying there, yeah, in that bed of yours, next to that sort of interesting lump in the mattress you have, I was thinking I could get used to this. Maybe this area isn't so bad. Over there, I was thinking, I'm going to put my telly . . .

Kyra Have you still got that big one?

Tom Oh no. It's much bigger now. I've got a home projection system. Enormous. It's going to take up most of that wall.

He points to her wall of books, then looks round contentedly, imagining the scene.

Yes. The football. Sunday afternoons with the lager . . .

Kyra Do you still support Chelsea?

Tom Of course.

Kyra How are they?

Tom They play the English game. My own game, you know. Kick it up the middle and hope for the best.

He is amused, knowing how perfectly the sentiment suits him personally.

And over there, the stereo. Maybe put Frank in a box room. He'd love it. We could make a life, you and me. Takeaway Indians . . .

Kyra Except you'd need the house next door as well to store all your clothes.

Tom Oh no, I've stopped all that rubbish. I haven't bought clothes . . . well, since Alice died. Do you think I've lost weight? A diet of suffering . . .

He does a little pirouette.

Kyra I didn't notice, in fact.

Tom No.

Kyra I wasn't thinking.

Tom I was thinking, whatever else happens, we always have this.

Tom has said this speculatively, but Kyra says nothing. She is curled up in the chair, at peace. She puts her bread back in the sauce and starts eating again.

I was wondering, you know, it can't be much longer. Your term.

Kyra No. There's only two weeks to go.

Tom Do you know what you're doing for Christmas?

It's just I've now got this place in the sun. It's at the water's edge. It's perfect. The steps lead down to the sea. The island has palm trees. Beaches. Great fish. Unless of course you'd made other plans . . .

But she still doesn't answer, just dipping her bread in the sauce.

I mean, I'm just saying. Think about it.

Kyra Yes.

Tom No pressure.

Kyra No.

Tom No hurry.

Kyra Of course.

Tom If you let me know, say, Friday . . .

At once he holds up a hand.

No, honestly, that's just a joke.

They both smile, liking his half-serious, half-funny tone.

For God's sake, I'm not totally insensitive, I don't think 'One fuck and everything's solved . . .'

She has got up to go to the kitchen to put the kettle on and now passes him.

Kyra Two, though, and that'll be different.

Tom (*smiles*) I mean, well, yes. That sort of thing.

He's pleased with the way this is going. He is at ease in the flat, casually looking at papers on her desk.

So it's good . . .

Kyra What?

Tom This teaching? You enjoy this teaching of yours?

Kyra I wouldn't say 'enjoy'.

Tom Ah . . .

Kyra It can be pretty stressful. But at least it does mean I feel stretched.

Tom Stretched?

Kyra Yes.

She smiles at him.

Surely that's a good thing, isn't it? Don't we think it's good to be stretched?

Tom Oh sure.

They both smile. She is very relaxed.

Kyra I know it sounds crazy, but I'm out at six-thirty – earlier.

Tom My goodness!

Kyra I get on the bus. That simple journey, Kensal Rise to East Ham, in many ways it's the thing I like best about the job. I take a good book. I take my sandwiches. Every day I sit there. Always the top. The top deck's better.

Tom Oh really?

Kyra Always. You hear better things.

She is becoming more expansive.

I've developed this passion for listening.

Tom Blimey.

Kyra It's like an addiction. I love it. I can't get enough. And the more I listen, the more it strikes me, you know . . .

67

what extraordinary courage, what perseverance most
people need just to get on with their lives.

Tom Huh.

Tom nods as if he's taking this seriously.

Kyra And at the start I actually got lucky . . .

Tom Lucky?

Kyra Yes, I met this fantastic Nigerian friend. Adele.
And she's introduced me to the group that she's in.

Tom (*frowns*) A group?

Kyra Yes. It's very informal. We meet every Friday after
work. We have a few drinks. That way you don't feel so
lonely.

Tom That's nice.

Kyra Because when you're working so hard, you're
working such ludicrous hours, the danger is you end up
losing sight of your aims . . .

She smiles at the idea.

And there's always something new. Like at the moment
we have this real problem. We have this private security
firm . . .

Tom At the school?

Kyra Yes. I mean, we've had them there lately. Just for
a few days. It's absolutely disgusting, the staff have
protested like mad.

*Tom is looking at her, amused by the depth of her
involvement.*

We had this problem with burglary. Lootings. A dinner
lady was mugged.

Tom She was mugged at the school?

Kyra Tom, that's not unheard of. Don't take up that Home Counties tone.

Tom I'm not. Just allow a moment of taxpayer's interest that dinner ladies now walk in fear of their lives.

He is making a joke, but she quickly corrects him.

Kyra One dinner lady.

Tom OK.

Kyra Only one incident. It happens. It happened once. But of course it's being used politically. There are – let's face it – certain elements. Partisan elements, who wish the school ill.

Tom For what reason?

Kyra Precisely because it is an enlightened regime.

He looks at her, saying nothing.

Tom, don't look at me like that.

Tom I didn't say anything.

Kyra I'm not a soft liberal. Far from it. My views have got tougher. They've had to. You grow up pretty fast. Education has to be a mixture of haven and challenge. Reassurance, of course. Stability. But also incentive.

Tom I'm not sure I actually know what that means.

But Kyra ignores his humour, really forceful and coherent, wanting to explain.

Kyra Tom, these are kids from very tough backgrounds. At the very least you offer them support. You care for them. You offer them security. You give them an environment where they feel they can grow. But also you make bloody sure you challenge them. You make sure they realise learning is hard. Because if you don't . . . if you only make the safe haven . . . if it's all clap-happy and 'everything the kids do is great' . . . then what are you creating? Emotional toffees, who've actually learnt nothing, but who then have to go back and face the real world.

She is genuinely carried away with this problem as she gets another piece of bread to dip in the sauce. Tom is watching her as non-judgementally as he can.

I mean . . .

Tom I see that.

Kyra I tell you, it's fucking interesting . . .

Tom I'm sure . . .

Kyra Finding that balance . . .

Tom Sure . . .

Kyra Finding it, keeping it there. Tom, there's nothing I've done in my life which is harder. Forty per cent speaking English as a second language!

She stands cheerfully dipping bread in the sauce.

Tom (*a little shocked*) You're really that involved?

Kyra You mean me personally?

Tom Do you go to staff meetings?

Kyra I'm not an activist, if that's what you mean. But I take it quite seriously. Because . . . apart from anything, I'm older than most of the teachers . . .

Tom Really?

Kyra It's a young person's area. A young teacher comes out of college. They think, this is the kind of work I want to do. Then pretty soon . . . well, they move house, they marry . . . They decide they want something a little bit easier.

Tom Mmm.

Kyra A little bit less arduous. Mostly.

Tom But that's not happened to you?

Kyra thinks a moment, then speaks thoughtfully, her tone hardening.

Kyra Early on, you know, I was spat on. Very early. Like maybe, the first day or two. In front of the class, this boy spat on me. He called me an arsewipe. A cunt. I tell you, I can still feel it. Here, on the side of my cheek. I realised I had no defences. That night I went home and I cried. Then I thought, right, this is it. No more crying. From today I learn certain skills – survival skills, if you like. I master certain techniques, if for no other purpose but that in the years ahead . . . maybe even after I've finished perhaps . . . I can say, right, it was a job and I bloody well did it. I learned how you have to survive.

Tom I see. It sounds like a challenge.

Kyra hesitates, deciding whether to risk saying what she actually believes.

Kyra I've seen the way things now are in this country. I think for thirty years I lived in a dream. I don't mean that unkindly. Everything you gave me I treasured. But the fact is, you go out, you open your eyes now, you see this country as it really is . . .

She shakes her head slightly, then waves her hand, as if to imply that nothing more can be said. Tom is watching, suddenly chilled, fearing he has lost her.

Tom But you have friends?

Kyra What?

Tom This life that you're leading? I'm asking, it's not

71

without friends? It's none of my business, but as you describe it . . . I suppose it all sounds a bit *bleak*.

Kyra Tom, the point is, we're mostly totally exhausted . . .

Tom I'm sure.

Kyra What are you asking? Do I go out? Oh yes, I go out! On Fridays, I go to Thank God It's Fridays. On Saturdays, Sainsbury's. And also, yes, I have a few friends.

Tom Well, good.

Kyra Adele is terrific. She lives downstairs. She's the woman who found me this place.

Tom You call that an act of friendship?

Kyra Oh very funny.

Tom It's more like she's trying to freeze you to death . . .

But Kyra's up to this, off to the kettle, and already off on a tack of her own.

Kyra It doesn't bother me. Not after my childhood.

Tom Being pushed by nannies beside stormy English seas . . .

Kyra My dreadful father had something he called heating-bill targets. He'd hold up the heating bills, he'd say, 'By all means, keep this place like a furnace, if that's what you want. But remember: turn it up in September, by February you'll have to be turning it down . . .'

Tom smiles at this.

You know he died?

Tom When?

Kyra Yes. A year ago. Dropped dead on the golf course.

Tom But, Kyra, I don't understand. I thought you were going to get lots of money.

Kyra Ah, well, yes, I thought so as well.

Tom *So?*

Kyra Tom, things are never that simple. This is also a man who kept cats.

Tom Oh come on . . .

He turns away in disbelief, but Kyra is laughing, somehow exhilarated by the account of her father's behaviour.

Kyra It's true. He gave me some money. Not much. In fact, very little. The RSPCA got nearly all of it.

Tom But for Christ's sake, how did you *feel*?

Kyra I didn't feel anything. What difference did it make?

Tom All the difference in the world.

Kyra What do you mean?

Tom frowns, as if it were obvious, not sure why she doesn't get it.

Tom If you'd had his money you would have been able to buy a new place.

Kyra Oh.

Tom I mean, *that's* what I'm saying. You would have been able to leave. You could have bought somewhere decent.

Kyra I mean, yes, I suppose so . . .

Tom You can hardly intend to live here the whole of your life? I suppose I'm asking, what are you planning?

Kyra Planning? Tom, I don't expect this to make any sense to you. But I'm planning to go on just as I am.

She has said what she wanted quite simply, but somehow in the very quiet of the moment there is a sense of challenge. She moves back to the kitchen, in order not to have to deal with his response. Neither of them mistake the fact that a crucial moment has been reached.

Do you want tea?

Tom What?

Kyra Shall I make tea for you?

Tom Tea? Oh, yes. I mean, yes. Of course.

Kyra is putting teabags in the pot. Tom is trying to keep his tone normal.

I don't know. I know it sounds silly. There's something . . . I suppose, an idea of the future. It seems to me important.

Kyra Why, sure. I have an idea of the future as well.

Tom Do you?

Kyra Yes. Yes, I mean loosely. A future doing a job I believe in.

She sees he is still unhappy, his pain undischarged.

Why does that bother you?

Tom Because of a feeling . . . it's to do with something that happened with Alice. Something which happened right at the end.

Kyra stands, milk carton in hand, seeing his pain, knowing she must let him speak.

Do you know how I first met her? I saw her modelling in a magazine. I thought, oh look, it's Audrey Hepburn.

Kyra You cut out her picture. That's what I heard.

Tom I sent her flowers. Red roses. I sent her these roses, day after day. After a month of this, she finally agreed to meet me. In a coffee shop. She was quite charming. Quiet, you know. But she said, 'I'm not a thing, don't you see? You can't buy me. Whatever you give me, I can't ever be bought.' I remember, even then, I was just laughing. I said, 'My God, do you not understand?'

He has become expansive, his old energy back as he tells this story, as well as a genuine indignation about his motives.

You see, by that time, I'd already started. I had a couple of restaurants, nothing too grand. But I'd already worked out – I'm not an idiot – you either run money or else it runs you. If you keep your money . . . if you're frightened to spend it, you become its prisoner. OK, sure, when you're making it, be as mean as you like. But when you spend it, just give. Give. Show your contempt for it. I said to her, there in that café, 'I give for the pleasure of giving. Just for the pleasure itself.'

Kyra But Alice understood that.

Tom No. She never accepted it. I promise you. Right to the end. She always thought if I was giving, then somehow I must want something back.

Kyra is beginning to understand now, instinctively knowing where he's heading.

Kyra You told me you built her that room to be ill in.

Tom That's what I'm saying. Exactly. That's what I mean. I gave it to her because . . . oh shit . . . I preferred it that she should be happy. What's wrong with that? I wanted her to die in a place that she liked.

75

He goes across the room and takes the whisky bottle.
He pours himself a scotch, which he does not yet drink.

While she was dying, every night I brought her these flowers. The very same flowers – red roses – that I'd given when we first met. Then one day she was lying, her head on the pillow, I thought asleep. She suddenly said, 'No. No more flowers.' I said, 'Why not?' She said, 'It isn't the same.' She said, 'The flowers were when you loved me. You and I were really in love.' She said, 'Now I don't want them.'

For a moment there are tears in his eyes, his grief almost overwhelming him.

She was one week from dying. Kyra, that's fucking hard.

Kyra Yes.

Tom I'd tried to explain to her . . . many times I'd tried to talk about you. But she'd cut me off. She'd made up her mind. She had her opinion. And believe me, she wasn't willing to change. She knew exactly what she was doing. The one thing she had was her moral authority. A wrong had been done. That was it. The last thing she wanted was to change her view of things, and certainly not by listening to mine.

He turns and looks at Kyra.

She used her death as a way of punishing me.

Kyra Tom . . .

Tom No, really. Really! You think I'm exaggerating. She treated me as if I were still some sort of schoolboy: you betrayed me; that's it. Now in my opinion that's not bloody fair.

Kyra Tom!

He moves away, bitter, his drink now in his hand, not looking at Kyra.

Tom What I'm saying: it wasn't one-sided. It wasn't simply that I was a shit. You have to deal with this – part of the problem was Alice. Right to the end, she couldn't forgive. And even now I feel out on a limb.

Kyra I see that.

Tom I get home from the restaurants – that's if I bother to go in at all – at ten-thirty I think that I'm tired, but then two hours later I'm sitting up, stock still in bed. I go for a walk on the Common. Sometimes. I go out around three. Just looking around, and thinking. Always the same thought. I find myself thinking: something must come of all this.

He knocks back his scotch in one, a wildness now starting to appear in him.

I try to go out. I try to enjoy myself. I think: oh tonight, I'll go out, I'll get drunk. But my foot's on the floor, I'm pumping, I'm flooring that fucking pedal, and nothing's moving. I'm getting no fucking pleasure at all.

Sensing where he is heading, she is nervous. But he is gaining in strength, as if the worst of this confession is over.

It's like, you know, like earlier you were saying, how all the time you felt you'd been loyal to her. You'd also been loyal to something inside yourself. I suppose I feel: what happens now? Do we just leave it? Just leave it completely? And if we did, isn't that like admitting our guilt?

Kyra Tom . . .

Tom No, look, isn't that like saying we did behave

shabbily? And, oh, it was just an affair! And then when she found out, it was over? Doesn't that seem to you wrong?

Kyra looks at him, then frowns, moving away a little. She is decisive, trying to be as serious as he was.

Kyra Tom, you know there's something which you do have to deal with. There is this whole world I'm now in. It's a world with quite different values. The people, the *thinking* is different . . . it's not at all like the world which you know.

Tom looks at her, saying nothing.

I mean, if we ever . . . if we . . . what I'm saying . . . if we can work out a way of keeping in touch . . . then you have to know that I have made certain decisions. And these are decisions you have to respect.

Tom Why, I mean, yes.

Kyra Good.

Tom Surely. I'm not a complete idiot.

Kyra No.

Tom You're saying you've made an informed and serious choice.

A note of mischief is beginning to be detectable. Kyra looks at him suspiciously.

You've chosen to live in near-Arctic conditions somewhere off the North Circular. No, really. Why should I have any problem with that?

He is beginning to get into his swing, exaggeratedly gesturing round the room now as he pours himself more scotch.

78

I promise. I'm deeply impressed with it. I assure you,
it gives me no problem at all. Put a bucket in the corner
to shit in, and you can take hostages and tell them this
is Beirut!

*There is suddenly some savagery in his voice, but Kyra
has decided to stay calm and not be bullied.*

Kyra Tom, I have to tell you, this place is really quite
reasonable.

Tom Oh really?

Kyra As it happens, I get it at a very cheap rent.

Tom I should hope!

Kyra It's you, Tom. The fact is, you've lost all sense of
reality. This place isn't special. It's not specially horrible.
For God's sake, this is how everyone lives!

Tom Oh please, please let's be serious . . .

Kyra I mean it.

Tom Kyra, honestly . . .

Kyra No, this is interesting, this is the heart of it. It
wasn't until I left your restaurants . . . those carpaccio-
and ricotta-stuffed restaurants of yours . . . it wasn't till
I deserted that Chelsea milieu . . .

Tom Which in my memory you liked pretty well . . .

She stops, not at all put off by his interruption.

Kyra I do like it, yes, that isn't something I'd ever deny . . .
but it wasn't until I got out of your limousines . . . until
I left that warm bubble of good taste and money in
which you exist . . .

Tom Thank you.

Kyra It was only then I remembered most people live in a way which is altogether different.

Tom Well, of course.

Kyra And you have no right to look down on that life!

Tom You're right.

Kyra Thank you.

Tom Of course. That's right.

Kyra waits, knowing this will not be all.

However. In one thing you're different. I do have to say to you, Kyra, in one thing you're different from everyone else in this part of town.

Kyra How is that?

Tom You're the only person who has fought so hard to get into it, when everyone else is desperate to get out!

Kyra All right, very funny. For as long as I've known you, you've loved this.

Tom Loved what?

Kyra Whenever I say anything serious, there's nothing you like more than winding me up.

Tom Yes, I'm afraid that is true. But it's hard to resist winding people up when they've little metal keys sticking out of their backs.

Kyra And what does that mean?

But Tom is already moving across the room to pour himself a whisky, feeling himself on top in the argument.

Tom OK, you're right. I know nothing about anything. As you would say, I'm pampered. I admit it. Frank drives me round. But even I know that East Ham is on one side

80

of London, and this place we're now in is somewhere quite else!

Kyra So? That is just chance.

Tom Oh really?

Kyra That's just how it happened. A friend found this flat! Adele was desperate. She was in the most desperate straits.

Tom just gives her a blank, sardonic stare.

All right, I admit it wasn't exactly convenient . . .

Tom It was sort of a sacrifice, is that the word? You work in one dreadful place. But of course for you, that's not nearly enough. You must punish yourself further by living in another dreadful place. And spend the whole day commuting between them!

Kyra Oh, for God's sake, that's not what I do.

Tom And, what's more, listening to the people on the journey, mopping up their every remark. As if they were Socrates, as if they were Einstein, just because they happen to travel by bus.

Kyra goes out to the kitchen to get the tea. But it doesn't stop him.

Remember? I come from bog-ordinary people, me. No solicitors hanging on my family tree! If you start out ordinary, I promise you, one thing you're spared, this sentimental illusion that ordinary people can teach you anything at all.

Kyra has been going to fill the teapot with hot water, but she is so provoked by him that she now comes out of the kitchen area, nodding vigorously.

Kyra I tell you, it's this, it's this that's so interesting. How you're threatened . . .

Tom Me, threatened?

Kyra Of course.

Tom By what?

Kyra I remember. As soon as any quite normal person is praised – a waiter, a chambermaid, someone who's doing a quite lowly job – you become like a dog on a leash. You can't wait for them to do something stupid, and great! You've found your moment to bite.

Tom That isn't true.

Kyra Oh, isn't it?

But now it is her turn to feel confident.

I remember once saying I thought that Frank did his best to hide it, but underneath he was really quite bright. You said, 'Oh come on, let's face it, Kyra, there's a *reason* he's a driver . . .'

Tom Well, what am I meant to say? You want me to lie? It's only the *truth*!

Kyra You don't talk to him. You don't even talk to him.

Tom Frank? I talk to Frank. He tells me how Tottenham are doing, he tells me who Cindy Crawford is sleeping with now . . .

Kyra Oh, really!

Tom I mean, please. I'm not saying that Frank was born stupid. Believe me, I wouldn't say that. But if you turned him upside down, his brains would come out on the floor.

Kyra Why do you think I'm working where I am? I'm
sick of this denial of everyone's potential. Whole groups
of people just written off!

*But Tom is moving away, drinking, now thoroughly
enjoying himself.*

Tom Oh I see, right, you've been reborn. Now I
understand you . . .

Kyra Tom . . .

Tom You see good in everyone now! How comforting!
Of course. But if I could be reborn as anyone, I'm not
sure Julie Andrews would be my first choice.

*Now it is Tom's turn to go through some sort of
barrier, suddenly losing patience, at last wanting to
put an end to things.*

I mean, Kyra, please! As you'd say: let's be serious! You
must know what's happening. Jesus Christ, just look at
this place! I mean, it is screaming its message. For
instance, I tell you, look at that heater! Sitting there
fulfilling some crucial psychological role in your life.
There are shops, I mean, you know, *shops*, proper shops
that exist in the street. These shops sell heaters. They are
not expensive. But of course they are not what you're
looking for. Because these heaters actually heat!

*Tom shakes his head, moving across the room to get
more scotch, reaching the real centre of his complaint.*

You accuse *me* of being a monster. You say that I'm
guilty. You tell me that I'm fucking up the life of my
horrible son. But the difference is, at least I *admit* it. At
least this evening I took that on board. But you! Jesus!
It's like talking to a Moonie. I've not set off like some
fucking missionary to conduct some experiment in finding
out just how tough I can make my own way of life.

Kyra You think that's what I'm doing? You really think that's what this is?

But Tom is already behaving as if it were all too ridiculous for words.

Tom I mean, I've been listening, I've been listening to this stuff you've been telling me – the bus! The school! Even the kind of place that you choose to live – and, I'm thinking, my God, my dear old friend Kyra's joined some obscure religious order. The Kensal Rise chapter! She's performing an act of contrition.

He suddenly laughs, the next thought striking him.

You say to me, Lord goodness, everything's psychological. I can't be happy because I've not come to terms with things that I've done. But you – you're like Page One. A textbook Freudian study! Your whole fucking life is an act of denial! It's so bloody clear. You know what it's called? Throwing Teddy in the corner! You're running so fast you don't even know you're in flight.

Kyra Running?

Tom Yes. Of course. Yes, it's obvious.

Kyra I suppose you couldn't tell me. I'm running from what?

Tom Do I need to say?

His look, half modest, half arrogant, infuriates her as much as his answer, and she turns away exasperated.

Kyra Oh honestly, this really . . . I mean, that is contemptible! Why do men always think it's all about them?

Tom Because in this case it is!

But Kyra never even reaches the kitchen before turning on him again.

Kyra I'll say this for you. You always understood procedure. You've always known the order in which things should be done. You fuck me first. *Then* you criticise my life-style . . .

Tom Now Kyra . . .

Kyra Doing it the other way round, of course, would be a terrible tactical mistake.

Tom All right, fair enough.

Kyra I mean, if you'd started by calling me weak and perverse, if you'd told me straight off I was fleeing from you . . . But the great restaurateur knows the order. You don't serve the pudding before the fucking soup!

She has said this with such venom that she now turns and goes to get their tea.

Tom I refrained from commenting only because it's so bloody obvious. I didn't actually think it needed to be said. You have a first-class degree, for Christ's sake.

Kyra Oh, really!

Tom You came out top of your year.

Kyra puts his tea down and stands by the table drinking her own.

I can't see anything more tragic, more stupid than you sitting here and throwing your talents away.

Kyra Am I throwing them away? I don't think so.

Tom Kyra, you're teaching kids at the bottom of the heap!

Kyra Well, exactly! I would say I was using my talents. It's just I'm using them in a way of which you don't approve.

She has put down her tea and now goes into the darkened bedroom, leaving the door open.

Tom (*carrying on as if she were still there*) God, you claim *I'm* dismissive of people, you think I don't give them a chance. But any of those people who work for me . . . when they saw what you were doing with the gifts that God gave you . . . they would be so bloody furious.

Kyra (*off*) Would they?

Tom Of course! They wouldn't understand you, any more than I do. They would simply say you were shallow and spoilt. You know you could be teaching at any university. They'd take you today! Anywhere you liked! But oh no! Of course not, for Kyra nowhere is good enough. Except of course somewhere that's no good at all . . .

He stands, satisfied by his own irony, now becoming a generalised bad temper.

Of course it's only this country, only here in this country, it's thought to be a crime to get on. Anything rather than achieve!

Kyra What you call 'achieve'!

She has appeared again in the bedroom doorway. She has dressed and put her jeans back on. He looks at her.

Tom Sitting in North London, just spinning your wheels. Out of stubbornness. Sheer goddamned female stubbornness.

Kyra 'Female'? That's a very odd choice of word.

He knows that he has betrayed a source of his anger and she at once has an ascendancy in the argument with him. She picks the books up off the floor and begins regretfully.

You see, I'm afraid I think this is typical. It's something that's happened . . . it's only happened of late. That people should need to ask why I'm helping these children. I'm helping them because they need to be helped.

Tom turns away unconvinced by the simplicity of the answer, but she is already moving back to the table with the books, her anger beginning to rise.

Everyone makes merry, discussing motive. Of course she does this. She works in the East End. She only does it because she's unhappy. She does it because of a lack in herself. She doesn't have a man. If she had a man, she wouldn't need to do it. Do you think she's a dyke? She must be fucked up, she must be an Amazon, she must be a weirdo to choose to work where she does . . . Well, I say, what the hell does it matter why I'm doing it? Why anyone goes out and helps? The reason is hardly of primary importance. If I didn't do it, it wouldn't get done.

She is now suddenly so passionate, so forceful, that Tom is silenced.

I'm tired of these sophistries. I'm tired of these right-wing fuckers. They wouldn't lift a finger themselves. They work contentedly in offices and banks. Yet now they sit pontificating in parliament, in papers, impugning our motives, questioning our judgements. And why? Because they themselves need to feel better by putting down everyone whose work is so much harder than theirs. (*She stands, nodding.*) You only have to say the words 'social worker' . . . 'probation officer' . . .

'counsellor' . . . for everyone in this country to sneer. Do you know what social workers do? Every day? They try and clear out society's drains. They clear out the rubbish. They do what no one else is doing, what no one else is willing to do. And for that, oh Christ, do we thank them? No, we take our own rotten consciences, wipe them all over the social worker's face, and say, 'If –' FUCK! – 'if *I* did the job, then of course if I did it . . . oh no, excuse me, I wouldn't do it like that . . .'

She turns, suddenly aggressive.

Well, I say: 'OK, then, fucking do it, journalist. Politician, talk to the addicts. Hold families together. Stop the kids from stealing in the streets. Deal with couples who beat each other up. You fucking try it, why not? Since you're so full of advice. Sure, come and join us. This work is one big casino. By all means. Anyone can play. But there's only one rule. You can't play for nothing. You have to buy some chips to sit at the table. And if you won't pay with your own time . . . with your own effort . . . then I'm sorry. Fuck off!'

She has said this with such shocking brutality and callousness that Tom is stilled for a moment.

Tom All right, very well, I do see what you're saying.

Kyra I should hope so.

Tom This work you're doing leaves you deeply fulfilled.

Kyra flashes him a look of contempt.

But, Kyra, are you also saying you're happy?

Kyra Oh come on now, Tom, that isn't fair!

Tom Why not?

Kyra That's a shitty kind of question. You know. It's a game! I'm not playing that game!

But Tom has already moved away to get more whisky, his poise back and amused.

Tom The funny thing is – do you see? – you talk about escaping your father. You were always telling us. The chilly, cold childhood you had! But here you are, building exactly the same kind of bunker that he did . . .

Kyra Nonsense!

Tom Living exactly the same kind of isolated life. You end up here in this room. With ice on the windowpane. The wind still blowing off the bloody English Channel. And no one allowed to get near . . . (*He is suddenly quieter.*) The only time you haven't been lonely, the only time you actually lived a proper life among friends, was when you lived in our family. And you know bloody well that is true.

Kyra doesn't answer, just looking at him as he moves away, sure of himself.

Kyra On no account must I be happy. On no account must I have succeeded in getting away.

This is so near the mark that Tom just looks guilty, as she smiles, amused now at being able to satirise him.

You walk in this room, and at once you're picking up folders . . .

Tom What folders?

Kyra Glancing at the bookshelves. Lifting my papers. Oh my God, does she have a boyfriend?

Tom Oh, really!

Kyra Is there any trace of a *man*?

Tom I never did any such thing.

Kyra Looking for any male objects. Any gifts. Any ties. Any socks.

Tom Oh come on now, that's ridiculous.

Kyra Is it? Your whole body language expresses it. Ownership! I think you've patrolled this room fifty times. Inspected its edges. You even smelt the fucking bed! Like an animal. The whole thing's about possession.

Tom Kyra, you know that's not true.

But she is having too much fun to stop.

Kyra I mean, apart from anything, there is the arrogance, the unbelievable arrogance of this middle-aged man to imagine that other people's behaviour – his ex's behaviour – is always in some direct reaction to *him*.

She laughs now, going to get herself more tea and knowing she is building a formidable case.

Tom Well, it is!

Kyra You were saying – my God! – you were telling me you don't think of us as objects.

Tom I don't.

Kyra We're not possessions, that's what you say! Yet you stand there complaining your wife omitted to forgive you.

Tom She did!

Kyra I have to ask you, Tom, why the hell should she? When all the time you were dreaming of somebody else.

Tom All right.

Kyra I mean, Jesus . . .

Tom All right!

For the first time he is badly rattled. She is shaking her head in disbelief now.

Kyra Earlier this evening you were telling me that all the time she was dying you were meanwhile thinking about me! That's right! Yet you're standing there seriously demanding my sympathy for the terrible hurt which you're claiming *she's* done to *you*!

She has blasted him with this last phrase and he can't answer. So now she wanders away, so sure of her point that she laughs.

I mean, even you, Tom . . . even you must see it. I know, being a successful businessman – sweet wife, me adoring you as well! – you're richly deserving of compassion, I know your life was really jolly hard . . .

Tom All right. Very well . . .

Kyra But even you must see the balance of sympathy in this case maybe . . . just *maybe* lies somewhere else.

Tom You only say that because you weren't around.

At once Kyra turns impatiently, going to the kitchen, riled by the old accusation.

Kyra Oh, that again!

Tom Yes. Because that's at the heart of it. That's at the heart of all this.

Kyra Is that what you think?

Tom You know what I'm saying is right. You simply walked out! You simply walked out on me! That is a fact.

He points a finger at her as if she were a wayward employee.

And what's more, you did not consult me. You made a decision which I never approved.

Kyra (*at once not able to take his indignation seriously*) Approved? You mean, you signed no consent form . . .

Tom (*at once catching her tone*) All right . . .

Kyra You took no executive decision? You mean you never 'discounted' me, was that your phrase? I was never filed next to Alice. Diminishing assets!

Tom Oh, very funny. Oh yes, very smart!

He is moving away, nodding as if this is all too familiar for words. But she is enjoying herself, into a riff now.

Kyra You did not downsize me, delayer me, you did not have a drains-up meeting to discuss the strategic impact of letting me go? You mean I just went and there was no management buy-out?

Tom Oh, is this your idea of satire? And I suppose it's meant to be at my expense?

He turns, only half joking, his sense of humour departing.

I knew this job of yours would make you a smartarse. Teacher! Of course. It's a joke. All teachers look down on business! They all mock business!

Kyra Tom, I'm just asking, but are you developing just a bit of a chip?

Tom Not at all.

Bad-temperedly he moves to get himself more scotch, but nothing will stop her now.

Kyra I mean, like earlier . . . earlier this evening, you were going on about 'business'. 'No one understands *business*,' that's what you said. Suddenly, I must say,

I hear it everywhere. These so-called achievers telling us they have a grievance. The whole of society must get down on their knees and thank them, because they do something they no longer call 'making money'. Now we must call it something much nicer. Now we must call it 'the creation of wealth' . . .

Tom looks at her uneasily, but she is really enjoying herself.

Putting money in your pocket. No longer the happy matter of just piling up coins. Oh no. We all have to say it's an intrinsically worthy activity. And the rest of us, we're ungrateful . . . we're immoral . . . we must simply be *envious* . . . if we don't constantly say so out loud. You have to laugh. It's this modern phenomenon. Suddenly this new disease! Self-pity! Self-pity of the rich! No longer do they simply accumulate. Now they want people to line up and thank them as well.

She moves towards him, more serious now.

Well, I tell you, I spend my time among very different people. People who often have nothing at all. And I find in them one great virtue at least: unlike the rich, they have no illusions that they must once have done something right! Nor do they suffer from delicate feelings. They don't sit about whining. How misunderstood and undervalued they are. No, they're getting on with the day-to-day struggle of trying to survive on the street. And that street, I tell you . . . if you get out there . . . if you actually have to learn to survive, well, it's a thousand times harder than leading an export drive, being in government, or . . . yes, I have to say, it's even harder than running a bank.

She nods at this gentle reference to what he said earlier. She is quieter now.

And the sad thing, Tom, is that you once knew that. When I first met you, you knew that full well. It marked you. That was the charm of you. It made you different. And I'm not sure the moment at which you forgot.

Tom looks at her.

Tom Well, thank you.

Kyra Not at all.

Tom I needed that lecture.

Kyra It wasn't a lecture.

Tom It was good of you. Henceforth I'll try not to complain.

He looks down, quietly self-mocking.

Of course I'm disqualified from having any feelings, because I've made some money.

Kyra I didn't say that.

Tom No, you said something near it. For you, people are no longer people, it seems. Now they're symbols. And I am a symbol of . . . what does it matter? Something you're plainly angry with.

Kyra Oh come on, you know it's not as simple as that.

Tom (*not worried by her irritation, going on unfazed*) I can see that you're furious. I'm not sure I wholly know why.

Kyra Come with me. Just spend a day with me. Then I think it will be pretty clear.

Tom Oh I'm sure. There's plenty of injustice. God knows, it's always been there. The question is why you've gone out to look for it.

*Both of them know a decisive moment has been reached
between them. Tom is quite calm, almost smiling.*

You see, it's a funny thing, you've always said yes to
everyone. It's something I noticed right from the start.
Everyone liked you for this very reason. The first time they
meet you, they always say, 'Kyra, what a nice person!'
Always. 'Kyra, no question, she's a good sort . . .' (*He
stops, gentle, knowing where he's going.*) It's typical.
Your friend needs a tenant. To you, oh, it's no problem.
You'll do it. There's no inconvenience. You're happy to
do it. That's who you are. Even for us, when you started.
You were happy to babysit when Alice and I wanted to
go out. It used to amaze me. I used to ask myself why
there was only one person, one person in the world my
friend Kyra ever said no to. And that is the man who
asked her if she'd be his wife.

Kyra sits silent, just looking at him.

I remember, I remember that morning so clearly. I
remember coming downstairs. Then you were at the
office. I rang you. I said, 'I'm afraid she's discovered.
This is our moment. It's finally possible. So now at last
we make a clean break . . .' You put down the phone.
For the rest of the day I couldn't find you. At the office
they said you'd simply walked out.

Kyra I did.

Tom Why? My marriage was finished. You knew that.
And Alice herself had no wish to go on.

Kyra doesn't move, just watching.

You could have had a thousand reactions. You could
have gone to try and talk to Alice. You could have come
to me. But no. You did something cowardly. You picked
up your bags and walked out.

Kyra looks at him darkly, not answering.

Oh, you always said you did it for Alice.

Kyra Partly.

Tom That's what you told me. When I finally found you, you said, 'I had to do it. I did it for Alice. And for the children as well.' But that wasn't so. Well, was it?

Kyra What do you want me to say?

She looks at him resentfully, as if cornered. Tom wanders away to get more whisky, having the concession he wanted.

Tom You didn't give a fuck about Alice's feelings. Alice's feelings were just an excuse. I mean, even tonight, you were telling me, you told me: an adulterous love is the best. Well, let me tell you it isn't. The best thing is loving with your whole heart. Yes, and what's more, out in the open. The two of you. That's when there's risk. Not the risk of discovery. But the risk of two people really setting off on their own. But that means all the things you've avoided. Really giving yourself.

He has no need to press his argument any more. His tone is sorrowful.

Even now you're doing it. You're telling me how much you love the people! How much you're in love with the courage of the people on the bus! Yes, of course you love them. Because in three minutes you can get off.

Kyra stays sitting, stubborn now, her mood darkening from sadness into resentment.

Do you think I don't see it? Loving the people's an easy project for you. Loving a person . . . now that's something different. Something that will take you right to the brink.

Kyra That isn't fair.

Tom Isn't it? I think it is. You love the people because you don't have to go home with them. You love them because you don't have to commit.

Kyra (*quiet, not moving, looking down*) You're very cruel. I've made a life here.

Tom Yes. You can't open a paper, that's what you say. You have banished papers, you tell me, you've banished TV. I mean, why? What's the reason? It's some kind of insanity. What, you feel the world is somehow *letting you down*? You go off to do what you call 'rebuilding'. 'Rebuild your life', that's what you say. Start again. But how can you? Kyra, look at you now! It won't even work. It can't work. Because it's built on a negative. It's built on escape.

He shakes his head, genuinely infuriated now by her apparent passivity, sitting unmoving in her chair.

What is it in you? This thing that you have. Why doesn't it yield? I don't understand it.

Kyra No. I honestly don't think you do.

Her tone is icy. At last something has hardened in her. Tom tries to backtrack.

Tom Look . . .

Kyra You never will, Tom. It's the difference between us. It's kind of a gulf.

She is deadly in her calm. She seems to be suppressing her strongest feelings.

You're right. I've become my anger.

She looks down.

And now I think you should go.

Tom Go?

Kyra Yes. You got what you wanted. You wanted me to say I never loved you enough. Well, plainly, in your view, I didn't. And so that's the end of it. Isn't it?

She moves to the other side of the table where she takes up the pile of books. She puts them down, puts on her glasses, and calmly takes the first one to work on.

And these are books which I have to mark.

Tom is so inflamed by her control that he suddenly loses his temper. He impetuously picks up the top book and throws it haphazardly across the room.

Tom Oh come on, these fucking books, these fucking children. Who are you fooling? Marking books in the middle of the night! Do you think that I'm fooled? You know what we had. Why can't you admit it?

He has screamed at her and picked up books and thrown them across the room. Because she does not respond, he picks up a couple more books. Then pushes over the pile. It is a gesture of mess and futility.

Kyra I think you should change.

Tom looks at her a moment, then he turns and goes into the darkness of the bedroom. Kyra is plainly shaken by what has just happened. She goes to the kitchen and pours herself a glass of water, which she drinks. She moves across to the sideboard and takes a small card out of a drawer. She then moves back to the telephone and dials a number.

(*On the phone.*) Yes, hello. I'm at 43 Cannon Road. There's a friend of mine going to Wimbledon. (*She listens.*) I understand that. A doorbell. Hollis. (*She waits a second.*)

Thank you. Yes, as soon as you can.

She puts the phone down. She stands a moment, then goes to sit down again at the table. She is still for a moment. Tom comes back into the room in his suit, but carrying his shoes. They ignore each other as he sits down in an armchair to put his shoes on.

I got you a cab.

Tom Oh, all right . . .

Kyra I didn't suppose you were going to call Frank.

She looks kindly at him, trying to sound natural. But they are both shattered. It's past three and nothing either of them intended has happened.

They say they're not sure, but they think they can get through the snow.

Tom By the time I get home it's going to be time to go into work.

He is now dressed. He looks a complete mess, his clothes flung on, crumpled and untidy. She looks at him, some genuine warmth in her voice.

Kyra You look ridiculous. I'm afraid you've forgotten your tie.

She goes out into the bedroom to look for it. He looks round the room for a moment, knowing it is the last time he will see it. She comes back in and hands him his tie. He takes it and goes over to a small mirror which hangs over the kitchen sink. She sits at the table.

You ask me if I remember that day. I remember the days before it. Why I wrote those letters at all.

Tom shifts. She looks directly at him.

Do you remember why I had written?

Tom Of course. You went off on holiday,

Kyra Yes. For once, on my own. Because you two couldn't come – I think a new restaurant was opening.

Tom That's right.

Kyra And I was exhausted. So I insisted. And you said, 'Kyra, you promise, whatever you do, you must write . . .'

Tom They were wonderful letters.

Kyra I'm glad you thought so. I can remember, the first day going down to the beach and thinking . . . I am going to make this man very happy. I am going to tell him what he really wants to hear. It was also the truth. Even now, I remember, I remember writing, 'You will never know the happiness you've given me. I'll never love anyone as I love you . . .'

She is so direct and simple that it is as if she is saying them right now for the first time.

After a few days, people on the beach were all looking and laughing. This strange English girl, I was chalk white, under a parasol, ordering just an occasional beer.

She seems lost in the memory, but now she once more looks him straight in the eye.

You say I can't give, that I've never given. I gave in those letters. I gave my whole heart. 'Just to think of you fills me with warmth and with kindness. All I want is that it should go on . . .'

Tom Yes.

Kyra I was on the beach, but I was in London, with you, as you tore at the envelopes, opening the envelopes with your big hands. I could see you. The overwhelming power of thought.

Tom stirs as soon as she resumes.

Then of course I got back. I said to you, 'Tom, those letters I wrote . . .' You said to me, 'Yes, don't worry, it's fine, there's a safe in our house. It's upstairs in the attic. There's no reason Alice would ever go near . . .'

Tom No.

Kyra Then, later, that morning. My first question to you on the phone: 'How did she find them?' 'Oh,' you said . . .

Tom Sure . . .

Kyra Just for the night, you'd left them tucked away in the kitchen.

Tom That's right.

He moves in, wanting to defend himself.

But I told you, the night before I'd got them out to read them. I admit, I'd had a few drinks. Alice was asleep. I thought, I'm going to wake her if I go up to the attic.

He stops a second, trying to make his explanation as smooth as possible.

So I thought, just for this evening, I'll hide them in the kitchen. Then later I'll put them back.

Kyra But?

Tom Oh, for Christ's sake, you know what happened. I was going out to work and . . . Look, I don't know . . . Frank had been waiting, he was bullying me, telling me I had to hurry up. For whatever reason . . . I went off to work, and yes, I forgot!

Kyra You left them in the kitchen.

Tom Look, I'm not saying it was highly intelligent. I mean, at the time, I said it was crazy. I told you: it was stupid. It was remiss.

Kyra No, it wasn't remiss, Tom. It was deliberate.

There is a sudden silence. You can see Tom thinking how he is going to respond, whether to protest, or to consent.

Please, please don't start lying! Whatever you do, don't start lying to me!

Tom stands, chastened by her reaction. Then her own anguish begins urgently to appear.

Of course. Do you think I'm proud of it? Do you think it was easy? Just to walk out of your lives? Every day, I've thought of the wreckage, of what must have happened to Alice and you. But I couldn't stay. I couldn't. Breeze in to Alice and say, 'Please understand, in my mind I never betrayed you. Really, I promise you, you have our everlasting love and respect . . .'?

She smiles bitterly at the absurdity of it.

Do you think we could have been happy? You and me? Happy like murderers, perhaps. And all the time I'd be thinking: the one thing . . . the one thing I asked him never to do . . . he went off and did it deliberately.

Tom Kyra, that just isn't true!

He turns away, knowing he cannot argue any more. And his concession calms her.

Kyra We had six years of happiness. And it was you who had to spoil it. With you, when something is right, it's never enough. You don't value happiness. You don't even realise. Because you always want more.

She is beginning to be upset by what she is saying. He knows it is true.

It's part of the restlessness, it's part of your boyishness. You say you knew that I loved and valued your family. You knew how much you were loved. But that can't be true. Well, can it? Because if you'd realised, why would you have thrown it away?

She looks at him, completely sincere.

I love you, for God's sake. I still love you. I loved you more than anyone on earth. But I'll never trust you, after what happened. It's what Alice said. You'll never grow up. There is no peace in you. I know this. For me there is no comfort. There's no sense of rest. The energy's wonderful. Oh God, I tell you the energy's what everyone needs. But with the energy comes the restlessness. And I can't live in that way.

Tom (*serious now, pleading, unflinching*) You wanted a family. You say what you loved was family. I'm happy to start a family again.

Kyra No. It's too late. And you know it.

Tom Do I? Yes, I suppose that I do.

The doorbell rings. She turns and looks to it. They are both standing, some way between them. Tom does not move.

Tom The point is, I lived a long time next to cancer. Apart from anything it fucks up your brain. You start thinking things are deliberate. That everything's some kind of judgement. And once you think that, you might as well die.

The bell rings again. She opens the window to call down to the street.

Kyra He's coming.

*But he does not move. She picks up the bag he
brought the whisky in, and puts the remains inside.*

Your whisky.

But he does not take it.

Tom I came here today, wanting forgiveness. I thought
you'd say, well, OK. Things do just happen, that's how
it is. The world's not a court. Most things are chance.
That's what I'm saying. A girl of eighteen walks down
the King's Road . . . And in that girl, there's infinite
potential. I suppose I just wanted some of that back.

*His appeal to her has been so sincere and from the
heart that she cannot answer. The bell rings again.
Tom smiles grimly, giving way to the inevitable. He
moves across the room and kisses her on the cheek.*

Goodbye.

Kyra Goodbye, then.

*Tom looks at her a moment, then moves to the door,
but turns back before he goes.*

Tom At least, if nothing more, come to one of the
restaurants. There are one or two which are really not
bad. I promise you, you know, on a good night, it's
almost as nice as eating at home.

*He turns without looking at her and walks out of
the room, closing the door behind. She listens to the
sound of him going off down the stairs. She looks a
moment round the room, turns out the lights, then
goes across to the little heater, and pulls the plug out.
The red glow dies.*

SCENE TWO

*From the darkness, morning light begins to shine at the
window. It is in a small white square, throwing eerie
shadows across the chilly room. Nothing has moved
from last night. There is a desolation of bottles and
glasses, the remains of the spaghetti, the abandoned
tray of cutlery on the floor and the schoolbooks still
scattered over the carpet. The room looks wrecked.
Already there is a loud banging, knocking and ringing
at the downstairs door. After a moment or two, Kyra
comes flying through from the bedroom, pulling on her
clothes as she comes. She has managed to get her jeans
on, and is now just piling on sweaters and shirts. She
has plainly been woken up by the racket as she comes
through at amazing speed.*

Kyra All right, for Christ's sake, what is it? I'm coming.
What the hell's going on?

*She goes out of the room. We can hear her going
downstairs and opening the door.*

(*Off.*) Oh, I don't believe it.

Edward (*off*) Surprise!

Kyra (*off*) What are you doing here? What have you got
there? Come on, don't stand out there freezing.

*The sound of the door being closed and them
scrambling together, laughing, excited up the stairs.
Their cheerful early morning vitality contrasts with
the sombre mood of the previous scene.*

Edward (*off*) It's kind of a joke. I just hope I can get it
upstairs.

Kyra (*off*) Well, I must say!

*There is a moment, and then the two of them appear.
Edward, wrapped in scarves, is carrying an enormous
styrofoam box which he has trouble getting in through
the door. It is a couple of feet wide and a foot high,
and appears to be heavy. Edward is talking as he
comes in. Kyra follows.*

Edward I don't know, at the time it seemed funny . . .

Kyra Just put it down over here.

*She is laughing as she closes the door and clears the
central table for him to put the box down.*

Jesus, what time is it?

Edward I was frightened I'd miss you. I was frightened
you'd already be gone.

Kyra Christ Almighty, I've overslept.

*She has found a little clock in the middle of the night's
debris.*

It's almost seven o'clock . . .

Edward I don't know. Perhaps this is a crazy idea.

*He has put the box down in the middle of the table.
Rather sheepishly he mimes a fanfare with a little
tooting noise.*

Kyra I don't know what it is.

Edward I've brought you breakfast. You said you missed
breakfast more than anything else.

Kyra Oh, Edward, I don't believe it.

Edward So here it is!

*He opens his arms like Dandini, a young man half full
of pride, half embarrassment.*

You make a wish and it's here.

*Kyra stands watching as at once he moves towards the
box to take its lid off. Inside the large box there are
various smaller ones, either for refrigeration or to
keep things hot. But first, Edward takes out a linen
tablecloth which he spreads over her table. There is a
lighthearted gaiety in his manner, which seems to have
changed from the previous night.*

I went to the Ritz. I've a friend. He's my best friend
actually. He was at school with me. He works in the
kitchen.

Kyra Is he in his gap year?

Edward He is.

*They smile at last night's joke. Edward is now getting
out a load of Ritz silver – knives and forks, pudding
spoons, salt and pepper pots, and an ornate butter dish.*

And he smuggled me this stuff. All this silver. Apparently
they lose thirty ashtrays a week. People put them in their
pockets. Still, that's how the rich stay rich, I suppose.
Look – a real butter dish with proper ice cubes.

Kyra Unbelievable.

Edward I'm afraid the toast's a bit hard.

*Edward has got out a silver toast rack with the toast
already ranged on it. He is working at great speed and
with considerable accomplishment. Kyra is so taken
aback that she does not move, just watches delighted as
he works like a professional waiter, laying the china now.*

Charentais melon. The orange has been freshly squeezed.
Marmalade. And there are croissants. At least I know the
coffee is hot.

*This, because it is in a silver thermos, which Edward
now opens. Then he takes another silver dish from the
hot box and opens it.*

The eggs are scrambled.

Kyra Fantastic.

Edward Well, they looked pretty nice when they left.

Kyra It doesn't matter. We'll eat them. Oh this is wonderful!

Edward Bacon. I thought you'd be pleased.

Kyra I didn't eat last night.

But Edward doesn't hear this because he has taken out the last pieces of linen and is moving towards her with them in his hand.

Edward And look, the *pièce de résistance*. Just smell the napkins.

Kyra Yes, they're incredible.

Kyra is suddenly overwhelmed and throws her arms round Edward, holding him close, the tears pouring down her cheeks.

Oh, Edward, thank you. Thank you so much.

She holds on to him, not wanting to let him go. After a few moments, he quietly detaches himself, and she wipes her cheeks.

Edward Hey, look, I mean, it's just breakfast. I've just brought you breakfast.

Kyra I know.

Now he puts a small vase with a rose in it between them as the last touch. The table looks perfect. It all seems to have happened in no time at all.

Edward Are we going to eat it?

She smiles. The light is growing all the time at the window. As Edward moves to the table, Kyra sets about getting ready for work, gathering her things together, her mood transformed into a purposeful high humour.

Kyra I have to eat quickly. There's a boy I'm late for. I'm teaching him off my own bat. Extra lessons. Early, so early! I sometimes think I must be going insane.

She laughs. She has thrown her things down on the chair and moved across to brush her hair in the little mirror in the kitchen area. She talks happily meanwhile as she does.

I wake at five-fifteen, five-thirty. The alarm clock goes off. I think, what am I doing? What is this all about? But then I think, no, this boy has the spark.

She throws him a nervous smile.

It's when you see that spark in someone . . . This boy is fourteen, fifteen. His parents are split. He lives in this place I cannot describe to you. It's so appalling he has to go to the bloody common to work.

The light is still growing at the window as she shakes her hair, and then starts putting things in her bag for the day's work. Edward watches, diffident, standing by the table, slightly awed at her energy and sudden access of cheerfulness.

I mean, to be a teacher, the only thing you really have going for you . . . there's only one thing that makes the whole thing make sense, and that is finding one really good pupil.

She has moved into the room, and seeing the abandoned schoolbooks on the floor, starts to pick them up and arrange them in a pile.

You set yourself some personal target, a private target, only you know it – no one else – that's where you find satisfaction. And you hope to move on from there.

She gathers the last books together on the floor. Then for no apparent reason she repeats what she just said.

And that is it, that's being a teacher. One private target, and that is enough.

She is kneeling on the floor, suspended for a moment, completely still, completely isolated in her own thoughts, as if there were no one else in the room, no one else in her life at all. After a moment, Edward goes to behind one of the chairs he has set out at the table. Hearing him move, she quickly gets up.

Edward Your chair.

Kyra puts the books down on a side-table and goes and stands where he wants her to sit in a little parody of waiters' manners.

Kyra Are you ready?

Edward Yes. Yes, I'm ready.

Kyra Then sit.

Edward goes round to his side of the table, Kyra standing behind her chair waiting until he is ready as well, observing the formality.

This looks terrific. Come on, Edward, let's eat.

They sit down opposite one another. He pours coffee. She reaches for some scrambled eggs and toast. They smile at each other occasionally, at ease, but saying nothing. Together, they start eating happily. The table looks incongruously perfect in its strange setting. As they eat contentedly, the light from the window fades to dark.

AMY'S VIEW

For Nicole
pour toujours

Amy's View was first performed in the Lyttelton
auditorium of the the National Theatre, London, on
13 June 1997, and transferred to the Aldwych Theatre
on 14 January 1998. The cast was as follows:

Dominic Tyghe Eoin McCarthy
Amy Thomas Samantha Bond
Evelyn Thomas Joyce Redman
Esme Allen Judi Dench
Frank Oddie Ronald Pickup
Toby Cole Christopher Staines

Director Richard Eyre
Designer Bob Crowley
Lighting Mark Henderson
Music Richard Hartley

This production transferred to the Ethel Barrymore
Theatre, New York, on 3 April 1999, with Anne Pitoniak
taking over the role of Evelyn Thomas, Tate Donovan
that of Dominic Tyghe and Maduka Steady that of
Toby Cole. Sound Design was by Scott Myers.

The play was revived in a new production by the Theatre Royal, Bath, where it opened on 3 October 2006, and toured to Brighton, Richmond-upon-Thames and Malvern before opening at the Garrick Theatre, London, on 20 November 2006. The cast was as follows:

Dominic Tyghe Ryan Kiggell
Amy Thomas Jenna Russell
Evelyn Thomas Antonia Pemberton
Esme Allen Felicity Kendal
Frank Oddie Gawn Grainger
Toby Cole Geoff Breton

Director Peter Hall
Designer Simon Higlett
Lighting Peter Mumford
Sound Gregory Clarke

Characters

Dominic Tyghe
Amy Thomas
Evelyn Thomas
Esme Allen
Frank Oddie
Toby Cole

Place
Near Pangbourne and in London

Time
Between 1979 and 1995

When shall we live, if not now?

Seneca

Act One

The living room of a house in rural Berkshire, not far from Pangbourne. The year is 1979. To one side there is a large summerhouse-cum-veranda, full of plants; at the back, a door leading to a hall and staircase. The room has an air of exceptional taste, marked by the modern arts movement of the 1920s and 30s. It is comfortable, with sofas and chairs decked in attractively faded French fabrics. Nothing new has been bought for years. By the biggest chair, discarded embroidery. This was once the home of an artist, Bernard Thomas, and all round the room is evidence of his work, which is rather Cézanne-like and domestic in scale. There are small sculptures dotted around. On one wall are some plates he designed. On another, a box of objets trouvés. Yet the art is discreet, part of the general surroundings, and plainly has been there long enough to go unremarked.

It is past midnight, it is mid-summer, and it is pitch dark outside. There are some warm orange standard lamps on around the room, and a lamp at a big table at the back. In the centre of the room a striking-looking young man, Dominic Tyghe, has turned a very old bicycle upside down on some newspapers, and is trying to mend its front tyre. He has a big kitchen bowl of water to one side. He is tall and thin, just twenty-two, with long black hair, carelessly dressed like a student. Some way apart, Amy Thomas, one year older, is sitting at the big table. In front of her is a big pile of manuscripts which she is assiduously working her way through, making tiny notations. Dark-haired, in jeans and a T-shirt, she is thin also, with an unmistakable air of quiet resolution.

They are already talking as the play starts, caught in the middle of a chain of action.

Dominic I think it's this next.

Amy Do you want me to help you?

Dominic I think it's under control.

Amy What do you do with the water?

Dominic You watch for the bubble. Once you see the bubble, then you're on to the leak.

Amy smiles across lovingly. Evelyn Thomas has come into the room. She is white-haired, in her late seventies, in good shape, but moving and talking in the self-contained rhythm of older people, on a course of her own. She is carrying in a pile of big books.

Evelyn I wanted to show him this album. Pictures of your mother when she was young.

Amy It is past midnight. Are you sure you shouldn't be going to bed?

Evelyn I wait every night.

Amy What time does she get here?

Evelyn It varies. She comes in a taxi.

Amy What, from the station?

Evelyn Oh no. From London.

Amy My God!

Evelyn has set the books down on the table, at the far end from Amy, and has started to look through them.

Evelyn Thank God your father never found this. Esme at RADA, some young man with his arm round her waist.

Amy You do know the pub is already closed?

Dominic It's no longer the beer. It's the challenge.

Evelyn is still turning the pages.

Evelyn Esme, with another young actress. Looking quite peaky.

Amy A taxi from London!

Evelyn looks up a moment.

Evelyn You did tell her you were coming?

Amy I left a message. Some woman at the theatre. She sounded sort of ginny. Three packs a day.

Evelyn Yes. That's her dresser. Tweed skirts. A voice like Alvar Lidell.

Amy That was her.

Evelyn Did you mention your friend?

Amy Not by name. But I did say I was two.

Evelyn She never sees anyone. Of course, she pretends that she does. I suppose she does see the neighbours. But I wouldn't count them.

Amy Nor would I.

Evelyn Horses and hip operations, otherwise you're wasting your time.

She turns another page.

Here she is again, looking sluttish.

Amy has gone over to see how Dominic's getting on.

Dominic Do you think it's just been in the garage too long?

Evelyn That's Bernard's bicycle.

Amy We thought it must be Dad's.

Evelyn For a start, he's been dead fifteen years. And he didn't cycle for another fifteen before that.

Dominic Oh then, I must say, no wonder.

Evelyn Overall, you may be looking back to the war.

Dominic laughs at the hopelessness of it.

Dominic Yes, well, whoever, they lost the instructions.

Evelyn Are you sure you have the right one? I could never tell the difference between the John Bull bicycle repair kit, and that little printing set they do as well.

Amy Oh yes of course, the printing set! The time I spent getting my fingers bright blue . . . with those little rubber ants . . .

Evelyn Ah yes. Your paper.

Amy, going back to the table, raises her voice for the older woman.

Amy You remember? I did it for years. You can't have forgotten. How could you? Surely. It was called *Amy's View*.

Evelyn So it was.

Amy You see. Infant journalist. Crosswords. Cartoons. Interviews. Mostly with my mother, I'm afraid. I used to hawk it round the widows of Pangbourne. I made a small fortune.

Evelyn has gone back to the album.

Evelyn Esme, smiling, at the seaside. Wearing an unfortunate jumper.

Dominic (*sniffing*) Do you think people used these things to get high?

Dominic goes to glue the rubber strip at the table.

Amy Dominic was spared all the pleasures of family. He was brought up by nuns.

Dominic Well, not exactly.

Evelyn What's she saying?

Dominic (*raising his voice*) I'm an orphan.

Evelyn I'm sorry.

Dominic There's really no need.

Evelyn speaks as if Dominic were not present.

Evelyn Does he know who his parents are?

Amy No.

Dominic I always thought they'd turn out to be frightful. And not to be interested in the same things as me. I'm not sure we'd know what to say to one another.

Evelyn Wouldn't you?

Dominic Apart from, 'Oh, so it's you.'

He seems unperturbed.

I don't think it's really such a big issue. They're strangers. I don't think they marked me for life.

Evelyn Don't you?

Dominic No. No, I don't think so. I just am who I am.

He frowns a moment at the table.

Evelyn What a strange thing for your young man to say.

Amy is unsettled by Evelyn's reaction.

Amy Is it? I understand.

Evelyn Do you?

Amy Of course. His family didn't want him. That's what they were saying by letting him go.

Evelyn More likely they weren't able to cope.

Amy Yes, that as well. Of course, that's part of it.

She suddenly stops, embarrassed.

Well, *you* say, Dominic.

Dominic Obviously, I can only guess at their reasons. But they made a choice. It's always seemed to me I should allow them that choice.

Evelyn looks at him quite sharply.

Evelyn What a depressing philosophy. Are you sure you're with the right man?

Amy Quite sure.

Dominic I don't think she's worried.

Evelyn Of course not. At her age, that's par for the course.

Dominic has gone back to the bike, not taking this mischief-making seriously.

Amy Grandma, we don't need your views on the subject . . .

Evelyn I'm saying nothing. I'm reading this book.

Amy Good. So I should hope.

Dominic is kneeling, putting on the blue strip.

All right, Dominic?

Dominic Why, sure. Everything's fine.

He spins the wheel, the job done.

Amy Dominic's editing a film magazine. That's his main interest. He writes about films.

Evelyn In my day we just used to watch them.

Dominic Ah yes, but things have moved on.

Amy Evelyn taught art . . .

Evelyn I did.

Amy In a school . . .

Evelyn In the same school. Quite near here. For over forty years. I always told the children: just do it. What is there to say?

Amy Ah well, Dominic doesn't feel that at all.

Evelyn No.

Dominic I think it's worthwhile to discuss the whole concept of cinema. I can't get past this extraordinary idea. That actually it's nothing. It's just beams of light.

He stands a moment, thinking it through.

All that complexity, that feeling. And it's all in the air.

Amy You should read what he's written. He has these extraordinary theories . . .

Dominic (*modestly*) Well . . .

Amy To do with psychology. The relation of cinema to dream? How we experience fictive narratives while sleeping. I know it sounds heavy, but when you read it, it makes perfect sense.

Evelyn is neutral, giving nothing away.

Evelyn What's it called, this magazine?

Dominic *Noir et Blanc.*

Amy It's in English. It's just the title that's French.

Evelyn Well, good.

Amy Dominic started it himself. I go round in the evening . . .

Dominic There's only two of us.

Amy I go round selling in cafés, in cinemas . . .

Evelyn I thought you'd got a job of your own.

Amy Yes. But this is the evenings. I go out and sell *Noir et Blanc.*

Amy stops, as if brought up short.

It's odd. It hadn't occurred to me. It's like *Amy's View.*

Evelyn Yes.

Amy Except this time the view is Dominic's.

Before she has time to be embarrassed she hears an approaching taxi.

Is that the sound of a car?

Evelyn Did you say she's coming?

Amy Dominic, I think it's my mother.

Evelyn I'll put her food in the oven. The pub sends something round.

Dominic I'll move the bike.

Evelyn It's usually disgusting.

Amy My goodness, she gets her food from the pub?

Evelyn has gone. Seeing Dominic about to move the bike, Amy stops him.

There's no need. You mustn't be embarrassed. She's terribly easy, I promise you that.

Dominic It's all right. It's not me that's embarrassed.

Amy No.

He kisses her lightly. They wait a moment, their backs to us, like children. Then we see her take his hand.

Esme (*off*) Hello. Is there anyone there?

Amy (*raising her voice*) Yes. Yes. We're in here.

Esme Allen comes in. She is forty-nine, in a simple dress and carrying a big bag. She is surprisingly small, her manner both sensitive and intense. Something in her vulnerability makes people instantly protective of her.

Esme Amy, how are you? How good to see you. Are you all right? You don't look very well.

Amy No, I'm fine.

Esme kisses and hugs her daughter warmly.

Mother, I promised I'd introduce you. This is my friend with a bike.

Esme We've never met.

Dominic No.

They shake hands. There is a slight hiatus.

Dominic.

Esme How are you?

Dominic Thank you. I'm very well.

*They both smile at their own awkwardness. Evelyn
comes in and starts laying a place.*

Esme I got your message. I'm thrilled at this privilege.

Dominic Just let me move this.

Esme Don't move it, please, on my account. I quite like
it there. What've you been doing? Rallying?

Amy No, Mother, he's just been mending the tyre.

*Dominic has turned it upright and is leaning it against
the wall.*

Esme I see. Is he freelance? Does he do fuses and plugs?
The tank in the attic's in a terrible state. Why did he
start with the bike?

Amy Very funny . . .

Esme I don't need to bother with supper, Evelyn.

Amy He fancied the pub for a beer.

But Evelyn is already on her way out.

Esme Tell me, how long are you down for?

Amy Oh, well that's up to Dominic. I got a couple of
days from my publishing house.

Esme Did you get some dinner? I'm afraid there's never
anything here. Evelyn's gone macrobiotic or something.
She eats pulses. She believes they're prolonging her life.
As if it hadn't gone on long enough.

Dominic There we are.

Esme I get in steak and kidney if I'm not to starve.

Amy smiles, in recognition about Evelyn.

Amy Yes, Evelyn's already cast an eye over Dominic.
Found fault with him.

all. No, you write as if you like them and suddenly, they're really responsive.

Esme Of course.

Dominic Yes, but it almost shocks me how much.

Esme is looking at him a little harder.

Esme So what are you saying?

Dominic I don't know. I suppose in my little way . . . just on this stupid diary, I mean . . . I suppose I've realised that writing is power.

Esme Uh-huh. Which you can use consciously?

Dominic Sort of.

Esme So you can start to advance your career?

She has not said it unkindly but it prompts a rush of denial from them both.

Dominic Well . . .

Amy Dominic doesn't mean that.

Dominic No. Not at all.

Amy Dominic'd never do that.

Dominic No. Not blatantly. But on the other hand, if you take what they say – which is often not interesting – and you make it witty, next day you give it some oomph, then I've noticed they call you. It's a hideous phrase, but you begin to make contacts.

Amy And that's something which Dominic realises he may have to do.

Esme Make contacts?

Dominic Yes.

Esme Goodness.

Dominic I can't avoid it. If I'm to make films. And why not?

Amy Yes. You're just getting access.

Dominic That's it.

There is a slight silence.

The mistake of course would be to take the stuff I write seriously. But what does it matter? As we say on the diary, it's gone in a day.

Esme Mmm.

Esme has grown thoughtful. Amy wants to dispel the atmosphere.

Amy I hadn't realised the play was still running.

Esme No, well, it was going to close. Then someone reopened it. In a smaller theatre.

Amy I see. And you're still in it?

Esme Oh yes. At least for a while.

Amy joins in the familiar complaint.

Esme *and* **Amy** There are no parts for women.

Esme I have a good death scene at least. The writer's not terribly present. Nor the director. They only stay for the opening.

Amy They wind you up and you go.

Esme Yes.

Esme tucks her legs up under her and looks absently at Evelyn, who has returned.

What on earth are you doing with that album?

Evelyn I got it out to show it to Amy's young friend. But he showed no interest.

Esme No, well, he's right. There's nothing to see.

Amy looks anxiously to Dominic.

Amy Dominic, you've never seen my mother acting.

Dominic No. It must seem ridiculous. I do know how famous you are. But my generation . . . by and large, we don't go to the theatre. To us it doesn't seem relevant.

Esme Now why should it? I quite understand.

Evelyn goes out again, saying nothing.

People say, oh, everyone should go to the theatre. Why should they? We don't want an audience being brought in by force. And for us, there's nothing more disheartening than playing to people who are there because they've been told it's doing them good.

Dominic Quite.

Esme Let's play to people who actually like it. And if there aren't very many, so be it. But don't come because you've been told to. No, that won't do at all.

She is thoughtful, so again Amy prompts her to cheer her up.

Amy Mummy is brilliant at playing comedy.

Esme I'm usually best at playing genteel. With something interesting happening underneath. Layers. I play lots of layers.

Amy She plays them wonderfully.

Esme Thank you. My Shakespearean heroines were not a success. I suffered with a gay Orlando. Amy remembers. Everything was fine when I was dressed as a boy.

Amy But then there's this bit . . . *As You Like It*, do you know? She has to reveal she's a woman . . .

Esme He was right. I don't blame him. I was sexier the other way.

Amy Nonsense!

Esme But oh dear! The look on his face . . .

Esme lights a cigarette.

Amy It was funny.

Esme Everyone's so young at the theatre. Theatre's a young person's game. Eventually it becomes undignified. Dressing up, pretending to be someone else. Then saying things which someone else tells you to. After a while, you start to think, where am I? Where do I fit in all this?

Amy consciously keeps things going.

Amy How are the rest of them? How is that actor? The one who plays the old man.

Esme Oh, they've changed him. Now Perry Potter is playing that part. You know Perry. He wears a scarf. And a sort of *pan bagnat* to cover his baldness.

Amy A *pan bagnat*?

Esme You know those things. Like this.

She swirls her hand round her head.

Amy What on earth are you talking about? A *pan bagnat* is a kind of a sandwich.

Esme Why . . .

Amy With olives and tuna. Mother, it comes in a bun.

Esme Of course I know that. I know that!

Amy She has such extraordinary gaps in her knowledge. She thinks a *pan bagnat* is a hat!

Esme Oh very satirical. You're all so superior. With your new universities. I don't have book learning, not the hyper-accurate type. But I have a different kind of intelligence . . .

Amy Oh yes, we all know that kind of intelligence. The kind that's kind of like just being thick.

Evelyn returns with salt and pepper and a half-drunk bottle of wine.

Esme I had irregular schooling. Ask Evelyn. Schools didn't teach in those days. It was considered vulgar.

Amy They taught. But you chose not to hear.

Dominic is politely interested.

Dominic Do you do television also?

Esme Oh, television, really!

Amy She hates it.

Esme I do.

Amy She doesn't even watch.

Esme Working your guts out while people do something else. There you are, working. What are they doing? Eating. Or talking. Just great! Being taken no notice of in ten million homes.

They all smile. Esme seems more comfortable now.

Dominic Do you always come back in the evening?

Esme When Amy was young, I just hated to leave her. She was such a sweet girl. She always filled this house with her friends.

133

Amy My girl friends used to sleep over.

Esme And then I suppose I got used to it. I still don't like sleeping in London.

Amy She doesn't like staying there after a show.

Esme That's right. It's the nature of my job. It's all opinion. People flitting round telling you, 'I like it, I don't. I thought this, I didn't think that.' There's nothing to get hold of. But at least if I come home in the evening . . . well, I just like the feeling. I look at this house and something is real.

She looks round a moment. Evelyn is still pottering.

I don't want to eat, Evelyn.

Amy Grandma, you should be going to bed.

Evelyn Why? I'll sleep when I'm dead.

Esme Television? No, I don't want to do it. For as long as London has its fabled West End . . .

She stubs out her cigarette. Evelyn goes out again.

And you?

Amy Oh, I'm fine. Really. We just fancied a visit. And of course for you to meet Dominic too.

Dominic responds tactfully.

Dominic Here. Let me take this bike to the garage.

Amy Well, thank you.

Dominic I'll be back in a mo.

He goes out. The two women are alone.

Esme You'd better say. I'm not such a bad mother.

Amy What?

Esme Not such a bad mother that I can't tell. Please, I don't think I can stand an engagement. Do people still do that?

Amy No. I promise that's not what this is.

Esme Well?

Amy It's not serious. I promise you, it's nothing serious at all. I'm wanting to borrow some money.

Esme Ah, thank goodness. Money, that's all.

She seems genuinely relieved.

Of course. How much do you need?

Amy I'd like five thousand.

Esme I'm sorry?

Amy That would be perfect.

Esme Say that again.

She suddenly looks at her directly.

Why on earth do you want five thousand? There's nothing in the world which costs five thousand pounds.

Amy If you don't mind, I don't want to say.

Esme I'm glad, in that case, it's not serious. What would have been serious? Ten?

Amy I will tell you. I promise I will tell you one day. But you've always said: if I needed anything I was to come to you.

Esme Why, surely.

Amy No strings attached. Well, Mother, I'm here.

Esme recognises a note of challenge and rises to it.

135

Esme That's fine. That's no problem. Now? How do you want it? Do you want a cheque?

Amy If you could.

Esme Sure. Yes of course. Let me do it. Now where exactly did I put my things?

Amy There. Behind you.

Esme Of course.

She takes her bag across to the table.

How much?

Amy Five thousand.

Esme You mean five thousand pounds? Do you mean, all in one go? Not in instalments? One day you will give it back?

Amy smiles politely at these jokes. Esme has opened her cheque book.

Amy You always said, if ever . . . if ever something came up, you wouldn't ask anything, you'd simply give me whatever I asked.

Esme Oh yes.

She pauses a second.

But first just tell me what this something is.

Amy Mum . . .

Esme No really, I'm joking. I trust you. You know I do. I'm not asking anything. Not a thing. I know if I asked you would tell me, but I'm not going to ask.

She starts writing. Amy just watches.

Which account is it? I have no idea. There's money from Bernard's estate. The ludicrous thing is, I don't make anything at all from the play. I'm losing. By the time I've got a taxi from London, I don't have anything left.

She looks up at Amy.

Now what is the date?

Amy June 25th. It's 1979.

Esme Well, I know that. Please, do you think I live in a dream?

She hands Amy the cheque.

Amy Thank you.

Esme How did I do?

Amy You did brilliantly.

Esme Aren't you proud of your mum? Cash it quickly before it can bounce. No, really. You're fine. It'll pay.

She kisses her.

The Trappist. I shan't say any more.

She starts opening doors and calling out.

Now, Dominic, are you all right? Are you lost in the garage? Evelyn, what's happened? What's going on?

Both Dominic and Evelyn have reappeared, Evelyn with shrivelled pub dinner.

Ah Dominic, right, there you are.

Dominic I am.

Esme Are you going to bed, the two of you?

Dominic Soon.

137

Amy slips the cheque among her things, and looks to see what Dominic is doing.

I have to write something first.

Evelyn (*putting down the plate*) Here it is.

Esme My God, what have you done to it? Vegetarian's revenge. The way she heats it! Every day less attractive, until I give in.

Evelyn It's pure crap.

Esme I know. I love it. Do we have any HP?

Amy has been looking to contact Dominic.

Amy Are you going up?

Dominic I'll just work a little.

Amy Shall I come with you?

Dominic Do you mind? Just give me ten minutes. For God's sake, I just need ten minutes, all right? Is that so unreasonable?

He has snapped at her. Suddenly the atmosphere is tense.

Amy No, of course not. No problem.

Dominic stops, trying to take the heat out of the moment.

Dominic I'll see you later. Goodnight, Esme.

Esme Goodnight.

Dominic goes out. Esme has her meal in front of her, but makes no effort to start.

Well, there it is. It's extraordinary. You've found yourself such a handsome young man.

138

Amy Why? Does that surprise you?

Esme Not in the slightest. Any man's lucky to end up with you.

The tone of this is light and friendly but Amy is ill at ease.

The theatre, of course, is full of these people. Good-looking young men who have yet to find out who they are. I see them all the time.

Amy Is that meant to be Dominic?

Esme Well, you know him better than me.

Esme waits but Amy says nothing.

But, on the other hand, you have come to ask my opinion . . .

Amy Have I?

Esme I think so.

Amy I'd say on the contrary. Didn't I ask you not to say a word?

Esme Amy, please, I wasn't born yesterday. When a daughter comes to her mother and says, 'Don't ask anything, I beg you, ask nothing at all . . .', isn't it just a way of saying: 'Quick, Mother, help! I'm desperate to talk'?

Amy can't resist smiling at this.

Amy Are you saying I did that unconsciously?

Esme Unconsciously? Hardly. 'Give me five thousand pounds.' As a way of getting my attention, it would take some beating. Well, wouldn't it?

Amy Yes. I don't know. Oh, perhaps. I'm confused.

Amy smiles, relaxing, giving in.

Esme After all that is the basic skill. That *is* my profession. You have to get that right, or you might as well give up. You say one thing but you're thinking another. If you can't do that, then truly you shouldn't be doing the job.

A look of mischief comes onto Amy's face.

Amy That reminds me, I did see that thing with Deirdre . . .

Esme Oh Deirdre!

Amy I saw that new play which stars Deirdre Keane.

Esme Well, Deirdre can't even manage the line in the first place, let alone the bit where you think something else.

Amy She wasn't very good.

Esme They tell me she's laughable. Apparently she comes on dressed like a lampshade, a great smear of lipstick right across her face . . .

Amy They're right . . .

Esme They say, rolling her eyes like a demented puppy dog and facing out front all the time.

Esme is shaking her head as if outraged.

Amy She got very good reviews.

Esme Deirdre? She practically goes down on the critics. You've seen her. She's craven. She's always trying to please.

Amy Is that such a bad thing?

Esme Of course not. But nobody's explained to her the basis of the whole project.

Amy Which is?

Esme Why, to please without seeming to try.

Amy Oh, I see.

Esme That's what one's attempting. Of course we all know it can't be achieved. But that's the ideal. To make it look effortless.

Esme looks at her a moment.

Perhaps it applies just as much in our lives.

Amy looks, knowing she cannot avoid things any longer.

Amy Look, Mum, I do know you're desperate to talk to me . . .

Esme Me?

Amy There's a thousand questions you're longing to ask . . .

Esme I can see you're in trouble. In a moment I'm hoping you're going to say why.

Amy It's not trouble. I wouldn't say trouble exactly . . .

Esme How's life in your publishing firm?

Amy Great. They're trying to promote me.

Esme I'm pleased.

Amy But one thing's bound up in another.

Amy stops dead. Esme speaks quietly.

Esme You're expecting a child?

Amy How did you know? Is it really that obvious?

Esme It isn't not obvious.

Amy When did you know?

Esme The moment I saw you, of course.

Esme pushes her uneaten meal aside. She gets up and takes Amy in her arms. Amy can barely speak through her tears.

Amy Oh God, I'm going to cry . . .

Esme Well, cry.

Esme begins to sob with her.

Please cry, cry all you want to . . .

Amy No, no, I mustn't . . .

Esme Oh Amy . . .

Amy I mustn't . . .

She tears herself decisively away.

Esme Why not? It's wonderful . . .

Amy I mustn't!

Esme Amy, this is wonderful news.

Amy Because . . . oh shit, I don't know how to say this. You're going to think I'm insane.

Amy is wild, raising her voice.

I haven't told Dominic. I know this sounds crazy but I don't think I shall.

Before Esme can react, Evelyn appears again, beating her usual path.

Evelyn You haven't eaten your supper.

Esme No. Why don't you go to your bed?

Evelyn What's wrong with her? Why is she crying?

Esme Hay fever.

Evelyn Do you want me to re-heat it?

Esme No thank you.

Evelyn has gone over to collect the plate. Esme raises her voice to Evelyn.

I don't think it can take any more.

Evelyn (*at Amy*) You know she doesn't eat anything.

Amy Oh really?

Evelyn She comes in here, looks at it, then pushes the plate to one side.

Esme has moved across to usher her out.

Esme Evelyn, you must go, you must go to your bed now.

Evelyn I'm not going to sleep.

Esme Very well then. Just lie. Just lie there. Think about family. Here we are. Under one roof. The whole of our family. At least such as it is. Think about that and be grateful.

She kisses her.

Evelyn Just promise me she's not going to marry the critic.

Amy He hasn't asked.

Evelyn Good. As long as she doesn't marry a critic, then I think I can sleep.

She goes out, pleased with having said it. They are both amused at the absurdity.

Esme Oh Amy . . .

Amy Well really! She never changes.

Esme No.

Amy She seems really well.

Esme Oh sure. She's going to outlive me. It doesn't bother me. I've known that for years.

She goes and gets her cigarettes.

It's become a marriage, like any other. If when I'd met Bernard, they'd said to me, you'll live ten years longer with Bernard's mother than you will with Bernard himself . . . I'm not sure I'd have jumped in so eagerly.

Esme lights her cigarette.

But you never know how things are going to turn out.

Amy No.

Esme looks at her a moment.

Esme So what is the problem? Dominic's the father?

Amy Oh yes. We can say that for sure.

Esme But you feel – what? – for some reason that now's not the moment for Dominic to know?

Amy Exactly.

Esme I see. Well, it's interesting. It makes for an original decision. But I can't help feeling there's some sort of flaw in the reasoning perhaps. You're hoping he's not going to notice?

Amy No. No, of course not . . .

Esme You don't feel it's possible he's going to find out?

Amy is amused, but Esme goes on.

I mean, I do see the man is an egghead. You just have to look at him. But even so you'd have to be pretty unworldly!

144

Amy You know very well that's not what I mean.

Esme Do I?

Amy now sees a way to explain.

Amy All right, look, he *is* an intellectual. But in some ways he's younger than me. In a sense, he's a bit like a child. In a good way. He's child-like, is that the word?

Esme Child-like is good. Childish is less good.

Amy Yes. In that case, the first.

Esme is just watching, not commenting.

But also the thing is . . . he's extremely attractive.

Esme Ah.

Amy It's something . . . well, it makes things different, I find.

Esme Yes I can see. The little-boy manner . . .

Amy For instance: we met at a publishing party. Dominic arrived with this girl. She was only eighteen. And she'd published a novel. I have to say, not a bad novel . . .

Esme Oh, novels!

Amy And what's more she had these incredible legs . . .

Esme Ah, well then . . .

Amy Jet black hair. This wonderful bosom. I saw him with her as soon as they walked in the room. All the time they were laughing together, her arm around him, like she didn't have a care in the world.

She stops a moment.

So yes, I admit, it slightly surprised me when he came over. When he started talking to me.

Esme And how did she take it?

Amy The teenage novelist? Well I think she felt pretty miffed. I think they all are. The tall one. The blonde one from Cambridge. Another one who sang in a band . . .

Esme And it's the thought of these ex's which is unsettling you . . .

Amy No, not exactly. Oh God, I'm explaining this badly . . .

Esme Don't tell me you think you can't compete.

Amy Not at all. No. I do know what I'm giving him. I'm giving something none of the others could give.

Esme What's that?

Amy Self-confidence. I give him some faith in himself. I build him up.

Esme Yes, I'm sure. And what exactly is he giving to you?

Amy begins to sound defensive.

Amy Look . . .

Esme No, I mean it . . .

Amy Now, mother . . .

Esme You're telling me you're flattered. As you describe him, he has women around him like flies. And you're thinking, 'And he's chosen me! Golly Moses! I'm going to do anything to hold on to this . . .'

Amy Mother, that isn't fair.

Esme To a point where you're frightened to tell him you're pregnant! Is that it? You're frightened you'll lose him. Is that how things are?

She turns away, deeply disturbed.

Oh Amy, I can't believe it. I'm shocked. This is terrible . . .

Amy Really, I promise you, that's not it at all.

Esme Isn't it? You've given me a list of his conquests. What am I meant to say? Me, I don't care who he's slept with. All I care is what happens to you.

Amy Of course.

Esme If he loves you.

Amy Of course.

Esme Does he say it?

Amy Oh really!

Esme I mean it. In those exact words?

Amy Yes. Yes, he has said it.

Esme Good. I know it's meant to be just the first step. You expect to go on from there. But the fact is, in my experience, it's quite alarming how few of them can even do that.

Now it is Amy's turn to be angry.

Amy All right, for God's sake, he says it! He says it. Why are you so worried?

Esme Why am I worried? Why on earth do you think?

Amy (*conceding*) All right . . .

Esme What a question!

Amy All right!

Esme You seem to think just because this man is attractive it somehow absolves him from doing what any normal, decent person should do.

Amy tries to give her a real explanation.

Amy No, that's not it. I have to explain to you. There are things . . . there's a background you don't yet understand. But the point is, Mother, you do have to listen . . .

Esme I'm listening . . .

Amy You have to sit down and promise to give me a chance.

Esme Well, of course.

Amy I've lived through this nightmare. Now I'm beginning to see a way through. But you must give me a hearing.

Esme Why, surely.

Amy Without interruption.

Esme Amy, I hope I've always done that.

Esme looks reproachful.

Amy The truth is . . . my relationship with Dominic has been pretty fragile. It's volatile, is that the word? He can be bad-tempered. He suffers from depression quite badly. At times he . . . well, he's like . . . he's a victim of moods.

Esme is silent, her disapproval clear.

So the point is, I thought, this is really tricky. Do I just go to him and tell him outright? No, that's going to shock him. And also . . . I know for a fact he will say to me . . . look, will I get rid of it?

Esme Amy . . .

Amy And for me, there's no question of that. So, all right. It's like solving a puzzle. I want to keep the baby and I want to keep Dominic as well. So I must work out a way of telling him so he doesn't feel pressured, so he doesn't feel, 'Oh God this is just what I feared . . .'

Esme is becoming restless.

He said . . . he has said from the start he wasn't ready for children . . .

Esme Oh really!

Amy Mother!

Esme All right . . .

Amy He said this. From the very first day. The point is, I made him a promise. No children. He said: 'Whatever else, I can't face starting a family . . .'

She stops a moment.

So you must see that does make things difficult now.

But Esme cannot stay quiet.

Esme What was this? Some sort of contract?

Amy Mum . . .

Esme Some sort of written agreement which he had you sign?

Amy No.

Esme Without any allowance for what might actually happen?

Amy Mother, you promised!

Esme Yes. I promised to give you a hearing. Not to let you throw away your whole life!

Esme stubs out her cigarette and gets up.

This stuff: no children! It's abstract! It's all in the abstract!

Amy I know.

Esme But something has happened. It's actually happened. An event which changes all that. You are actually having the baby. Whether he likes it or not, the baby exists.

Amy Yes, of course. So?

Esme *So*, I'd have thought it was obvious, the sooner you face him, the sooner you tell him . . .

Amy No. That's where you're wrong. Because I just know – I can feel in my stomach – it's going to seem like it's blackmail.

Esme Oh come now!

Amy For him it'll be like I'm springing a trap.

Amy suddenly raises her voice.

It's everything he's feared! I know him. You don't. I tell him now and at once he's going to feel cornered . . .

Esme That is ridiculous! What kind of man is this?

Amy And when Dominic feels cornered, I tell you, I've seen him, he turns just incredibly stubborn and ugly . . .

Esme Well then, you've answered my question.

Amy Mother, I'm sorry, but I'm very clear about this.

Amy is reluctant, not wanting to go on.

The fact is, you know, I'd not wanted to tell you . . . the girl from Cambridge . . . the one who was with him before . . . the point is she also . . . she also got pregnant.

Esme Ah. Now I see what you're telling me.

Esme has stopped as if at last seeing to the heart of Amy's problems.

And I suppose we can guess what happened to her.

Amy shifts uncomfortably.

Amy Oh look, I mean it's not . . . it wasn't immediate. It wasn't like 'She's pregnant, I'm off . . .'

Esme No?

Amy But it's true. He stopped her having the baby. Then he told me things did start to sour between them. And, pretty soon after, he felt that he'd had enough.

Esme looks hard at Amy.

Esme But Amy . . .

Amy I know . . .

Esme You do have to ask yourself . . .

Amy I know, Mother. I know what you're going to say. But the answer is: yes. He is the right man for me. I know this. I know it profoundly. In a way which is way beyond anything.

Esme is silenced by Amy's conviction.

So it's just a question of what I do now.

Esme sits down quietly at the table.

That's why I came to you and asked for the money. The money will mean I can be by myself. That means . . . well, if I have to, I can bring up the baby alone. Of course I will tell him. I'll tell him eventually. After some months. But what I will not do is bully him into some sort of disastrous alliance – out of sheer circumstance – when the point is, it's not what he wants.

Esme And what you want, does that count for nothing?

Amy Yes, of course it's important. I promise you, I've thought this thing through. I charge in, I frighten him.

Where does that get me? All that happens is, I destroy the whole thing.

Amy reaches across and takes Esme's hand.

You always said I was the rational one in the family. I was blessed with certainty, that's what you said.

Esme Yes, I did.

Amy So please, you must trust me. It's a matter of timing. And the timing is something which I must decide.

Dominic appears at the door. He has a pad of paper on which he has been writing.

Dominic Oh I see. Lord, you're still talking . . .

Amy Dominic, my goodness . . .

Dominic Have I butted in?

Amy No. Not at all. Not in the slightest.

Amy looks nervously to Esme. Dominic is aware of the atmosphere.

We were just chatting. Discussing old times.

Dominic I realised I can't find the books that I needed. Do you know if they're in your case?

Amy Oh sure. Let me get them.

Dominic No, don't be silly.

Amy No really, I know where they are.

Dominic If you're sure.

Amy It won't take two seconds. All right, then, Mother? I'll be back in a sec.

Amy squeezes her hand, then goes out. Esme doesn't move. The wine is unopened in front of her. Dominic starts to look round the room.

Dominic It's nice here.

Esme I'm sorry?

Dominic The house.

Esme Oh . . .

Dominic It's beautiful. The pictures. Your husband did these? What is it, this one? Oil on canvas?

He is looking closely at one of the oils.

The crosshatch technique. Is that what it's called? Eggshell. Amy told me he was an artist. I like the style very much. What is it called?

Esme 'Called'?

Dominic What school was he part of?

Esme What school?

Dominic What movement?

Esme I suppose he gets lumped as an English impressionist. At least, when they auction him that's what he's called. But Bernard didn't call himself anything.

Dominic Oh really?

Esme No. I don't know to explain this, but it's simply not how he thought.

Amy appears, with a couple of film reference books under her arm. She looks to see nothing untoward has occurred.

Amy Here we are.

Dominic Oh thanks.

Amy I'll come up with you. You don't mind if I read?

Dominic No.

Amy I'll say goodnight then.

She leans down to Esme and kisses her.

Amy Mother, goodnight.

Esme gets up and moves towards the door.

Esme Dominic, my daughter has something to tell you. In my view, it's essential she speaks to you tonight. So I'm leaving you here and I'm going to bed.

She stops for a split second at the door.

She's pregnant.

She goes out. It has all happened so quickly that Amy is lost for a response. Then she runs out into the corridor where we can see her calling upstairs.

Amy Why did you tell him? Mum, what the hell's going on?

End of Act One.

Act Two

The same. Six years later. It is a Saturday afternoon in late July. The year is 1985. It is towards the end of a perfect summer day. Benign sunshine is flooding into the room from the windows and from the greenhouse and veranda at the back. Although so much time has gone by, the room appears identical.

Esme comes through the door, wearing a slightly ostentatious satin outfit with a floral motif, and a rather extravagant hat. She is carrying gloves, a bag and a huge bundle of flowers. Although now fifty-five, she is also little changed. Amy is immediately behind her, once more in jeans and a simple shirt. She is only twenty-nine, but motherhood and the passage of her twenties has made a mark on her. She is more confident but her hair is tied more austerely, and there is a wariness, a sense of strain.

Both of the women are in exceptionally high spirits, an ordeal behind them. As at the beginning of the first act, the action is already in train as the lights come up.

Esme Let me take off this hat.

Amy Oh, the hat was just crazy.

Esme Oh, flowers! What flowers!

Esme puts the flowers down on the table to take off her hat. The room is muggy with the day's heat, so Amy goes to open the greenhouse doors.

I knew from the start the hat was *de trop*.

Amy Well, it was. People could hardly see past it. All

155

they could see was this enormous saucer on top of your head. Bright green. Even your face looked iridescent.

Esme Well, thank you.

Amy kisses Esme.

Amy Nobody can say you don't give it a go.

Esme But I carried the gloves, did you notice? I never put them on. That was the clever touch.

Amy I should hope not. Who are you? The bloody Queen Mother?

Esme No. Just auditioning.

They both smile at the truth of this.

Did you see Evelyn?

Amy It's all right. She's sleeping.

Esme Well, come on, then, Frank, are you going to come in?

Frank Oh, thank you.

Frank Oddie is hanging around the doorway, but now comes in. In his early fifties, he looks easygoing and amiable in his shirtsleeves, tie and flannels. He carries his jacket. His manner is a touch apologetic, as if out of his natural habitat. Esme passes him as she goes out to hang up her hat and kick off her shoes.

Esme (*from the hall*) Did we lose Dominic?

Amy He's taking care of the children.

Esme For once.

Frank, in the middle of the room, loudly addresses no one in particular.

Frank Oh God, all that lemonade!

Amy I told him he had to. For once he's bloody well got to.

Esme I just hope he wasn't too bored.

Esme has come back barefoot and is unwrapping the flowers on the table.

I couldn't tell behind those dark glasses.

Frank Now can we drink something serious?

Esme He has wonderful dark glasses.

Amy Oh yes.

Amy, still opening doors, laughs, while Frank holds up some whisky he has found.

And what's more, they never come off.

Frank Anyone?

Amy Not even at night.

Esme throws a caustic look towards Frank.

Esme It's all right. I've already warned Amy.

Frank What, that your nearest neighbour's a soak? I admit I have been drinking a lot. I know. But there you are. I know.

He holds up his hands as if defending himself against an unseen critic.

Esme No one's worried!

Frank My life has been simply unspeakable. I'm allowed the consolations of drink.

Esme Mmm.

She goes out to the kitchen.

Frank At least at the weekend. I drink more at the weekend. And today after all was a very special day. And you did wonderfully.

Esme (*off*) Thank you.

Frank (*to Amy*) Didn't she do wonderfully?

Esme reappears now, carrying two vases.

Esme Almost fifty-five and opening my very first fête. 'Our thanks to the people of Pangbourne . . .'

Amy Oh God!

Esme happily sets about arranging her flowers. Frank is pouring three scotches.

Esme I think now I've done it, I actually quite like it. It's easier than acting. I think I might do it full time.

Frank You wouldn't know the problems I had persuading her . . .

Esme I wasn't sure I was right for the role.

Amy has now aired the room and joins her mother, fetching scissors for the flowers' stems and handing them to her, one by one.

Frank But you pulled it off brilliantly.

Amy Perhaps just a touch of hauteur. The famous actress, among us, briefly, just briefly . . .

Esme Well, I had no intention of loitering.

Frank Among us, and then she was gone!

He hands Esme a whisky.

Esme Thank you. I was touched. I hadn't expected it. The fruit, the vegetables, all the little cakes. These people who turn out and sit at their stalls. All those ridiculous pickles. And those incredible wines!

Amy Did you try them?

Esme I did. That disgusting elderberry. And something – what was it? – parsnip cordial, or something like that.

Amy Rows and rows of jam. Jam coming out of their ears.

Esme Yes I know. And you look at the flowers, the trestles, the tents and you think: just what is this? What *is* this occasion?

Frank What *is* it? What do you mean, what *is* it?

Esme I mean, you do wonder: is anyone fooled?

Esme has filled one vase and is deciding where to put it. Dominic has come downstairs. Now twenty-eight, he looks tidier, more prosperous, at ease in his fashionably casual clothes, and still wearing dark glasses. He is already speaking as he comes in with books in his hand.

Dominic Ah, there you are, Esme . . .

Esme Oh Dominic . . .

She laughs and accelerates across the room to avoid him.

Oh God . . .

Frank Fooled?

Dominic At last, now I've found you!

Esme Oh Lord, I've been dreading it.

Dominic There's no reason we shouldn't do it right now.

Frank What do you mean, *fooled*?

Frank is standing in the middle of the room, but they all ignore him.

Esme Can't you see I'm exhausted?

Amy What have you done with the children?

Dominic Don't worry. They're happy upstairs.

Amy looks tolerantly at him, then goes to the stairs to listen out for them.

Esme Dominic wants me to give him an interview, you know, for that programme of his.

Frank Oh yes. I may have seen it.

Dominic Today it's research. It's for filling in background.

Esme They were thrilled at the fête. They knew you were someone. They knew you were far more famous than me.

Dominic Oh come on . . .

But Frank can't let go.

Frank I'm sorry, look, I know that I'm stupid . . .

Esme Frank isn't stupid.

Dominic They didn't think that.

Frank But I do have to point out: the village fête happens. It happens. By everyone's good efforts. People work to get it ready for most of the year . . .

Esme I'm sure they do.

Frank It means a great deal to us all.

Esme Yes, of course.

Amy returns and touches Dominic's arm.

Amy They seem to be quiet, it's OK.

Dominic What's all this about?

Frank So what are you asking when you say that you stand there and wonder if anyone's actually *fooled*?

Esme has gone to work on a second vase where Amy now joins her, cutting stems.

Esme Why surely, it happens. Frank, I know that it happens. I think we can agree it takes place. And, what's more, I admit, I found myself moved . . .

Frank There you are.

Esme But I'm also aware the whole thing is some sort of fiction . . .

Frank A fiction?

Esme Yes. Miss Marple! Thatched cottages! Congratulations to Mr Cox on the size of his enormous courgettes! It's Heritage England. It's some sort of fantasy theme park, but don't tell me it actually still makes any sense.

Frank I don't see why not.

Esme suddenly raises her voice.

Esme Because this is a suburb!

Frank Oh I see, now I get it . . .

Esme It's become a rich suburb, like any other, from where people like you, Frank, go to the City all day. You take the train to a place which enshrines your real values . . .

Frank Oh really now, Esme. 'Real values'!

Esme And there you do your real work . . .

Frank So?

Esme So this place is not what it claims to be, this kind of organic community, rigged out with horses and jodhpurs and church choirs and such . . .

Dominic smiles to himself and sits down with his book at the side of the room.

Dominic Is this some sort of serious argument?

Esme I mean, why get an actress to open the proceedings unless the proceedings are kind of a fake?

Esme has dealt her coup de grâce, *but Frank is ready to counter attack.*

Frank You know, she says something like this every evening. I come round every evening . . .

Amy You do?

Frank Well, nearly every evening.

Esme He comes pretty often.

Frank All right, but be fair, we have things to discuss.

Amy What things?

Frank Well, business.

Esme Frank comes to talk business, that's right.

Frank And always she's saying this isn't real countryside.

Esme It isn't.

Frank She says that life in the country is finished.

Esme It is!

Underneath the banter, real feeling is beginning to show in Esme.

Oh yes, of course, when Bernard was born . . . even by the time I first came . . . you could still look out over Berkshire. The glittering Thames. But now . . . it's basically Surbiton. But with the extra inconvenience that things are that much further apart. I walk a little bit *further* to Sainsbury's. I walk a little bit *further* to the garden centre. But otherwise, no. I'm living in Surbiton! And it's only the memory of what has now vanished that has me believing I still live where I did.

She sits down and lights a cigarette.

Frank But that isn't fair. Everyone's here in the evening. At weekends they make their life here. And they try to continue traditions which – let's face it – have lasted for hundreds of years.

Esme Yes, well, they go through the motions.

Frank is beginning to sound quite angry.

Frank And so what is the purpose? Why on earth do you think people persist with these rituals – these things that you say are just shams?

She pauses a moment. She is quiet.

Esme Because they know no alternative. Because they no longer know who they are.

Frank looks shocked at this answer. Esme stubs out her cigarette and makes to move.

Frank Well, I'm not sure I quite follow that one . . .

Esme Now who wants some supper?

Amy I'll do it. No, please let me, Ma.

Dominic Supper? Why, sure . . .

Frank I'd say it's outrageous in fact.

Dominic But wouldn't it be better . . . I don't want to press you . . . but wouldn't it make better sense to do this thing first?

Esme Yes, of course.

She stops at the door, looking round.

I mean, yes, if you want to.

Amy Mum's been avoiding this moment all day.

Esme Nonsense. What makes you say that?

Dominic Because you'll do anything rather than sit down and talk!

Dominic has burst out, exasperated.

We came down last night, I keep asking. Every time I look at you . . .

Esme Oh really!

Dominic You flit from the room.

Esme It's just not my métier!

Dominic Well I wish you had said so.

Esme I did. I said so to Amy. The whole thing was Amy's idea.

Amy I just thought you'd enjoy it.

Esme Well, thank you. It's like going to the dentist for me.

She leans down and kisses Amy.

Dominic Look . . .

Esme This ridiculous costume! I need five minutes to change. You must admit, I do look like a tree. It's simple. Just give me five minutes and then I promise I'm yours.

She has gone before anyone can protest. Dominic looks ironically at Amy.

Amy All right . . .

Dominic Amy . . .

Amy I know. I know. I did warn you.

Dominic I know you warned me.

Frank She's impossible! She's like this every evening. She's truly impossible!

Frank is grinning, proud of her.

Amy Come here.

Dominic What?

Amy Just come over here.

Amy is at the flowers. Dominic goes over to join her. She kisses him.

You did very well. No, really. You're being very patient.

Dominic Thank you.

They smile at one another, then Dominic moves away, the bond between them secure.

Anyway, as long as she doesn't start on her stories . . .

Amy She won't.

Dominic Those god-awful theatrical stories of hers . . .

Amy I've told her.

Dominic How Perry dropped his props! How the set wobbled in Barnsley. How Deirdre can never remember her lines. If there's one thing that puts people off theatre, it's those meaningless stories they tell all the time.

Amy She knows that.

Dominic looks at his watch.

Dominic You know, I could still be in London. That's what's so crazy. I could still be in London right now. There's this big media gathering . . .

Frank Oh really?

Dominic This conference. People coming in from all over the world . . .

Frank And I suppose you feel you should really be with them?

Dominic Believe it or not – I'm not being arrogant – but some people are flying in specifically because they know I'll be there!

Frank I see.

Frank frowns at his drink, as if contemplating the problem.

Dominic It's a big thing. This country is changing. I work in independent production. It's a field where the British can well take a lead. And I have to wait while this – no offence – but this middle-aged actress decides when she's willing to favour me with ten minutes' chat.

Dominic knows he has gone too far.

Frank Well I think . . .

Dominic Look, I'm sorry. That came out pretty ugly. If I'm angry, the truth is, I'm angry at myself. This is familiar behaviour from Esme. Amy, you know what I'm saying.

Amy just looks at him.

I think we've seen this before.

Frank looks between them, wanting to help.

Frank Perhaps . . . I don't know . . . perhaps you could call them.

Dominic Call who?

Frank These big media people of yours.

Dominic Call to say what? That I'm stuck in the country? That I have no idea when I'll get back?

Amy controls her anger, low, suppressed.

Amy Dominic, I never ask you for anything. Just do me this favour, all right?

Esme returns in slacks, carrying a couple of plates of hors d'oeuvres.

Esme All right, here I am, now I'm ready for your questions.

Dominic Good.

Esme Salami? Go ahead . . .

Dominic Thank you.

Esme Ask any questions you like.

Dominic I was thinking perhaps we might do this in private.

Esme Oh, do you think so? I was hoping that everyone might want to join in.

Frank Not me.

Esme Dominic's planning this programme. We all sit under spotlights. In a studio. Debating.

Frank And what is the subject to be?

Esme looks sweetly at Dominic.

Esme No, really. It's your idea. Tell him.

Dominic We're discussing the question of whether the theatre is dead.

There is a slightly sticky moment.

Amy Dead?

Frank Oh I see.

Dominic I told you that, Amy.

Amy I didn't realise it was quite as dramatic as that.

Dominic Well, we might as well face it. It is a real question. To people of my generation at least. In the old days it seemed like theatre was really exciting. In those days, it still had something to say . . .

Esme offers the salami to Amy, who takes the chance to put her hand on Esme's arm.

Esme Amy?

Dominic But now . . . I don't know, we're all watching video. I believe human beings have changed. They've evolved. They have different priorities.

Frank My goodness.

Dominic The image is much more important. The image has taken the place of the word.

Frank nods and tries to look intelligent.

Frank Uh-huh.

Dominic You know, you go to the theatre. A character comes in the door. You think, oh my God! He's going to cross the room. Jump-cut, for Christ's sake, just jump-cut! And then next thing – oh Christ, you just know it! The bastard is going to sit down and *talk*.

He shakes his head pityingly.

And it's so slow. They do it slowly. And the way they act! It's so old-fashioned. In these big barns and they all have

to shout. Why don't we admit it? It's been superseded.
It had its moment, but its moment has gone.

*Amy looks nervously across at her mother, but Esme
is not remotely concerned.*

Dominic Of course I defer to you, Esme . . .

Esme Thank you . . .

Dominic You understand it all much better than me. But
who does theatre reach? Who is it talking to? Obvious.
To me, it's just wank time.

Esme I see. Well it's good that at least you've not made
up your mind . . .

Dominic Look . . .

Esme No, really, that famed objectivity. He's open-
minded . . .

Amy (*smiles*) Yes . . .

Esme Wouldn't you say? Dominic has no agenda or
anything.

Dominic All right, very funny . . .

Esme There's no question of you boys having to work
to a script!

*Esme seems oddly cheered as she moves round with
the plates.*

Have you noticed? It's always the death of the theatre.
The death of the novel. The death of poetry. The death
of whatever they fancy this week. Except there's one
thing it's never the death of. Somehow it's never the
death of *themselves*.

Dominic Esme . . .

Esme The death of television! The death of the journalist! Why do we never get those? It's off to the scaffold with everyone except for the journalists!

Amy It's true.

Esme Now I wonder why can that be?

Esme moves away laughing as Amy begins to clear the table for supper.

Amy It's pointless arguing with Esme. As she says, she doesn't do argument.

Esme I don't.

Amy She only does instincts. The worst thing, I tell you . . .

Esme My instincts are usually right!

Amy Usually! Usually!

The two women laugh together, happy.

Esme Though I must say it's kind of unfortunate, Dominic happening to ask me right now . . .

Amy Why?

Esme I've been thinking about giving up acting.

Amy Oh really? Yeah? I wonder where I've heard that before.

Esme I'm thinking of leaving the field free for Deirdre. She gave an interview – did you see it?

Amy No . . .

Esme The usual rubbish. The cover of the *Radio Times*. She claims she's never been interested in sex. 'It bores me,' she says. I thought, in that case, I know for a certainty, you've been bored stiff for most of your life!

But Amy is frowning now.

Amy But Mum . . .

Esme What? Am I serious? Is that what you're waiting to ask?

Amy Yes.

Esme I do have a problem.

Frank Oh really!

Esme How can I say I'm an actress when the point is I no longer act?

Frank That isn't true.

Frank has given her a second drink.

Esme In my head I'm an actress. But what have I actually done? A radio broadcast from Birmingham. A voice-over. For a green disinfectant, in fact. I played a germ. And meanwhile it's . . . what? Three years? No, four since I actually appeared in a play.

Frank Well . . .

Esme So you might say it's hardly the moment for me to hold forth on your programme.

But Dominic is beginning to get excited.

Dominic No. On the contrary, it seems to me perfect. 'There are no parts for women,' I've heard you say that . . .

Esme Oh . . .

Dominic Well now here's your chance to say it in public.

Esme Yes, maybe that's what's putting me off.

Dominic Why?

Esme A natural diffidence. 'There are no parts for women.' Another way of putting it: 'I'm out of work!'

She shares the absurdity of it with Frank, but Dominic persists, vehement.

Frank No, you're right.

Dominic Exactly! No women – that's part of what's wrong with the theatre. It's one of the reasons why I never go.

Amy Dominic, you are so full of shit. You never go anywhere where you're meant to switch off your telephone . . .

Dominic Now, Amy, that is just stupid . . .

Amy And also where you have to shut up and sit still.

Amy has suddenly come to life.

Dominic Look . . .

Amy I never see my friends. I know no one in publishing any more. I said, 'At least can we go to the opera? Just once?' On comes this dying diva. All round the deathbed. *La Traviata*. Act Three. She opens her mouth. Beep beep from Dominic's pocket!

Dominic All right, but at least it rang a High C.

Amy Oh sure. A call from America! From someone to say they'd call back later on. 'I'm calling to let you know I'll be calling you later . . .'

Dominic Amy hates them.

Amy It's the only way the children know he exists.

Esme Really?

Amy Chloe did a drawing of her father. She had him with a phone to each ear!

Dominic Chloe exaggerates. Chloe is a child who exaggerates.

Amy No she's not. The tragedy is, she draws what she sees . . .

Esme has sat down quietly watching this argument develop between them.

Every evening the phone rings at seven. Then again at eight. Then at nine. It's always Dominic. 'Oh I'm held up at work.'

Dominic Well, I am!

Amy Then it's midnight. I'm sleeping. Always in a bed of wet nappies, of course. 'Oh Amy, can't speak.' If you can't speak why call me? Why call me? 'I'm with this producer.'

Dominic is suddenly quiet, lethal.

Dominic Well, what do you want? Do you want I don't call you?

Amy No.

Dominic Do you want I never call you at all?

There is a moment. They have fallen into a real, disastrous row. Amy turns away.

Amy Oh please, let's leave it. Just leave it.

Esme watches from the side, quite still.

I want to ask Mum how she'd manage to live.

Esme Me?

Amy Yes.

Esme I suppose, on my income. Remember, I always have Frank.

Frank I control her portfolio.

Esme Frank is my saviour. He allows me to ignore all that nonsense. I never read any of that stuff myself.

Frank She doesn't!

Esme I don't even take in the figures . . .

Frank It's true. They just pass before her eyes!

Esme I don't care. As long as there's food in the larder . . . I know! I'm just lucky that Frank came along.

She throws a warm glance to Frank, who basks in her approval. Amy watches, trying to understand what is going on.

Frank And I must say, you know, since my wife died, I admit, my evenings had been fairly bleak. With no Sarah. So to come round and talk about Esme's investments . . .

Esme Drink whisky.

Frank That too. For me, it's been very healing. It has. I owe Esme everything. Yes, in her quiet way, she's nursed me back to good mental health.

Frank seems almost overwhelmed. Amy is tentative, a little confused.

Amy And you think she could manage . . . she could get by financially?

Frank Why yes. Not to live like John Paul Getty, of course. But surviving. Managing to live with some sort of dignity.

Esme And God knows dignity's not nothing these days.

Amy But what would you *do*?

Esme Oh there's far too much talk about 'doing'. If I gave up, then I'd just have to get on and 'be'.

She is half satirical. But Amy is dismayed.

Amy Well, I'm just stunned.

Esme Why?

Amy It seems so extraordinary. Dominic.

Dominic Hmm?

Amy What do you think?

Dominic Oh. I've always thought the theatre was boring. So I quite see why you want to get out.

Esme is amused by this, but Amy is not.

Amy That's not quite what she was saying.

Dominic No. She said something like it.

Esme Oh Dominic! Making mischief again!

Dominic Is that what I do?

Esme A professional passer of judgements!

She makes a little mock-swipe with her hand at Frank.

Frank, you're not really saying you've missed this little programme of his.

Frank Well . . .

Esme Dominic's our cultural arbiter. He exists to tells us what's good.

Dominic Not at all.

Esme He informs the public what they should be seeing.

Dominic On the contrary! 'Should' isn't in it. It's to get rid of 'should' that the programme exists.

Frank 'Should'?

Dominic We all know that art is encrusted in snobbery. People feel frightened. The arts establishment tries to make them feel cowed.

Frank I see.

Dominic So we say to them: 'Don't be bullied. Just follow your own instincts. Don't let anyone dictate to you. Make up your own minds.'

Esme is eager to join in.

Esme At the end . . .

Dominic Yes . . .

Esme They have a small item.

Dominic Very brief.

Esme What's it called?

Amy It's called *Not Up to Snuff*.

Esme That's right. Where they kindly bring the public up to date on art which they feel has been over-praised.

Dominic is beginning to feel goaded.

Dominic Why not? I don't apologise.

Esme There's a little animated figure . . .

Dominic This drawing . . .

Esme This little cartoon bloke in a cap, and he takes the work they discuss. Then he throws it . . .

Frank Oh yes, now I remember. I've seen it!

Esme He throws it into a bathroom.

Dominic Splash!

Esme And you then hear the sound of a loo being flushed. It's wit.

She smiles.

Dominic All right, but why do we do it? Because there's so much hype, there's so much palaver, there's so many people claiming to be artists these days.

Esme Is that right?

Dominic So why not invent some sort of decent corrective, in which you say: 'Hold on, let's just be serious. Is this thing as good as everyone makes out?'

Esme watches from the side, glass in hand, pleased with the bonfire she's lit.

Frank Interesting.

Dominic Like a book . . . you buy a book. What is it? Twelve pounds? Thirteen? We're there to say: now let's just be careful. Is this really all it's cracked up to be?

Esme Ah, you're performing a public duty, you mean?

Esme moves round the room with her drink.

Ah yes. Like a hangman. Reluctant, but responsible. 'It's a dirty job but it's got to be done.' Is that it? You're – what? – *public-spirited*? But that doesn't quite explain the relish you show.

Dominic What relish?

Esme When something is awful.

Dominic I say so.

Esme Yes.

Dominic What's wrong with that?

Esme Oh nothing. Just that glint round the eyes. That smile. 'Oh God be praised, I've got a real stinker. What happiness! Now I can really rip into this . . .'

Dominic is beginning to get angry.

Dominic Look . . . What . . . so what are you saying? Do you think I've some kind of personal axe to grind?

Esme Oh, seriously now, Dominic, come on!

Dominic *What?*

She has turned away, laughing.

Esme It's not for me to say, but years ago, remember, when I first met you – with Amy – you wanted to make your own films.

Dominic Well, I do!

Esme I mean real films! Not people wittering about other people's work. I mean, actual new-minted stories. Showing people. In the grip of real passions.

But Dominic is already shaking his head.

Dominic Oh that's simply old-fashioned. It really is nonsense! I don't accept that distinction at all.

Esme No?

Dominic That whole old-fashioned notion! Criticism can be just as creative as making up *stories*, you know. Sometimes more so. Seeing things clearly, placing them, giving them context: that work is just as important as art.

Esme You think so?

Esme grins conspiratorially at Amy.

Dominic Oh I suppose you think it's all down to jealousy. Of course! Isn't that what actors and writers all say? I must somehow be jealous. The perpetual excuse! Critics only hate you because they've not had the guts to make crappy British features or churn out turgid middle-class novels themselves.

Esme just smiles, as if his tone proved her case.

Esme Well . . .

Dominic I suppose you think critics are all fuelled by jealousy?

Esme Not all of them, no.

Dominic But you think that I am?

Esme looks at him a moment, serious.

Esme I think you're aware of your power.

Dominic I most certainly hope so. Because the point is, I try to use it for good.

Dominic in his view has won the argument.

And the result is, the programme's almost absurdly successful . . .

Esme I know that.

Dominic Its ratings are way beyond what anyone hoped. Because it actually puts itself – unlike all the others – on the side of the consumer . . .

Esme The consumer?

Dominic Yes. By which I mean ordinary people like me . . .

Esme Oh . . .

Dominic And this whole, you know, arty flim-flammery, this whole elitist nonsense of 'bloody-well-like-this' and 'we-know-what's-what' – I tell you, that attitude's over. It's finished.

Esme Well, thank God at least we're clear about that.

Dominic looks at her warily.

It is the most wonderful casting. The country's most famous, most influential programme which lays down the law on the arts. And it's run by a man who seems to have only one small disadvantage. What is it? Remind me. Oh yes, I remember.

She suddenly looks across the room at him with real savagery.

It turns out he doesn't like art!

She has lit the blue touchpaper but before Dominic can react, Evelyn comes into the room. She is now eighty-four. She is still physically firm, in one of her tartan skirts and pullovers. But when Esme gets up to usher her to her favoured chair you see that she is being treated differently.

Ah Evelyn. All right?

Evelyn I thought I heard voices.

Esme You did.

Evelyn There are people here.

Esme Yes, that's right. This is Dominic.

Evelyn Dominic?

Dominic Evelyn.

Esme You remember? And Amy.

Amy Grandma.

Evelyn Yes, I remember. And you? Who are you?

Esme I'm your daughter-in-law. I'm Esme.

Evelyn And Bernard? Where's Bernard?

Esme I'm afraid to say Bernard's not here.

Evelyn Not here?

Esme No. Bernard is dead.

Evelyn Dead?

Esme Do me a favour, Frank. Can you just get her a drink?

Evelyn has sat down, very confused now. Dominic is restless, wanting to interrupt.

Dominic Look . . .

Evelyn He's dead and nobody told me?

Esme Nonsense. We told you, it's just you forget.

Evelyn How could you not tell me?

She is beginning to cry. Esme is signalling urgently to Frank.

Esme More. More. Just keep pouring.

Evelyn You didn't even tell me. How could you? Why did nobody tell me?

Esme ignores Evelyn's crying.

Dominic I'm sorry, I'm aware that somehow you all think it's funny . . .

Amy Oh God, now that *is* the children this time . . .

She goes to the hall, as Dominic goes on.

Dominic There's some sort of hidden agreement in play . . .

Frank holds up a huge measure of scotch.

Esme Yes, that's fine.

Dominic You think you can all just dump on my programme . . .

Esme (*taking it*) Thank you . . .

Dominic 'Oh it's all just this trivial rubbish on telly. So it doesn't matter, we can say what we like . . .'

Esme Oh really now, Dominic . . .

Dominic Whereas – please! – just imagine the horror if I decided that this was a two-way privilege. Oh, if I decided to tell the truth about you!

Frank looks puzzled, but Esme turns, at last giving Dominic her whole attention.

Frank What truth?

Esme Dominic, you're highly successful. You've no reason to worry. You now have the power you craved.

Dominic But of course in your view that's vulgar and nasty . . .

Esme I haven't said anything!

Dominic Because you think it's wrong to want to get on!

Amy is returning through the hall and Dominic is prompted by the sound of her.

Evelyn It's good. Can I have some more?

Esme No, not now.

Amy is at the door, unaware of what has gone on.

Amy Dominic, you did say you'd bath them.

Dominic I will bath them.

Amy Well, when?

There is a new determination in his eye.

Dominic I will do it. I will bath them just as I promised. And then – I'm sorry – but I'm going to take them back home.

Amy What?

Dominic Yes. I'm just tired of this snobbery . . .

Amy What snobbery?

Esme Oh really!

Frank Now steady on . . .

Dominic This unspoken assumption. You know what I'm saying. Always! This permanent leer of good taste! Whenever I come here, I walk into this household . . .

Amy Oh . . .

Dominic I just have to take one look at the walls. And suddenly I'm back in short trousers. I feel like I'm back to being fifteen years old.

Amy looks, but Esme is not reacting.

And you two go into a huddle. The two of you. Smiling and giggling like schoolgirls in each other's ears. And at once I'm no better than some sort of dustman or servant.

Amy Dominic, I think you exaggerate.

Evelyn has been peering at Dominic.

Evelyn Is that man Bernard?

Esme I think we can safely say that he's not.

*Dominic is expressing years of grievance and he's not
going to let go.*

Dominic And I do understand. Yes of course, you resent
me. You're right. I work in a medium which you look
down on. You pretend it's not good. But in fact that's not
your real reason. You really don't like it because television
brings you bad news. Because actually, in some crude
way, it does belong to the people . . .

Esme Oh Dominic, 'the people'!

She laughs out loud, mocking him.

What do you know about 'the people', indeed?

Dominic Yes, the truth is: you fear it. Because in its
awful, gaudy vitality, television reminds you of what
people think. And when you hear their opinions, when
you see the evidence of their real taste, then it's pitifully
obvious: the sheer downright irrelevance of this self-
enclosed arty little world that you've made.

Esme Oh . . .

Dominic People love things which you think are vulgar.
They've no time for the stuff which you think so great!

He smiles, anticipating his own joke.

Forgive me, but a lot of people love Deirdre Keane. They
think she's a very fine actress.

Esme Dominic, there's no one in the world who really
thinks that.

Amy Look, Dominic . . .

Dominic What?

Amy Can't you just leave it?

Dominic Why should I?

Amy Not everything is directed at you. You always do this. It's one of those stupid, meaningless arguments . . .

But Dominic is only fired more by her challenge.

Dominic I'm swamped in this bloody English gentility! It's typical. She opens this absurd bloody fête! But the question is, will that stop her doing it? Oh no, not her. She wants it both ways. Both to do it and mock it.

Amy Dominic . . .

Dominic It's classic. The English attitude to their own institutions: defend them to strangers but laugh at them yourselves! The privilege of not seeming to take anything seriously. But still making sure that nothing is changed!

Esme is quiet. He knows he has hit home.

If you don't want to do the programme, then say so! Instead of just trying to get me provoked.

Amy She's not trying. I'd say she's succeeding.

He looks unforgivingly at Amy.

Dominic I've always thought this. Whenever we've visited. I've had the same thought. She is permitted to look down on how I make my living. But I'm not permitted to look down on hers.

There is a depth of feeling now which silences the others. Frank tries to help.

Frank I'm sorry, I've been standing here. But I haven't heard anything – not one single syllable – to cause you such desperate offence. All right, you were arguing about culture. I know nothing about culture. I'm the first to admit. The last film I saw was *Doctor Zhivago*. In my opinion, it was pretty good. But even if someone came along and said, no, you're wrong, it was bollocks, it

DAVID HARE

hardly seems to me important. It's not worth risking a friendship for that.

Dominic But we're not. That's not the argument. We're not talking about art. Isn't that right? No, we're discussing something quite different.

Frank What's that?

Neither Esme nor Dominic want to answer.

What are you discussing?

Dominic Whether I deserve her daughter or not.

Evelyn Her daughter?

Amy makes to intervene, but Dominic overrides her.

Amy Dominic . . .

Dominic You know she once told me Amy was pregnant. She told me before Amy herself. Yes. You remember that evening? When your mother blurted it out?

He looks now at Amy.

I wonder, do you know why she did that? Did you believe her when she said it just sort of slipped out? 'Just sort of *slipped out*'? No, I don't think so. She said it in the hope I might then go away. She's never come to terms with the fact Amy loves me. She thinks that Amy is wrong to share her life on my terms.

Amy She's never said that.

Dominic Hasn't she? She thinks you shouldn't have taken me. She hates the arrangement we made.

Amy Please.

Dominic It was clear. I would always put my work first. Well, it's true. We did agree that. Didn't we? Esme disapproved.

Esme's face is set like a mask.

You see, she can't answer. She won't. That's Esme. To her credit, she'll never say the kind thing. But why don't we stop this dancing round each other's feelings? Why don't I simply stop coming down?

Esme Fine.

Amy Mum . . .

Dominic I didn't want you on the programme.

Esme No. No, I can see that.

Dominic The whole thing was Amy's idea.

Esme Yes.

Dominic Because . . . well, we know Amy . . . it's Amy's view that everyone should try to get on.

There is a moment's silence.

Well, I say no, actually, let's really not bother. The mistake is to try and be kind. Like employing actresses to talk about theatre for no other reason but they're down on their luck.

Amy looks down, embarrassed by this now.

I didn't think it was sensible. I didn't want my girlfriend's mother, you see. Because I knew I'd be having her for the wrong reasons . . .

Esme Yes.

Dominic And things always go wrong when they're done in bad faith.

He moves towards the door.

It's up to you, Amy. I can take the children or not. Please. Either stay the weekend with your mother. Or else why not come back with me?

*He goes out and up the stairs. We hear him calling
to the children. Evelyn has fallen asleep. Amy takes
a step towards Esme, who is giving nothing away.*

Amy I wonder . . . do you think you could go and see if
he'll talk to you?

*Esme looks at her as if she doesn't understand the
question.*

Mum, I do know it isn't your fault. But if you . . . I don't
know . . . if you just went up and talked to him . . .

Frank You could at least talk to him, Esme.

Esme Oh, so you think that as well?

She walks across the room. She lights a cigarette.

What, I'm meant to apologise?

Amy No.

Esme I'm meant to pretend I've done something wrong?

Esme shrugs slightly.

He's right. There are people who are simply not meant
to get on. Amy, you do it from kindness. I know that. I
know it's your view that love conquers all. But it doesn't.
Or at least, that's what I've learned.

*At once from upstairs the sound of Dominic calling
down.*

Dominic (*off*) Are you coming, Amy? Are we taking the
children? They're ready. They can go back.

Amy (*calls*) Just give me a minute.

She looks all the time at Esme.

(*Calls.*) I just need a minute.

Dominic (*off*) We're going.

Amy takes a step towards Esme.

Esme Come on, it's not so dramatic, it's not so disastrous as that. We'll see each other. I'll see the children.

Amy You've never understood. You know that I love him. You never see the man who I love.

Esme No. And if I was going to, I fear the moment has passed. Now I'm getting supper.

She has suddenly moved dismissively, but Amy is infuriated by her answer.

Dominic (*off*) Amy!

Amy Why do you say that? You still can't forgive me. You can't forgive the choice that I made.

Esme It was wrong.

Amy It isn't your business. And the reason you make it your business is because you have no life of your own!

Dominic (*off*) Amy! Let's go!

Amy turns and goes out. Esme is suddenly stilled by what Amy has said. She stands at the table where she had been headed.

Amy (*off*) Are you ready?

Dominic (*off*) Yes. I've got all your things. Come on, we're going. Just give me a hand.

There is the sound of them on the stairs. Then it goes quiet.

Esme Frank, I wonder, perhaps now this evening . . .

Frank Of course. Tomorrow I'll give you a call.

Esme Would you? I'd like that.

He nods and moves out through the veranda, patting his pockets as he goes.

Frank Are you all right, Esme?

Esme I promise I'm fine.

Frank goes out. It is nearly dark outside. Esme moves to clear up the glasses and plates. From outside the sound of the children and the adults. Then the door slamming and the car driving away. As Esme collects the last plate, Evelyn wakes.

Evelyn Where's Bernard? Somebody tell me. Where's Bernard?

Esme Evelyn, I've told you. Bernard is dead.

Evelyn Yes.

There is a short pause.

Evelyn And so tell me one more thing. Where's Bernard?

Esme goes into the veranda. She sets down a chair where she can sit with her back to us and stare at the night sky. Then after a while she answers.

Esme Bernard's not here. Bernard is dead.

End of Act Two.

Act Three

The same. It is eight years later. A summer night in 1993. It is very dark. A single lamp burns at the table, throwing big shadows all over the room. Frank is sitting in shirtsleeves and corduroys, working alone. The table is piled up with books and documents. He has glasses on and has been working for many hours. His customary bottle of whisky is beside him. At some distance from him Evelyn is asleep in a wheelchair. She is ninety-two. She is very thin with an astonishingly pale face and a shock of white hair. She sleeps with her mouth open.

After a few moments, Frank looks up at the sound of someone moving outside. Amy appears through the veranda entrance. Now in her late thirties, she looks thinner than ever, and quite aged, almost gaunt. She comes quickly into the room, like a refugee, not realising there is anyone there.

Amy My God, you surprised me.

Frank I'm sorry.

Amy The veranda was open.

There is a moment's unease.

I didn't know you'd be here.

She hesitates, then kisses him, just brushing his cheek.

Frank.

Frank Hello, Amy. Are you looking for your mother?

Amy Well, yes. Is she always this late?

Frank No. But today there's a big operation . . .

Amy Oh right.

Frank She's been building up to it all week. And they can be quite tricky.

Amy nods, understanding.

I wish she would learn to drive herself back.

Amy looks at him a moment.

Amy And you?

Frank Me?

Amy Are you actually living here?

Frank Oh . . .

Amy Are you living here now?

Frank Do I really live here? I think you'd have to ask Esme. And will you please let me know what she says?

Amy puts her car keys down on the table.

Amy And do you bring her supper?

Frank Oh well, meals can be quite chaotic.

Amy Does she still get her stuff from the pub?

Frank Surely you noticed . . .

Amy No, I didn't see anything . . .

Frank No pub any more.

Amy Really?

Frank is trying to put her at ease.

Frank They've made it a wine bar. Everything's changed. You can only get wind-dried yak meat. Native Berkshire dishes like that. Served with alfalfa sprout salad.

Amy Good gracious.

Frank Oh Lord yes. All washed down with Aqua-Libra on draught.

Amy has begun to move round the room, looking at the walls.

Amy And how's Mum?

Frank Bearing up. Considering. I've been trying to persuade her to move out of here . . .

Amy Ah.

Frank After what's happened. It's frankly too large. She could even live in London. Why not? But you know your mother.

Amy Stubborn.

Frank Yes.

Amy I was expecting the walls to be stripped.

Frank Not yet.

Amy Has she sold any paintings?

Frank I'm not even sure she would if she could.

He grimaces slightly.

Your father isn't collected. Except by people who loved and remember the man. And now even they are all turning seventy.

Amy Yes. I suppose.

Frank Bernard's almost completely forgotten. Except by one or two students. One of them came here, said, 'I'm not really interested, if you want to know the truth. But Bernard Thomas is perfect for a thesis. He's just the right degree of obscure.'

He smiles wryly, but she doesn't respond.

I wonder . . . can I get you anything?

She shakes her head.

Did your mother know you'd be here?

Amy No.

Frank I must say . . . she didn't mention it . . .

Amy We haven't spoken for a while.

He waits a moment.

Frank It's funny. In some way she's carefree. After such a disaster. I know it's perverse. But in some way it's made her much happier.

Amy Yes, I can see that.

Frank A burden's been lifted.

Amy frowns at him, concentrating now.

Amy You've been with her a lot?

Frank Well, I do have a pair of pyjamas. There's a pair I keep in this house.

Amy But where are they?

Frank Oh, sadly they're in the guest room. But, remember, the guest room is not far from Esme's.

Amy I see.

Frank She wakes in the night, to be honest. Her dreams are very intense. I sit by the bed till she sleeps.

Amy She's always alone?

Frank does not answer.

Frank I think you know what I feel for her, Amy. I can't help it, I've felt the same way for years. Perhaps even before my wife died. People say to me, 'You're crazy, you can't go on doing this. You've waited such a long time.' I say, 'And I'll wait longer.'

Amy Yes.

Amy looks beyond him to Evelyn.

And Evelyn?

Frank Oh, Evelyn. Does she hear? She no longer speaks. The fretting is over.

Amy passes a hand right in front of Evelyn's face but there is no reaction.

You can never tell. Has she accepted her fate?

Esme appears, stopping at once at the sight of Amy. Now in her early sixties, she is carrying a bundle of envelopes.

Esme Well, Amy, good gracious.

She has spoken quietly, and Amy turns in surprise.

Amy Mum. I didn't hear you.

Esme Oh no? I'm afraid I did take a taxi. I know I shouldn't, but I thought what the hell? Frank doesn't like it.

Neither of the women know what to do. They stand a moment, lost.

Amy Are you all right?

Esme Yes. I'm exhausted. It's been a tough day. Why haven't you called me?

Amy Oh . . .

Esme makes a useless gesture with her hand, and the dam bursts. She moves and embraces Amy, weeping.

Esme Oh my God, Amy. Amy, how I've missed you, my darling . . .

Amy I know.

Esme It's been so awful. No, really . . .

Amy Oh Mum . . .

Esme is crying, overwhelmed and running her hands through Amy's hair.

Esme Really, no really, I'm fine . . .

Amy Oh Mother . . .

Esme is deliberately pulling herself away to try and recover from her outburst.

Esme Honestly it's . . . oh, it's . . . oh it's so silly, forgive me, I can't even speak.

Amy Don't worry.

Amy holds her mother's head in her hands a moment and looks into her eyes.

Don't worry!

Esme It's also . . .

Amy Go on.

Esme What does it matter? You're here.

Impulsively she hugs her daughter again.

Amy It's all right. Go on, say . . .

Esme Oh Lord, I know I sound selfish . . .

Amy You don't . . .

Esme But, the fact is, the truth is: I have had one hell of a day.

They both laugh at the absurdity, and Esme moves away to recover from the emotion.

Amy Well, I'm sure.

Esme I can't tell you, we had this patient . . .

Amy What patient?

Esme Oh, you know . . .

Frank Do you want a drink?

She waves a hand in dismissal.

Esme An old man of seventy. It was awful. He needed a new aorta.

Amy An aorta?

Esme Yes. There's no question, if we hadn't done it, he would have died.

Amy Well . . .

Frank Sit down.

Esme You've probably heard, there's this new operation . . .

Amy No. No, of course not. How could I have heard?

Esme You take a valve from a pig . . .

Amy A pig?

Esme You extract it, you keep it in ice. You take this little rounded ring of pig's muscle . . .

Frank It's true.

Esme And you sew it into the heart of the patient. It serves to replace the patient's own valve . . .

Amy I see.

Esme No, really it's almost standard procedure. But the point is, you're working very intensely – well, you can imagine – you're at this very high pitch . . .

Amy Sure.

Esme There's blood everywhere, great thick pools of it . . .

Amy My God!

Esme Crimson! Then there's the lasers, the burning . . . the flesh being cut . . .

She shakes her head.

I turn round, I'm passing the scalpel, I look down at this hand next to mine. This little nurse has actually got a ring on her finger. And what's more she's wearing this awful clunky paste bangle . . .

Frank looks nervously at Amy, as if fearing where this story is going.

I simply think: no, I cannot believe this. I'm sorry. No, really!

Frank I can imagine . . .

Esme And the fact is . . .

She pauses for a moment.

Well, I'm afraid I just go.

Amy Go?

Esme Yes, what I mean is, I started to shout at her. I was shouting! Amy, I do know it's wrong. But it's so unhygienic. What, I'm meant to say nothing?

Frank This isn't the first time . . .

Esme I say, 'What the hell's going on?'

Frank smiles uneasily at Amy.

Frank What does she say?

Esme I say, 'This is serious.' This nurse, she's just so weedy, she's like this weedy little thing. I've never even seen her before. I say, 'For Christ's sake it's a major operation. The cameras see everything.' She just stands there. She looks at me like I'm going mad.

Frank Well, I'm sure.

Esme So now the whole studio's stopping. The director – oh, he's coming down from on high! This little idiot starts sulking. She says, 'Oh come on, it's only TV.'

Esme pauses, furious.

Well . . .

Frank My God!

Esme No, I'm sorry, but to me that's unforgivable. You can say anything but you must never say that.

Frank smiles again at Amy.

Frank This has happened before.

Esme 'If we do it, we make it authentic, or else let's not do it at all . . .' Well, it's true! That's the whole principle. Do it properly! You have to ask yourself, 'Is it real or is it not?'

Amy frowns, not able to answer.

Anyway, by now – oh, bloody chaos! The surgeon's dropped the scalpel in this awful prop pool of blood. The patient's sitting up on the table, he says, 'I'm sorry to ask this, but do I get a new aorta or not?'

Frank That's funny.

Esme People are gathering. They're saying, 'Look, we know you've been under great strain.' I'm screaming, 'It's not me, for Christ's sake. Why are you getting at me? It's that little tart with her sugar daddy's jewellery, she's the one who's destroying the show . . .'

She has suddenly become quite vicious.

Frank (*to Amy*) What about you? Will you have a drink?

Esme Apart from anything, just think of my character . . .

Frank Nurse Banstead . . .

Esme From her point of view – well think of it, you've seen the show . . .

Amy looks non-committal.

It's obvious. She's called a disciplinarian. You could say. Or you could say she's just one tough bloody bitch.

Frank Oh she is!

Esme Whichever. Do you really think she'd permit it? It's inconceivable! It's just unprofessional. I'm sorry, forget it, but that's what I think.

Frank seems nervous of his next question.

Frank But . . .

Esme But what?

Frank You did resume shooting?

Esme What? Well after an hour or two, sure. We had to get a new valve.

She looks angrily at Frank.

Oh Frank, please, I do know what you're asking. I'm not stupid! The only thing that concerns him . . .

Frank Well . . .

Esme Will I get thrown off the show?

Amy is frowning, not really understanding what's going on between them.

With Frank it's all about money, there's nothing but money. Every night he tells me, 'You must hold on to this job . . .'

Frank Well, you must!

Esme 'For your own sake,' he says, 'just keep your head down . . .' That's Frank! Anything rather than let me speak out!

Frank turns to Amy silently to ask what choice he has.

And I say, 'What? I'm just meant to endure these conditions? When the theatre is filthy? When people's lives are at risk?'

Frank Esme . . .

Esme I'm meant to say nothing? When basic medical procedure is flouted in front of my eyes? I'm sorry, I don't care, I'm not going to do it. I do have a conscience! There are times when it's simply too much.

Frank Of course.

Esme has picked up the envelopes she has earlier put down on the table.

Esme He never lets me forget the white envelopes . . .

She makes a fist of them in her hand.

Oh, I'm not opening them. I'm going to talk to my daughter instead.

Frank Do you want me to do it?

Esme No. They're my bloody envelopes. Thank you. I'll open these bastards myself.

Frank stands rebuked.

It's the post . . . the post is so frightening. I try to leave it until I get back. So that way . . .

Frank It makes no difference.

Esme I don't go to work in the morning . . .

Amy I can imagine . . .

Esme Simply not able to think.

Frank is enjoying this.

Frank She used to put them under the cushions . . .

Esme Oh really!

Frank It's true. I'd go round in the day, just feeling all the cracks in sofas to see if I'd come across more!

Esme All right, but it isn't actually as stupid as you think it is. You get the same letters again and again. So for God's sake . . .

She suddenly gives up.

Oh, stuff it! I actually don't want to discuss it. Not tonight. Can we please not discuss it? I haven't seen Amy for months.

Amy No.

Frank looks between them.

Frank Perhaps I should go. I'll make you both cocoa. Esme always has a cup before bed.

Esme That's great. Yes, will you?

She waves a hand ironically.

My domestic servant.

Frank If it was meant as a joke, then perhaps I would laugh.

He goes out closing the door.

Esme Oh really!

Amy He's funny. He is so devoted.

Esme Yes. I'm afraid he is desperate to marry me though. What's worse, it's getting more urgent. If I don't do it, he says he's going to give up.

Amy But he just told me the opposite . . .

Esme Did he?

Amy He told me he'd wait for you.

Esme Oh, I wish it were true. In fact there's a deadline. Yes, by Christmas.

Amy And what will you do?

Esme Oh, Christmas! I can't even see beyond Wednesday. I don't know. One day I'm afraid I may have to give in. I'll get into his Ford Granada. Drive cross country. Do it in some county town with nobody there. Spend the honeymoon in one of those phoney ivy-clad riverside hotels.

She gets a cigarette, suddenly exasperated.

How did it happen? I never foresaw this! Never!

Amy is unimpressed by the theatricality of her complaint.

Amy Oh come on, it isn't that bad.

Esme Isn't it?

Amy Of course not.

Esme I'm sorry. You're right.

She has suddenly conceded, and now she looks tearfully at Amy, not able to believe that she is back in the house.

I see you there, Amy, and for the first time ever I am feeling nervous . . .

Amy Mum . . .

Esme I mean, I'm nervous, but I'm also relieved.

The tension is resolved. Esme speaks more gently.

I've missed you . . .

Amy Me too.

Esme I've missed you so terribly. How long is it? It must be over six months. I keep reading in the papers about all your problems. And I've so longed to be able to talk. The whole thing's left me feeling so helpless.

Amy Yes, I've felt pretty helpless myself.

Amy manages a brave grin but her eyes are beginning to fill with tears.

I suppose you could say I've behaved like a coward. I couldn't help it. I went into my shell.

Esme Yes.

Amy It never lets up. Never. In fact, throughout it, I've not talked to anyone. I've just stayed with the children.

Esme How are they?

Amy The children are fine.

Amy waves a hand impatiently.

Oh we just hide all the papers. We hope the other kids say nothing at school.

Esme She's some sort of Swedish film star?

Amy Yes.

Esme I'm afraid I'd never heard of her.

Amy You're in a minority of one. That's why the media has been so enthused. We've had them on the doorstep with cameras.

Esme Is it possible? She is really Swedish?

Amy I think so.

Esme Swedish!

She looks away in disgust.

How low can you get?

Amy She has this throaty sort of gurgle. A tan and tons of blonde hair.

Esme You've met her?

Amy (*nods*) She's kind of a brainless Heidi. This big open grin. A lot of 'Why can't we be friends?'

Esme Please!

Amy 'Why can't we be friends? Because you're sleeping with my husband. I think that's one thing that might just get in the way.' I don't buy her dewy-eyed innocence.

Esme How could you?

Amy Oh, but she does have quite a good act.

Amy looks at Esme a moment.

But what's worst is that Dominic's bewildered. He's guilty.

Esme I'm sure he is.

Amy No. Truly. It's much, much worse than you'd think. Because he's lost. It's true. It's like he's spun off his axis. Most of the time, he acts like he's crazy. What's sad is, he doesn't even know what he wants. Things had been so much better. I promise. Since our wedding, it was odd, for the first time we were almost at peace. Deciding to marry . . . it helped to resolve things. And then this woman came out of the blue.

Esme is watching her, quiet, respectful.

Also he's now this media monolith. Music. And chat shows. And videos. So he sets out at dawn and escapes to his work.

Esme Is he living in the house?

Amy Oh sure, yes, we're living together. 'For the sake of the children.' Is that what they say? Not that it makes any difference. I never see him. Unless I walk by a telly. I can watch him on telly, if I so choose.

Amy is in agony, paler than ever.

I'm trying, but it's hard to stay steady. In any relationship you get cast in a role.

Esme I understand.

Amy Yes, I've played the strong one. And after a while that starts taking its toll.

Esme is about to reply. Amy interrupts, as if she doesn't want to hear.

Esme Well . . .

Amy And meanwhile you and I were no longer speaking . . .

Esme Darling, whose fault is that?

Amy And then I got wind of what's happening to you . . .

Esme (*dismissively*) Oh . . .

Amy I spoke to some people I know. The word is you're now in serious trouble. Well, tell me!

Esme Oh sure, but mine's only money, that's all.

She smiles blithely at Amy.

Amy Debts?

Esme Yes of course.

Amy And are they substantial?

Esme I've really lost track of them . . .

Amy Mum . . .

Esme They change all the time.

Amy looks at her, not letting her off.

The last time I opened one of those envelopes, then, yes, it was quite a large sum.

Amy How much?

But Esme has already got up and is heading for the discarded envelopes.

Esme Hold on, now where are my glasses? Let's look at this one which just came today. Look, yes, it's not so unusual.

She is holding the letter from the envelope some way from her glasses.

It seems to be round about five.

Amy Five? Five what?

Esme Five hundred thousand.

Amy Mum . . .

Esme Five hundred thousand – or so. There are lots of smaller figures as well. Not *exactly* five hundred thousand. Something a little more jagged than that.

> *She is peering in a rather actressy way which plainly irritates Amy.*

Or perhaps it's a six. It's all academic. It isn't the largest I've had. One morning, I simply couldn't believe it. I looked at it. It was eight! It was over eight hundred thousand. I thought this is just like being poked in the eye.

Amy Why are you laughing?

Esme My dear, what else can I do? The whole thing is just so totally . . . well, it's an out-of-body experience. What is the point of pretending it's real?

Amy But it is real.

Esme Yes. But – sorry – I simply don't have it. So what on earth do they want me to do?

> *Frank comes in triumphantly with a tray of hot drinks and biscuits.*

Frank Cocoa!

Esme I mean of course they can have what I give them . . .

Frank It's thick, how you like it.

Esme I give them every penny I have.

Frank She does love it thick.

Amy But surely you don't have to go on paying for ever?

Frank Oh Lord, are we on the forbidden subject again?

Frank grins cheekily across the room.

Amy Is it true it's all down to asbestos?

Esme Asbestos! You name it. There's also this silicone they stick in women's breasts . . .

Amy Silicone?

Esme Millions of American housewives . . .

Frank It's crazy . . .

Esme All suing their doctors. There's hurricanes.

Frank Called Hugo. Elyse. Victoria.

Esme That's right. Speeding through America, turning houses to matchsticks. In spite of their sweet little names.

Frank smiles up from stirring cocoa as Esme becomes more extravagant.

I tell you, whenever there's a serious disaster – you fall down, fall over, your house is burnt to the ground – in every country in the world, the procedure's the same, you turn to the victims and say: 'Don't fret, don't worry, there's really no problem. Just fill up a form and this weird British actress will pay!'

But Frank now wants to dissent.

Frank Oh please now, my dear, you slightly exaggerate . . .

Esme Do I?

Frank There are plenty of syndicates doing much worse than yours.

Esme How can they do worse? I'm losing everything! How can you lose more than everything?

Frank Well . . .

Esme It simply doesn't make sense.

Amy But . . . I'm sorry . . . who chose these syndicates? Who actually decided which ones you were in?

Esme The man with the cocoa.

Frank is stirring the milky drinks. There is a moment's silence.

Frank It's true.

Amy You?

Frank Yes.

Esme You didn't know that?

Amy I suppose I'd never quite grasped it. You personally?

Esme Frank is a commissioning agent for Lloyd's.

Frank I am. I bring them their business. I find them their clients.

Amy I see.

Frank waits for what Amy will say next. It is a delicate moment.

I knew you did something financial . . .

Frank No, no, specifically.

Amy I knew you advised her.

Frank I did. I advised her in all sorts of ways. I took charge of her money. That's what I did for her.

Esme He has that unhappy distinction.

Frank That's right.

There is an awkward silence.

It was my job to place it. So you might say, in one sense, the whole thing's my fault.

Amy Yes.

Frank smiles as if this idea were absurd.

But I mean . . . you did warn her?

Frank Of course.

Amy You did explain all the risks?

Frank Please. There's no question. I did everything right. I did behave ethically. Impeccably.

He leans in to Amy.

Biscuits?

Amy No thank you.

Frank It's a matter of simple bad luck.

Esme has sat down, content to let Frank explain. Frank seems equable, undisturbed.

Amy But the point is I also . . . I read in the paper there are certain people . . . it seems there's no limit to what they may owe.

Frank Yes.

Amy Is my mother one of them?

Esme Old Muggins. Wouldn't you know?

Frank seems unfazed.

Frank You have to understand: Lloyd's is a great British institution. It may be said to have existed for hundreds of years. It is, you might say, without peer. But it does have one special characteristic which makes it different from any other business in the world. Unlimited liability. As an investor you put up money and then in return . . . your exposure may literally be open-ended.

Amy I see. And my mother knew this?

Frank Oh certainly, I'd say she was fully aware.

Amy's tone is lower, more dangerous.

I don't think it actually occurred to her . . . it didn't occur to any of the investors in fact . . .

Amy Quite . . .

Frank An eventual disaster might one day transpire. There were few signs.

Amy But I don't quite know how to ask this . . . I suppose we can take it for granted . . . presumably you're in the same boat?

Frank looks to Esme.

Frank Well . . .

Amy Aren't you?

Frank Certainly I do have some problems. I've taken bad losses. It hasn't been an easy period for me.

Amy But?

Frank But I was in a different spread of syndicates. This is all highly technical, but I do have a slightly different portfolio.

Amy I see.

Frank's manner is still mild. Esme is like a sphinx.

Frank It's a question of return for your capital. For a higher return you do take higher risks.

Amy And?

Frank Well, in my own investments I admit I was always more cautious.

A decisive moment has been reached. A few seconds pass before Amy speaks.

Amy More cautious with your own money, you mean?

At once Esme gets up.

Frank Now look . . .

Amy All right, I understand now, I understand what's happened . . .

Esme Frank, perhaps you should leave us. I was wondering, why don't you sleep here? We can talk again in the morning.

She kisses him on the cheek.

Frank Yes. Whatever you say.

Frank moves off towards the door. But when he reaches the door he turns back.

Believe me, we all know that people are angry. When something goes wrong like this, it's human nature: you want to lash out. But these things happen. There it is. They're part of experience. Now if you'll excuse me, I'm going upstairs.

He takes his cocoa and goes. As soon as he closes the door, Amy explodes.

Amy Oh come on, I'm sorry, but this is outrageous . . .

Esme Oh Amy.

Amy You know it is.

Esme Do I?

Amy Mother, it's just simple theft. You know what he's done to you.

Esme He hasn't done anything. No, it's simply too easy!
I refuse to start saying that everything must be Frank's
fault.

Amy It isn't his fault? When he's lost all your money . . .

Esme So?

Amy He's taken every penny you had! And did he ever
mention . . . did he ever once mention that he was too
nervous . . . no, he was too *clever* to take all the risks he
was making you take?

Esme is trapped by the question.

Esme No. But, be fair, it's not something I ever asked
him . . .

Amy Oh!

Esme The subject never came up.

Amy I bet it didn't!

Esme I refuse to start saying the whole thing's deliberate.

Amy My God, and this man who's destroyed you . . .
you still let him sleep right here in the house!

Esme Why, of course. I'm allowed a companion.

Amy Yes, and, what's more, being Esme, you choose one
who's actually ruined your life!

But Esme is already on the attack.

Esme I'm sorry, but the fact is, I did take their money.

Amy So?

Esme I used to get a cheque. I never refused it. It came
in year after year. And – all right, you may think me
contemptible – but I always just thought of it as money
for jam.

She looks at Amy, unabashed.

I would just sit there. Open the envelope. I got all this money. I loved it. I never thought twice.

Amy So?

Esme So – please – perhaps you'll excuse me if now I refuse to blame others. How can I blame anyone except for myself?

Amy frowns.

Amy But occasionally you must have had your suspicions . . .

Esme Oh . . .

Amy When the money just flowed in like that? Did you never think, hang on, there must be a catch here?

Esme Well, now you say it.

Amy Did you never think this is too good to be true?

Esme shrugs, insouciant.

Esme The stuff just rolled in like the ocean. The truth is, you do start to think it's your right. You get so you don't even notice. You just sort of think, 'This is nice. This is bound to go on.'

Amy But then when you started to lose some . . .

Esme Ah . . .

Amy Yes, when the losses began . . . then you must at least have considered, you must have thought it was time to get out?

Esme On the contrary. Frank used to say, 'Oh good, look, there's been another plane crash, it helps remind everyone they ought to insure.'

Esme takes advantage of Amy's silence to try and make a joke of it.

The only thing I would say . . .

Amy Yes?

Esme I actually noticed when I was a girl, all the thickest people one bumped into always seemed to be working at Lloyd's.

Amy Oh, really!

Esme There was one chap I knew, even the Church wouldn't take him, but Lloyd's – oh Lord yes, no problem at all.

She laughs, stubbing a cigarette out.

Amy But all right, the point is, you knew you might one day lose *something* . . .

Esme Yes.

Amy You knew there was always that chance.

Esme Oh sure.

Amy But did they actually stop and explain to you, 'Look, you can lose every penny you have?'

Esme seems exhilarated by the question.

Esme Oh, not just every penny. Amy, I don't think you've grasped it. I'm losing much more than that. If it was only everything I had at the moment, then – let's face it – that would be nothing at all.

She stands, triumphant at her own logic.

No, this is . . . well, this is more awesome.

Amy How?

Esme This is everything I'll ever earn. For ever. This is my whole working life. Whatever I do – whatever! – it doesn't make any difference. Do you really not get it? There's simply no end to the money I owe. I can work for the rest of eternity, but the simple fact is: I'll always be broke.

Amy tries to keep her focused.

Amy All right, but did anyone explain to you? Was this explained to you when you first joined?

Esme Oh sure. I mean yes, very loosely.

Amy Mother, please tell me, was it or not?

Esme Yes. I mean, yes. Frank took me to London.

Amy And?

Esme We had a very good lunch. A really good lunch in the actual boardroom at Lloyd's. And the Chairman . . . the point is, he'd seen my Ophelia. And . . . well, he'd just loved it.

Amy moves away, really furious.

Amy I cannot believe this!

Esme And pretty soon after he gave me this form.

Amy This form?

Esme A consent form.

She shakes her head, irritable.

Fair enough, I admit I was flattered. I can't say I read it.

Amy You mean you just signed on the spot?

Esme I will swear to this day: this man really did love my Ophelia. He loved it. In that he was genuine. Whatever else may have been going on.

And now Esme is angry too.

All right, I can see! It's partly pure snobbery. If a cockney had said to me, 'You'll make all this money and you don't do a thing,' I would have said, 'Hold on, I wasn't born yesterday.' So in a way, yes, I don't like to admit it, but it does boil down to a question of style.

She waves helplessly round the room.

You should see it. There are these big silver candlesticks. There is all this china and glass, stretching way down this fabulous oak-panelled room. All right, I can see it's England as sheer bloody theatre. But there are times when theatre's pretty hard to resist.

Amy But, Mother, it's no longer theatre. You might as well face it. Those days are gone. You yourself say it: that England is finished. This is the moment you have to fight back.

Esme looks at her, not understanding.

Esme Fight back? How?

Amy Well . . .

Esme Oh, no doubt you want me to start signing petitions?

Amy Yes . . .

Esme Start saying I'm not going to pay?

Amy Well yes, to begin with. I mean, that would be quite a good start.

Esme Go and sit on some awful committee? Go to meetings in London where people talk about their money all the time?

Amy Mother, for the rest of your life you'll be talking about money. Why not talk about getting some of it back?

Esme Join an action group? No, I don't think so. I don't think I want to be seen on a picket line with a load of judges and Tory MPs. No thank you. I'd much rather just take my punishment. I'll take my punishment and shut the hell up.

Amy Oh, I suppose you think that's so noble . . .

Esme No, I just think it's sensible.

Amy I suppose you think there's some kind of principle here.

Esme Well, I do. I do think principle comes into it. Yes.

Amy Then of course we all know there's no question. We have to accept it. Because we know what part principle plays in your life!

Esme looks at Amy suspiciously now, not sure what she means.

Esme Of course I might do something if I thought it was worth it . . .

Amy Good.

Esme I'd start campaigning if I thought it would actually work.

Amy Well, it will.

Esme So what should I do?

Amy The same as all the other victims.

She pauses a second.

You sue your agent.

Esme Sue Frank?

Amy Of course. It's essential.

Esme Oh please, I do hope that's a joke.

Amy Why?

Esme Oh come on . . .

Amy Even I . . . I've read in the papers . . .

Esme That's just the most crazy idea . . .

Amy Literally, half of Lloyd's members are suing the bastards who got them into this mess. Why shouldn't you?

Esme I'd have thought it was obvious.

Amy Why should you be so different?

Esme Well, I suppose I'm just slightly inhibited by the fact we're meant to get married quite soon.

Esme has shot this joke at her, but now she turns and points at Evelyn.

And also . . . just think. Who looks after Evelyn? Who do you think pays for her nurse?

Amy Well . . .

Esme If it wasn't for Frank and his generosity, Evelyn would have long been living in one of those homes.

But Amy is not letting go.

Amy So what are you saying? That you're going to be Frank's prisoner for the rest of your life?

Esme No, of course not. I'm not Frank's prisoner.

Amy Aren't you?

Esme And Frank, may I remind you, is a very nice man.

Amy Oh yes, a nice man who's lost all your money.

Esme That's not who he is. It's just what he did.

Amy looks at her, amazed.

Amy We are what we do, for Christ's sake. Have you never grasped that? We are nothing else. There's no 'us' apart from the things that we do.

She suddenly raises her voice, infuriated by Esme's unwillingness to fight.

Mother, they're playing you. Do you not understand it? These people are crooks. They have posh manners, but at bottom they're just common criminals. And they feed off people like you! You know full well this is your moment. This moment isn't going to come twice. In your heart I think you do know that. You have to take control of your life.

Esme is suddenly provoked by this phrase.

Esme 'Take control'?

Amy Yes.

Esme What is this claptrap that all of you spout nowadays? Take control! As if our lives were like motor cars. Remember, I've never driven . . .

Amy Exactly!

Esme And what's more I never shall.

Esme is blazing now, full of contempt.

What a meaningless cliché! If you ask me why men always make such fools of themselves, it's because they're in love with the ludicrous notion that there's such a thing as to be in control! And now you want women to try it, you want them to peddle this same silly myth! Oh you all say it so easily, so glibly! 'Take control of our lives.' Who's in control? Finally? I ask you. The answer is no one. No one! If you don't know that, you know nothing. It's children who shout, 'Look at me, I'm in charge . . .' Well, I just won't. I'm refusing. I hate the idea of whingeing. I hate the idea of not taking your medicine and saying, 'All right, I've had some bad luck. But that's life.'

She goes across the room and sits down as if the matter were finished.

You're not going to persuade me. So please let's change the subject.

There is a short silence.

Why are you looking like that?

Amy What, I'm meant to be charmed? Is that it? Is this some performance? My mother putting on this brave and gutsy display. Well, forget it! I'm not bloody charmed by it.

Esme Amy . . .

Amy Not in one single degree!

Amy is moving towards her accusingly.

On the contrary, I don't find it charming. I find it pathetic, you see. I've found it pathetic for the whole of my life. Because as long as I can remember you've done this.

Esme I've done what?

Amy You've pretended it's funny to live in a dream.

Esme is shocked at the depth of her daughter's anger.

'He just loved my Ophelia'! 'It's an out-of-body experience!' 'Oh Lord, I suppose I never checked my accounts!' For Christ's sake, Mother, you're now in your sixties. Do you not think it's time you grew up?

She gestures round the room.

This incredible privileged existence! This exhausting performance! 'I'm an actress. Oh Lord, I know nothing at all!' This prize-winning comedy with my cheerful, lovable mother. 'Oh, just show me the document. Where do I sign?' How long did you think you could do this? This refusal ever to admit or face the problems you have. When the means of solving them are there if you choose.

Esme Oh really?

Amy But no, of course you won't seize them. And why? Because you'd think it demeaning. Because you'd have to behave like everyone else.

Esme sees her chance to retaliate.

Esme Oh I see, and you mean you've done so much better . . .

Amy No . . .

Esme You've lived your life so much better than me? This control you're so keen on – oh yes, you've mastered the rhetoric – sure, the rhetoric's easy! – but I've never noticed you actually exert it yourself. My God, you live with this man, this child, this figure who you think merits your love – and you let him run off with a slice of teenage Scandinavian charcuterie and even then – forgive me! – you don't even leave.

Amy Do you think I don't want to? Do you think I don't want to leave him today?

Esme Then please explain to me, tell me what's stopping you?

Esme smiles at the obviousness of it.

Is it the children or what?

Amy No. No, it isn't the children.

Esme What is it? Is it just dogged persistence? Is it because of Amy's famous view that love conquers all?

Amy No, it's not that.

Esme Then tell me what is it?

Amy What do you think it is?

Suddenly Amy is in real distress.

Because I can't face admitting you're right.

Esme stops, stunned.

Why do you think I've not called you? Why do you think we've not spoken for six months or more?

Esme I don't know.

Amy Because the moment I realised that I was in serious trouble with Dominic, then guess what? I realised I didn't want to speak to my mum.

Esme is silenced, shocked.

You never gave him a chance. There's a side of Dominic that you never saw. That you never wanted to see. From the very first day you were determined to judge him. And now you've got what you want.

Esme That isn't fair.

Amy Isn't it? Do you think I haven't wanted to ring you? Every day I long to ring up the best friend I have . . .

Esme Oh Amy . . .

Amy But every day I think I can't stand that moment, that look of pure triumph which I know I'm going to see in your eye!

Amy smiles bitterly.

You kept saying you looked down on Dominic. He worked in television, that's what you said . . .

Esme All right!

Amy You hated television because its values were poison . . .

Esme That's what I thought then.

Amy Oh, you'd have nothing to do with it . . .

Esme What do you want? I have to live somehow . . .

Amy But don't you see it's all so unfair?

She suddenly laughs outright.

You talk about your bloody TV show. Have I seen it? Have I seen it? I have. But only by wearing dark glasses, and with earplugs stuck in both ears!

Esme turns away.

It's so typical. You lay out your principles. 'The theatre!' Oh, and television's such a low form . . .

Esme Very well.

Amy And I swallow this stuff! And then your principles turn out to be much more like prejudice . . .

Esme All right! Isn't that true of everyone?

Amy But because I believed it, I actually suffered.

Amy shows sudden satirical relish.

At least with Dominic, there's something discussable. In what he does, there's something there you can like or dislike. But Nurse Banstead . . . my God, Nurse Banstead exhibits almost no human features.

Esme Now Amy . . .

Amy The show's beyond anything you can actually
debate. You stand there seriously arguing about whether
an operation's hygienic. Whether the show is authentic
or not. That doesn't depend, you know, on medical
procedure. It depends on whether anyone has learnt
how to act!

Esme It's not bad. It's not badly acted. Some of the scripts
are a little bit weak.

Amy 'Nurse, I think I need an immediate tonsillectomy!'
'Doctor, I'm losing my amniotic fluid.'

Esme Now, Amy, this is just needlessly cruel.

Amy Is it?

Amy is kind now, quieter.

You never saw it. Dominic was funny and gentle.
Ambition's destroyed him, that's all. Because he thinks
that the world of the media matters. He actually thinks
that it's real. So it's been harder to talk to him . . . for
years it's been harder to reach him. It's true. So he's gone
off with someone who cares about photos in magazines,
and opinion columns, and all of those dud London things.
But that doesn't mean the man was always contemptible.
It doesn't mean I shouldn't have been with him at all.
It just means . . . Oh look . . . the odds were against us.
But I happen to think it was well worth a try.

*Amy's anger has turned to distress, the tears starting
to run down her cheek.*

Of course I knew . . . do you think I'm an idiot? I always
sensed: one day this man will trade up. He'll cash me in
and he'll get a new model. I always felt it would come.
These men, they wait. They wait till they're ready. You
make them secure. Then of course when you've built the
statue . . . that's when they kick the ladder away. But I
did know it. I did it knowingly. It was my choice.

Esme looks at her a moment.

Esme And are you parting?

Amy Why? Would you be satisfied?

Esme No!

There is a silence.

Amy You want us to part because then you're proved right.

There is a second's pause. Evelyn stirs and lets out a cry in her sleep. At once Esme gets up and tries to move to Amy.

Esme Oh Amy, Amy, please come and hold me . . .

Amy No, Mother . . .

Esme Amy, please, Amy . . .

Amy I can't . . .

Esme has reached her, wanting to put her arms round her, but Amy is backing away.

No . . .

Esme Come on, darling, you've always held me . . .

Amy I know . . .

Esme Since you were a child you've hugged me . . .

Amy I know but . . .

Esme Please come and hold me . . .

Amy I can't . . .

Amy has moved away. Esme, not really knowing what she's doing, pursues her.

I can't even sleep, I can't think, I'm in agony . . .

Esme Amy . . .

Amy What sort of mother? I want a mother who I can ring up.

Esme Please. Please come and hold me.

Amy Who I can call, who won't judge me . . .

Esme Amy, please stop this!

She has now put her arms round her, but Amy is struggling. For a moment the two women seem to be fighting, Esme holding on to her, Amy trying to escape her embrace.

Amy All you will say, all you'll ever say to me, 'Well guess what, my darling? I was right all along . . .'

She suddenly shouts.

I can't! I can't do this! Please let go of me.

Esme Amy!

Amy Please let go of me! Please!

It is suddenly shocking to both of them. Amy has thrown Esme violently off and stands, shaken by the passion of the moment. Evelyn stirs, groaning. Amy starts to gather up her stuff.

Now I have to go . . .

Esme Please stay . . .

Amy No . . .

Esme Please stay.

Amy I'm sorry, Mother, I can't. Not tonight. I have to go back to London.

Esme I beg you, Amy, please stay.

Amy I can't.

Amy looks, still unable to go near her.

Esme Please stay. Just tonight. Just stay here and comfort me.

Amy I can't. I have to get back. I have to . . . I have to just try and be steady. I have to.

They are rooted to the spot.

Please let me. Mother. Please let me go. I have to.

Then Frank opens the door, and at once Amy moves quickly back towards the veranda.

I'll see you. I'll call you.

Esme Amy. Amy . . .

Frank I heard shouting. I heard you shouting downstairs.

Amy Goodbye.

Esme runs out towards the veranda and disappears, calling out.

Esme (*off*) Amy! Amy!

Frank What's happening?

There is a silence. Then the sound of a car starting outside. Its headlights sweep through the room. Frank stands helpless, just waiting. After a few moments Esme returns. She does not look at him, but walks past him to go upstairs.

Esme Good night, Frank. Please lock the place up.

She is gone. Frank stands alone.

End of Act Three.

Act Four

London. 1995. The backstage of a small Victorian West End theatre. A small dressing room with a row of mirrors framed in lightbulbs. Esme has not done anything to decorate it at all, so the effect is painfully bare. There is just a stool and a surface for all her make-up. There is a small sofa and a screen. Some period costumes hang on a rail.

As the act begins, Toby Cole is already appearing. He is in his early twenties, rather tousled and blithe. He has a Walkman round his neck, and a T-shirt, but he has not taken off his period breeches nor his dark make-up, so the effect is quite curious. He approaches the dressing room door nervously and calls in.

Toby I'm sorry. Do you mind?

A pause.

Am I disturbing you, Esme?

A pause.

Are you sleeping?

Esme (*off*) If only.

Esme appears from behind the screen. She is now in her late sixties. She has been resting, with her face covered in white cream so that it makes a mask. She looks like a kabuki player. She wears a pink dressing gown. She seems withdrawn, as if she has retreated into herself. She goes to the door and opens it to let Toby in.

Oh Toby, do you want to come in?

Toby I thought you might like a sandwich. I'm going to get a sandwich, that's all.

Esme smiles to say no, then goes to sit at her stool to begin getting ready for the next performance.

You never eat anything.

She throws a smile at him. Toby doesn't want to leave.

I was wondering what you thought of the matinee?

Esme Oh . . .

Toby I was pleased. It felt pretty good. I think I'm beginning to get the hang of that last scene. The rhythm. You always bang on about rhythm. And I thought this afternoon . . . well, actually the rhythm wasn't too bad.

Esme No.

Toby In that first scene, I wanted to ask: when we come from the shipwreck, do I look too eager when you give me the apple?

Esme No, I think you do it just right.

Toby is hanging around the door, at ease.

Toby Did you hear the director's coming this evening?

Esme No.

Toby I'll be interested to hear what he thinks.

Esme says nothing.

I still can't believe it. It's incredible. I was thinking, I mean really . . . this honky little show. I stuck my nose out in the alley just now. There's already a great long queue for returns. I mean no disrespect to anyone, but it is quite amazing. Isn't it? I'm not being offensive, but I never imagined it could happen to us.

Toby smiles artlessly.

I didn't dare tell you. I was telling my mother – this was weeks ago – you were going to star in this play. When she came to see it, she said – I didn't like to tell you – well, she said it was the best thing you'd ever done.

He holds a hand up to avoid offence.

You were always her favourite actress, I mean, not to be rude, but when she was young . . .

Esme It's all right.

Toby But she said . . . well everyone says this . . . it's like now you've got something extra.

Esme Perhaps.

Toby You should have heard her. She really meant it. She was really laying it on . . .

Esme carries on preparing.

Esme Do you get on with your mother?

Toby My mother? Oh sure. I mean, my mother? Yes, absolutely. She's more . . . well, I never think of her as being like a relative. In fact I don't think of her as being my mum. You know, perhaps I'm lucky. Perhaps it's my generation, but to me my mum is more like a mate.

Esme Hmm.

Esme is thoughtful a moment.

Toby Lately, you know, I've taken to watching you . . .

Esme I've seen you . . .

Toby I know. I just watch. When I'm not on, I stand in the wings and observe. I think . . . I don't know . . . it may be presumptuous but I feel I'm beginning to understand your technique.

Esme Good.

Toby You never play anything outwards. I've noticed, you keep it all in. So you draw in the audience. So it's up to them. And somehow they make the effort . . .

Esme Yes.

Toby They have to go and get it themselves.

Toby is embarrassed by his next question.

What I don't know is, how do you do that? This sounds stupid. Do you learn it? Is there a secret? Some particular thing.

Esme No, I don't think so.

She looks down a moment.

It comes with the passage of time.

Toby Yes.

Esme You go deeper.

Toby Exactly.

Esme You go on down to the core.

She shrugs slightly.

There it is.

Toby I wish . . . I don't know . . . there were some way that we could all do it. Just do it, I mean.

Esme I shouldn't worry. I promise, for you it will come. Come here.

Esme is very casual, but she has invited him over to kiss him lightly on the cheek.

Maybe a small cappuccino.

233

Toby Of course. No really, this one's on me.

She has reached into her purse, but he is already on his way out. Esme goes out to her small bathroom beyond the screen. As Toby goes he passes Dominic, who has come into the corridor outside. Dominic is nearly forty. His boyishness has gone, and his manner is more sober. He has thickened out to fill the smart, dark blue coat he is wearing. He is carrying a parcel the size of a shoebox, wrapped in brown paper. As he enters the room, Esme comes back, a slip showing underneath her untied dressing gown.

Esme Dominic . . .

Instinctively she wraps the dressing gown tight round her, holding herself.

Dominic I'm afraid I wandered in from the street. You seem to have no security.

Esme No. I think he goes off for a drink.

Dominic Ah.

Dominic shifts.

I'm aware you don't want to see me. I've been hanging around for an hour. Just plucking up courage. I brought you a present.

Esme What present?

Dominic This.

He puts the parcel down on the side. It is tied with string and sellotape.

Esme I need to prepare for the show.

She sits down at her desk to start taking her mask of face-cream off and to put on her make-up.

Dominic Actually I came to the matinee . . .

Esme Oh really?

Dominic Yes.

Esme No doubt you found it ridiculous.

Dominic Well . . .

Esme When did you last see a play?

He shrugs.

Dominic Oh . . .

Esme I didn't hear you shout out 'Fast forward!'

Dominic No, to be honest, I was kind of intrigued.

Esme Just kind of? Not wholly?

Dominic Plainly the writer's so young.

Esme Yes, he is.

Dominic That means it's absurdly pretentious. But then in a way I quite like that. I liked the play's youth.

Esme So do I.

Dominic That scene when you talk to the stars.

Esme throws a quick glance at him.

And somehow it's become this extraordinary phenomenon. Out of nowhere, it seems. Is that the appeal of the theatre, in fact? This weird arty evening . . .

Esme Yes.

Dominic No one could ever predict it. And yet they fight to get in.

He smiles at her a moment.

What do you put it down to?

Esme What, this one?

Dominic The success of this particular play.

Esme Well, you're right, it's pretentious, it's true. And it's young. But I knew when I read it, it had something special.

Dominic You saw that?

Esme People like it because they feel it's sincere.

Dominic shifts, knowing he must somehow get past her coolness.

Dominic The children were saying you're in a small flat now . . .

Esme Yes.

Dominic You've moved back to London.

Esme looks at him sharply.

Esme But you knew that.

Dominic I did.

Esme You've sent me all those cheques . . .

Dominic Yes.

Esme I'm afraid they're no use to me.

Dominic I realised it must be in the terms of the settlement . . .

Esme I burnt them.

Dominic I guessed.

He shifts again, uneasy.

Well, the bank said they hadn't gone through.

Esme They couldn't.

Dominic No.

Esme The Hardship Committee gives me an allowance. That's all I'm permitted. They seize all the rest. So unless you actually slip me a fiver, illegally . . . Whatever you give me, it goes back to Lloyd's.

She is beginning to put her make-up on.

I sold up the house, all my property, my furniture, my letters, my paintings. Everything I had. They take my wages. At the end I'm still short by two million. So, one way or another, your cheques aren't much use.

Dominic shifts again, moving towards what he has come to say.

Dominic I had thought it was personal, I'd feared you were angry . . .

Esme Oh really?

Dominic I feared you resented the money I sent.

Esme Yes, well, as I can't take it, I'm afraid you'll simply never find out.

This comes out so cold that Dominic tries to move onto the attack.

Dominic Look, Esme, I do know that you blame me . . .

Esme Blame you, you think?

Dominic You think in some way everything's that's happened is somehow my fault. I know that. I know you hate my new marriage. In your shoes, that's something I well understand.

Esme I don't think of it, Dominic. I promise you. I do my best not to think about you at all.

Esme smiles slightly in anticipation.

Except when I see all your posters . . .

Dominic Ah yes . . .

Esme When I go down the tube. This film you've directed. Everyone says it's been winning all sorts of prizes.

Dominic Some.

Esme So it seems like at last you've done what you want.

Dominic is now slightly desperate to get through to her.

Dominic Look, the point is, I really am trying. I really am trying my best. Do you think I'm not changed by what happened? Do you think it hasn't changed me?

Esme says nothing.

You think I don't have any conscience?

Esme No.

Dominic You think it doesn't hurt me when the children tell me what they've seen of your life?

Esme My life?

Dominic Yes! They say you've completely retreated. Since Evelyn died, they say you see no one at all. You refuse to go out.

Esme So?

Dominic begins to get more forceful.

Dominic All right, you think I'm indifferent, I'm callous, you think I don't care, but somehow the thought of you suffering . . . The children say it's like you've given up trying.

Esme Oh really? They told you that? Is that how it seems?

But Dominic persists, not willing to be put off so easily.

Dominic They say you called off your marriage.

Esme Yes.

Dominic You were going to marry Frank?

She throws a glance at him.

Esme Since you ask. That was some time ago. A long time ago. But I did what Amy was always telling me.

Dominic I see.

Esme I decided to take my life in my hands.

There's a moment's pause.

There we are.

Dominic But you're alone now?

Esme Do you think this is really your business?

Dominic Well as a matter of fact, I'm afraid that I do. Why do you think I've come here to see you?

Esme To be honest I have no idea.

Dominic I came because everyone's worried. I wanted to see you were coping.

Esme Well now you've seen me, so that's OK.

She waits a moment, then goes on preparing.

What, you're concerned for my welfare? Why? You have what you wanted. You've got a great family. The children tell me you've got a great wife. Why should it matter what on earth I am feeling? Dominic, do I really matter at all?

She gestures vaguely outside the room.

Any more than that dog out there in the alley. The sound of that train going by. That's all it is.

Dominic That is just nonsense.

Esme Oh, is it? The last thing that maybe might stop you sleeping. A source of minor discomfort in the otherwise perfect life you now live.

She gets up and looks him straight in the eye. All her hostility towards him suddenly comes out.

I did see the film. I'm appalled by the violence. I know in some way it's important to people like you. All that shooting and bloodshed. But I don't understand it.

Dominic We don't call it violence. We call it action.

Esme Whatever. It isn't how life is. Perhaps I'm just getting old.

She looks at him, unrelenting.

I'm tired of it, Dominic. This need you all have to get out the guns, and bam! and wham! and 'Kill the little fucker' and 'Shoot off his stupid bloody head.' What is it? What is this need you all have now? What happened? Are you just bored?

Dominic just looks at her, not answering.

Or is it that you just don't dare to deal with real experience . . . with the things that really go on in real life? Like grief . . . and betrayal . . . and love and unhappiness . . . and loss . . . the loss of people we love . . .

Her eyes now have filled up with tears. She is disturbingly out of control.

Dominic Esme . . .

Esme No . . .

He has moved towards her in an instinctive gesture of sympathy, but she puts up her hands to prevent him.

Loss. Yes, let that be your subject. Not childish games with explosions and guns . . . Which have nothing to do with anything . . . nothing to do with things that are real . . .

She cannot look at him. She turns and goes into the bathroom.

Dominic You know Amy's view: you have to love people. You just have to love them. You have to give love without any conditions at all. Just give it. And one day you will be rewarded. One day you will get it back.

Esme returns. She has put on a pair of ragged trousers and is buttoning a blouse. She is carrying a pair of shoes. She sits and starts to put them on.

At the end, the fact is – I don't expect you to like this – but Amy and I were getting on well. No, truly. We were. We came to some real understanding. Of course it's not . . . it wasn't like it was any longer a marriage. But we did manage some sort of real love.

She is silent, tense now.

After we'd split, admittedly. You may say it's easier. But it lasted, I don't know, three months. Or four. We were closer than at any time in our lives. So now . . . perhaps this is mad to you . . . but somehow the story just doesn't seem finished. Do you understand me?

Esme Of course.

Dominic I feel that now I must try and help you.

There is a silence.

Esme You want Amy's death to be of some use.

Dominic Yes.

He waits a moment.

Because she just died – one day she walks down a street, for no purpose, for no reason at all – one day she's there, then she's not. I've felt since that day, I have to see Esme.

Esme Why?

Dominic I do have to talk to her.

Esme So that I can tell you it wasn't your fault?

Dominic No!

Esme Tell you you didn't betray her? That none of it mattered? Is that what you want?

Dominic No, of course I betrayed her.

Esme Well then.

Dominic I really don't think that's the point.

Esme No?

She waits for him to go on.

Dominic I want you to say, all right, that was one chapter. And now that chapter is closed.

She sits down, saying nothing.

It's just . . . it's ever since the funeral . . . I've had this feeling, this instinct, it's much more than grief. It's to do with what Amy would have wanted.

Esme looks down in as much pain as him.

Amy would have wanted that we should be friends.

She cannot answer him.

Surely? I mean, with time that is possible. For Christ's sake, you know what she felt. More than anything she wanted that you and I should somehow get on.

Esme Oh I see . . .

Dominic Yes . . .

Esme You're saying you left her, you're saying you know you did let her down. But because Amy was good, because she was decent, somehow you shouldn't suffer? I have to forgive you because she was so much nicer than you?

He doesn't respond.

Some people rise. Well, don't they? They rise at other people's expense. For them to rise other people go down. We have to endure that. But please don't expect us to like you as well.

Dominic You don't understand. I'm saying something much simpler. Something for your sake too. Something which means we'll both be forgiven.

He looks down.

Because hating me now is a waste of your life.

She looks at him a moment, as if genuinely considering this.

Esme I have my life here in this theatre. My life is when the curtain goes up. My work is my life. I understand nothing else.

She waves a hand slightly to fight tears, but Toby is already back with two cappuccinos. They are both piping hot and he is juggling them slightly.

Toby Coffee.

Esme Oh Lord . . .

Toby I think it's still hot enough.

He puts the cappuccino down on the surface. Esme resumes getting dressed.

Esme Do you know Dominic here?

Toby Are you Dominic Tyghe?

Dominic Well, yes.

Toby I can't believe it. Wow! It's just incredible. I saw that film you just made.

Dominic Oh yes.

Toby The scene where the man's skull exploded! That shot of the flying blood and the bone . . .

> *He mimes shooting himself, and the effect of the back of his head exploding.*

I thought it was absolutely fantastic.

Dominic Oh well, thanks very much.

> *Esme looks at Dominic, but Toby, drinking his cappuccino, does not notice.*

Toby You're an old friend of Esme's?

Dominic I married her daughter.

Toby Ah yes.

Dominic We go back a long way. But she died very tragically. Without any warning.

> *Toby waits a second, respectful.*

Toby Esme did mention. Do you have children?

Dominic We do.

Toby How are they coping?

Dominic By and large, they cope very well.

> *He throws a glance at Esme.*

And they both love their granny.

Toby Yes. Well, we all love her here too.

Esme does not want this attention. She busies herself with getting ready.

Look, you know we only have three minutes.

Esme What? I don't believe you.

Toby It's true.

Esme I didn't hear the call. I must have missed it.

Toby Excuse me.

Toby slips out of the door.

Esme Dominic, you will have to go now.

Dominic Will you think about what I've been saying?

Esme I'll try to. Yes. If I can.

He waits patiently. She moves towards her coffee and takes a sip.

That day I remember so clearly. The day I walked in. You'd been mending the bike.

Dominic Yes.

Esme What was my reaction? Was it just fear of the stranger?

Dominic Only you know. Is that what it was?

Esme My daughter was lost to me. One look at you. Everything I had left to me was gone. Do you think it was pure blind instinct?

Dominic No. To be fair, you did dislike me personally too.

They smile together, some real warmth between them for the first time.

Esme It was just chance. It was chance I met Bernard. I was promiscuous. I was also nineteen. But I met this man. And from then on, everything seemed to be different. What if I hadn't? It was pure luck.

She stands, lost in thought.

Life with Bernard wasn't actually spectacular. It wasn't as if we were always in each other's arms. It was just calm. And we laughed at everything. That's all. Nothing crazy. But always with him, I felt whole.

*There is an offstage call of 'Beginners, please.'
Dominic takes a couple of steps backwards, pointing to the parcel.*

Dominic Remember, open your present.

Dominic stops at the door.

Esme, will you promise to call me?

Esme If I could, then why would I not?

He goes out. Esme is alone. She reaches up to the Tannoy, and the sound of the waiting audience is heard. She adjusts her costume in front of the mirror. She looks a moment at herself, then, curious, she takes the parcel he's left. She opens a drawer and takes a knife out. She cuts the string. She pulls back the paper. It's a shoebox. She opens it. Inside it are bundles of five pound notes – thousands of pounds' worth. Toby returns with a jug of water. He sees the box of money.

Toby What's that?

Esme It's money. Nothing else. It's a gift.

Toby looks puzzled.

My daughter's ashes. We should go up.

She puts the box down on her dressing-room table, and leaves it casually open. Then briskly she closes the door. She checks herself once more and leaves the room with Toby and they walk together towards the stage. The dressing room disappears. When they get to the stage, silently without any prompting from her, she leans down, half forward, and he pours the jug of water over her head, soaking her hair and the top half of her body. She smiles at him.

Thank you.

He starts taking off his T-shirt.

Toby Oh, by the way, the director's not coming.

Esme Oh really?

Toby No, he's changed his mind. So he's not coming.

He has taken off his trousers. He just has a strip of cloth round his middle, barely covering him, and he looks pitiful, like Poor Tom in King Lear. *She pours the rest of the water from the jug over him, and he shivers. She hands the jug to a stage manager. Then they stand together a moment, he blue with cold, she already focused on the task ahead, both of them curiously innocent in the silence.*

Esme Fair enough then. So we're alone.

The light begins to go down, until it is only on the two of them, glazed, nervous, full of fear. Suddenly there is the overwhelming sound of a string orchestra and the light goes down to near-blackness. Then they turn towards us, and the curtain goes up.

End of play.

THE JUDAS KISS

Pour mon amour

The **Judas Kiss** was first presented by the Almeida Theatre Company, in association with Robert Fox and Scott Rudin, at the Playhouse Theatre, London, on 12 March 1998. The cast was as follows:

Oscar Wilde Liam Neeson
Lord Alfred Douglas Tom Hollander
Robert Ross Peter Capaldi
Arthur Wellesley Alex Walkinshaw
Phoebe Cane Stina Nielsen
Sandy Moffatt Richard Clarke
Galileo Masconi Daniel Serafini-Sauli

Director Richard Eyre
Designer Bob Crowley
Lighting Mark Henderson
Music George Fenton
Sound John A. Leonard

This production was subsequently presented on Broadway at the Broadhurst Theatre, New York, on 29 April 1998.

The Background to the Play

In 1895, the Marquess of Queensberry, enraged by rumours of his son Lord Alfred Douglas's relationship with the Irish playwright Oscar Wilde, entered Wilde's club and left him a note accusing him of 'posing as a sodomite'. When Wilde decided that he could not ignore the challenge, and that he must bring a prosecution against Queensberry for criminal libel, the Marquess retaliated by searching London for a list of young men willing to testify against Wilde. Knowing of this list, Wilde nevertheless persisted with his case. After his private suit collapsed in two days, Wilde himself became liable for public prosecution under Section 11 of the Criminal Law Amendment Act of 1886, which had made 'acts of gross indecency' between men a criminal offence.

On 19 May 1897, Wilde was released after two years in jail. He went abroad at once, and never returned to England before his death in 1900.

Characters

Oscar Wilde

Lord Alfred Douglas (Bosie)

Robert Ross

Arthur Wellesley

Phoebe Cane

Sandy Moffatt

Galileo Masconi

ACT ONE: DECIDING TO STAY
is set in London in 1895

Scene One Lunchtime
Scene Two Teatime

ACT TWO: DECIDING TO LEAVE
is set in Italy in 1897

Scene One Dusk
Scene Two Dawn

Some say a cavalry corps
some infantry, some, again,
will maintain that the swift oars

of our fleet are the finest
sight on dark earth; but I say
that whatever one loves, is.

Sappho

Every man contains his own death
as the fruit contains the stone.

Rilke

Act One: Deciding to Stay

SCENE ONE

Friday, 5 April 1895. Romantic orchestral music. A streak of light falls near a bed on which a young couple are making love in a curtained room. The bed is in considerable disorder, a riot of counterpanes, blankets, sheets, and materials in rich brocade. The young woman, Phoebe, is seventeen, milk-white and beautiful. The young man, Arthur, is only a little older, short, sturdy, blond and handsome. In the shadows, she is seen dimly to climb away from him, his face pressed deep into her as she rises. Standing on the bed, Phoebe is now spreadeagled, her arms against the wall, in a gesture of crucifixion, as Arthur kneels against her. The stage picture is Renaissance: abandoned white flesh against rich patterns, passion expressed as religious torment.

The light spreads. The outline of an ornate hotel room becomes clearer. To the left of the bed, a huge window is swagged in rich material. To the right, a door. As their excitement grows, a discreet knocking begins. It goes unremarked. The knocking becomes louder. Arthur's name is called urgently. Then louder. Finally Phoebe hears it. Then Arthur hears it too. The music fades.

Phoebe Oh Lord God Almighty.

Like a frightened animal, she pulls free and runs across to the bathroom. Arthur holds a sheet against himself as he goes to unlock the door. He opens it a crack to check, then opens it further. Mr Moffatt is a refined, feline Scot in his fifties, wearing tails.

Moffatt Ah Arthur, I thought it was you.

Arthur Mr Moffatt.

Moffatt You will forgive me if I let in some light.

Moffatt has come into the room and is heading to the window. Arthur has closed the door, but seems unperturbed. Like Phoebe, he is quite strongly cockney.

Arthur You'll see, sir. I haven't yet started . . .

Moffatt has drawn the curtain. Light floods from the window onto the floor. The scene is of late-night abandon. Draperies strewn over the room, flowers, bottles, old meals uncleared from tables.

Moffatt My goodness. You have had some reckless enjoyment, I see.

Arthur Hardly, Mr Moffatt. This wasn't our doing. We were just about to start clearing it up.

Moffatt I would hope. Who was helping you?

Arthur Oh, the new maid.

Moffatt Where is she?

Arthur She's in the bathroom.

Moffatt I see.

Arthur Her name's Phoebe.

Moffatt Thank you. I am apprised of her name.

Arthur She's settling in nicely.

Moffatt Yes, Arthur. I think I had worked that out for myself.

Moffatt seems untroubled by the scene.

Does she want to come out of the bathroom?

Arthur I think she may want to, sir.

Moffatt (*raising his voice*) Phoebe, do you want to come out?

Phoebe (*from the bathroom*) I need my clothes, sir.

Moffatt Very well. I shall turn my face to the wall.

Moffatt stands facing the wall. Phoebe comes out of the bathroom, still naked. Arthur helps her, as she searches, unamused.

What are you doing?

Phoebe I'm looking for my smaller garments, sir.

Arthur holds up a pair of knickers.

Arthur Here.

Phoebe Thank you.

Moffatt If you avail yourself of the bathroom, we can make headway in here.

Phoebe Thank you, sir.

She goes out to the bathroom. Moffatt turns. Arthur has had a sheet round him, but now he opens it, showing himself to Moffatt. Neither man moves.

Arthur I'd not thought Lord Alfred would need his room quite so quickly.

Moffatt That is apparent. You will now get on and continue your work.

After a moment Moffatt moves across the room to start work. Arthur goes to pull his undergarments on.

Arthur Lord Alfred doesn't normally get back till the evening.

Moffatt That may explain your behaviour. It hardly excuses it.

Arthur No, sir.

Moffatt Lord Alfred has had to make a sudden change in his plans.

Arthur Oh, I see.

Moffatt Hence the urgency.

He lifts various silver lids on a side-table.

Too much champagne, by the look of it. The remains of a lobster. Plainly he has no respect for crustaceans. This looks like Chef's *moules marinières*.

Arthur, naked to the waist, goes to help Moffatt stripping the bed.

Did you visit any other rooms this morning?

Arthur Oh yes, sir. I've cleared out the dishes from most of this floor.

Moffatt Alone?

Arthur Phoebe was helping me.

Moffatt Really? And did you christen each room?

They work on at the bedclothes. Phoebe comes back, adjusting her maid's uniform.

Get me the baskets.

Phoebe I'll get them.

Moffatt Ah Phoebe, yes, right.

She goes, intending to open the main door.

And also . . .

THE JUDAS KISS

Phoebe Yes, sir?

Moffatt Tell your friend Arthur: the least he can do is put on the rest of his clothes.

Arthur smiles and moves towards his abandoned clothes. Phoebe goes into the corridor.

Arthur, I shall need to speak to you later. You have indulged in behaviour the hotel cannot possibly condone. I shall need to reprimand you in person.

Arthur Yes, sir.

Moffatt That's clear?

Arthur goes on dressing.

Arthur When do you wish this act of discipline to take place?

Moffatt After work. When exactly do you get off?

Arthur Five-thirty.

Moffatt Right after.

Arthur Yes sir.

Moffatt I'll wait for you outside the kitchens.

Arthur The kitchens it is, sir.

Phoebe comes back with a basket for the dirty laundry.

Moffatt The hotel has standards it must maintain.

Robert Ross has appeared at the door. He is a short man, not yet thirty, with a puck face, Buster Keatonish, and beautifully dressed. He is in obvious distress.

Ah good afternoon, Mr Ross.

Ross Good afternoon.

Arthur is now dressed. He and Phoebe bow and bob to Ross.

Arthur *and* **Phoebe** Afternoon, sir.

Moffatt Lord Alfred's room is not quite ready, I fear.

Ross There's some luggage.

Moffatt Of course, sir. Arthur.

Arthur goes out to get it, leaving the door open.

Ross I am expecting Lord Alfred presently. My fear is our presence is already known.

Moffatt Sir?

Ross I came through the lobby. Has someone been talking?

Moffatt Impossible.

Ross I'm grateful.

Moffatt It is out of the question. The Cadogan is a steadfastly private hotel.

Phoebe goes out again with dirty sheets.

Ross That is its reputation. That was the purpose in choosing it. You know why we came here.

Moffatt Indeed, sir.

Ross Lord Alfred needed somewhere discreet.

Moffatt Discretion is something we pride ourselves on.

Arthur appears smartly with a big bag.

Arthur The bag, sir.

Ross Please, just put it down where you will.

Arthur If it's Lord Alfred's, sir, then I'll unpack it.

Ross No. It isn't Lord Alfred's.

Moffatt now smoothly intervenes.

Moffatt That's fine, sir. We quite understand.

Phoebe reappears urgently at the door.

Phoebe Sir, there are people . . .

Moffatt What people?

Phoebe They do look like reporters . . .

Ross turns away in panic.

Ross It starts! It starts even now!

Phoebe Somehow they've got up the stairs.

Ross Mr Moffatt, this is what I most feared.

Moffatt I apologise. Have no concern, sir. You will not be inconvenienced, you have my assurance.

Ross Well, please.

Moffatt Excuse me and let me now go and deal with it.

Ross I would be most grateful. Thank you.

Moffatt I will do it.

Phoebe Back in a tick.

Moffatt has gone. Phoebe follows. Arthur opens new sheets for the bed. Moffatt can be heard admonishing the journalists outside: 'Gentlemen, this is a private area . . .' Ross looks uncomfortably across to Arthur.

Ross I'm sorry. It's our fault. We caused all this upset.

Arthur Sir?

Ross Last night a group of us ate in this room.

Arthur It's fine, sir.

Ross I'm afraid we only parted at five.

Arthur Did you have an enjoyable evening?

Ross No, I could not say enjoyable. Why no, not at all.

Arthur continues his work, the soul of politeness.

Arthur I've noticed Lord Alfred is addicted to company. He rarely likes to be on his own.

Ross No. No, he is companionable.

Arthur Yes, sir. That's what I meant. Since he came here, what is it? five weeks ago – I've seen him with a whole range of companions.

Ross Yes. Yes, Lord Alfred is always sociable.

Arthur Indeed, sir. It would be a dull world without company. Are you fond of company yourself?

Ross I?

He looks at Arthur thoughtfully a moment.

Ross Oh yes. Within moderation. Sometimes. Occasionally. But always at my own choice.

At once, Lord Alfred Douglas ('Bosie') arrives, followed by Moffatt. He is a startlingly handsome young aristocrat, twenty-three, fair-haired and volatile.

Bosie It is simply absurd, it is unendurable . . .

Moffatt (*bowing*) Lord Alfred . . .

Ross Bosie, you must calm down.

Bosie I cannot believe what has happened.

Ross I know.

Bosie Even now I cannot believe it.

Ross Where is Oscar?

Bosie He is on his way here.

Ross What are you saying? Do you mean you have left him?

Bosie I could not endure that solicitor!

Ross Oscar is travelling alone?

Bosie I simply got up and walked out.

He turns, anticipating Ross.

It's all right, Oscar and I had already decided. It was better we travelled apart. Somebody spat at him. It is known throughout London that his case has collapsed. The crowds all yell at him. The indignity is beyond all description. To have our names in their mouths!

He turns to Moffatt.

I need a glass of cold water. Get it!

Moffatt Yes, sir.

Bosie From a bottle! A bottle! None of that filthy sewage that flows from your taps.

Moffatt turns to Arthur, who has been working on, quietly ironic.

Moffatt A bottle of water for Lord Alfred.

Arthur At once, sir.

Bosie Why is this room in such vile disarray?

Arthur goes out. Phoebe joins Moffatt to continue tidying up.

Ross Oscar has finished the letter?

Bosie Yes. It is written.

Ross Is it dispatched?

Bosie To the *Evening News*. Saying the reason he was forced to abandon his case is he could not allow me into the witness box. He had to protect me!

Ross He is making that clear?

Bosie is shaking his head in anger.

Bosie He would not allow me to dispute with my father in public. It drives me to distraction.

Ross I know.

Bosie I, who was better placed to denounce my own father than anyone! And yet it is Oscar who forbids me to advance my own cause.

Ross is uneasy of this talk in front of the staff.

Ross He has explained to you. It would not be advantageous . . .

Bosie Not advantageous?

Ross He thought it would do you no good.

Bosie looks at him wildly, as if he's mad.

Bosie Oh well, how brilliant! What a brilliant decision! And how exactly could things have worked out worse than they have? My father, this disgusting little man, this vandal, who has pretty well ruined my life. And I am not allowed to speak of his appalling behaviour!

He turns, addressing the whole room.

And the result? It hardly needs saying: the case is in ruins. The two of us face equal disgrace. He made this fatal mistake. He did not call me!

Ross No.

Ross looks round, wanting to get rid of the staff.

Just one minute . . .

Bosie And now – through his own stubbornness, *now* he is paying the price!

Ross Yes. If you could allow us one moment . . . is it Phoebe?

Phoebe is carrying Bosie's books across the room.

Bosie Leave those things there! Just leave them! I asked for some water.

Phoebe Yes.

She stands, taken aback by his outburst.

Ross I apologise. Lord Alfred is under great strain.

Bosie Robbie, you always speak for me. In everything. Even with the servants, you speak as if I were not in the room. Always I am not allowed to speak! From this habit of silencing, from the way you have all made me silent, from this our present predicament stems.

Arthur comes back with a silver tray.

Well, I'll be silent no longer!

Arthur Your water, sir.

Bosie What?

Arthur The water you asked for. It's here.

Bosie frowns as if not understanding.

Bosie So? Set it down. Come on, what are you expecting? Tribute? What are you waiting for? Praise?

Arthur No, sir. Do you want me to pour it?

Bosie Pour?

Arthur Do you want me to pour it, sir?

Bosie Yes, of course. Do it, Arthur. What is the alternative? It pours itself? Hardly. Mr Moffatt, this staff you employ! Where do you find them? The music hall? Robbie, do you have some money? Will you give young Arthur here a penny or two?

Ross Yes, of course.

Bosie I'll repay you.

Bosie's mood has changed, so he is almost skittish to Moffatt.

What are they, music-hall comics?

Moffatt You told me before, sir, you'd been very happy with everything the staff had done for you here.

Bosie is already bored and wanders away. Ross tips Arthur and Moffatt.

Bosie Yes, oh yes. If you say so.

Ross Mr Moffatt, thank you. Here's something for you.

Moffatt The room is not yet ready, I fear.

Ross As long as you guarantee us security, we shall truly require nothing else.

Moffatt has opened Wilde's case on the bed. Phoebe bobs insolently, and they are all gone. The room is roughly restored to order.

Bosie, you realise I do have to speak to you.

Bosie I know you must speak to me. You have adopted your headmaster's tone. 'Come into my study!'

Ross Only because what I must say is important. We have little time. It is vital.

Ross pauses.

You know I have been to his house.

Bosie Yes.

Ross I have picked up his luggage.

Bosie Have you?

Ross At his instructions, I have also cashed him a cheque. Protest all you like, you know what is happening.

Ross is holding up Wilde's pocketbook.

He will come here only briefly. It is essential. He must not stay long.

Bosie No, first I suggest he must stop and take stock.

Ross No!

Bosie Robbie, Oscar has given me everything. He's a man I love, I admire. There is no one in the world I admire more than him. But to see him take up the challenge . . .

Ross Yes.

Bosie And then not to give it the care it deserves.

Ross stays quiet, patient.

Yesterday, making that joke in the courtroom – even you must see that did him no good . . .

Ross Plainly.

Bosie That says it all! This need to perform!

Ross Yes. But just at this moment, it's scarcely important.

But Bosie is ignoring him.

Bosie Finally that instinct is lethal. When asked of an Oxford college servant if he had kissed him. 'Oh no, I did not kiss him. He was far too ugly.' In front of the jury!

Ross I know . . .

Bosie It was not a good joke. Not even a good joke! There was no reason except to show off.

Ross No.

Bosie I had warned him. Yet from the moment he said it . . .

Ross I know. I know. You have said this.

Bosie From the moment he said it, our case was finished. We abandoned all chance of victory.

Ross I know. All of us said all this last night.

But Bosie takes no notice.

Bosie I had said to him, I had told him one thousand times, 'Be modest.' I said, 'I am English, you are not. The English people do not like wit. They abhor those who are cleverer than they are.' But he did not listen. No.

He suddenly raises his voice again.

Robbie, he has not listened throughout!

Ross tries to be precise to gain Bosie's attention.

Ross Bosie, your father's solicitors have passed on the papers. We know this. We've been told this for sure. They were dispatched to the Attorney General over two hours ago.

Ross has tried to calm him, but Bosie seems to miss the point.

Bosie Oh Robbie, come on, why do you think I sent for my cousin? This is exactly what I foresaw!

Ross steps towards him, still quiet.

Ross In a moment Oscar will come here. We will only have a short time. In conditions of calm and absolute seriousness, he will have to settle his resolve on the path he must take.

Bosie Of course.

Ross The Attorney General is even now speaking to the Home Secretary. It is assuredly only a matter of time. Asquith will give his consent. Pretty soon the local magistrate will issue his warrant for Oscar's arrest on a charge of gross indecency.

Ross puts up a hand.

Yes. You heard us this morning with Oscar's solicitors. If we stop and examine the evidence, if we look at that list – that disastrous list of young men – well, is it wise . . . is it truly courageous to stay here? Fight on when he has no chance to win?

Bosie Who says?

Ross Listen. Or rather, is it simply foolhardy? In open court, these men will bear witness. They will say the most terrible things. Things no one will ever forget. Whether he wins or he loses, Oscar's reputation will be destroyed for all time.

Bosie You say that.

Ross Very well.

Bosie I deny it.

Ross You may well deny it. That is your right. But your denial is not of the essence. Nothing now matters save Oscar's own view.

There is a silence. Bosie looks cannily at Ross.

Oscar has looked into the abyss. He has seen all the dangers. He will now leave the country. Yes. That is his decision. To leave it for ever. And you must respect this choice he has made.

They both look, neither man relenting.

By his nature, we both know Oscar can be excited. How do I say this? He can be swayed. I recognise this truth about Oscar. He is always available to your point of view. I am not seeking to silence you. Be assured. You may say what you like. I ask you, simply take care. There must be no hysteria. You may argue, but you must not dictate. This is the point I am making. On this occasion, because his whole future depends on it, I beg you, let Oscar set his own course. I know I can trust you, Bosie. Behave in a way which gives Oscar a chance.

The room is silent. But Bosie seems more amused than sobered.

Bosie Oh Robbie, you always speak prettily.

Ross Thank you.

Bosie Considerate. Modest, as always. Well-tempered. Does it never occur to you? Life has handed you the easiest role.

Ross What role?

Bosie Third party. Robbie, anyone can play third party. It requires no real talent. You play it to perfection, but bear this in mind: it is a role of no consequence. That's him!

He moves across the room because Mr Moffatt can be heard in the corridor, beckoning Wilde to follow him.

The role can be taken by anyone at all.

Oscar Wilde comes through the door. He is just over forty, with long hair, not at all the languid pansy of legend. He is solid, tall and fleshy, six foot three, a mixture of ungainliness and elegance. Mr Moffatt is behind him carrying two small bags.

Moffatt In here, sir, please, come in, the others are waiting . . .

Bosie Oh Oscar.

Ross Oscar, you're here.

Wilde What is this? Oh Bosie, dear Bosie . . .

Bosie Oscar . . .

They fall into each other's arms, hugging.

Wilde Bosie . . .

Bosie Oscar, oh Oscar! Thank goodness, thank goodness you're here.

Ross and Moffatt stand quietly waiting.

Wilde Forgive us, Mr Moffatt, Lord Alfred and I have been parted for almost an hour.

Moffatt I quite understand, sir.

Wilde We have survived the shock of separation. The strain has been awful. On my side at least. And reporters now seem to be holding some sort of professional convention in your lobby. Mr Moffatt has kindly guided me through.

Arthur has arrived with an ice bucket and bottles on a tray.

Arthur Wine, sir.

Wilde Robbie, can you give Mr Moffatt some money?

Ross Why yes, of course.

Wilde Please put my bags on the bed. Thank you.

Ross Oscar, remember, you do not have long.

Ross tips Moffatt, who puts the three bags together on the bed.

Bosie Robbie is desperate that nothing should detain you.

Ross Bosie . . .

Bosie He's given me a lecture on how I am to behave.

Wilde Oh Robbie, that was superfluous. Bosie at all times behaves impeccably.

Ross I have not said otherwise. Oscar, just tell us, what is your news?

Wilde My news?

Ross Yes.

Wilde My news? I have none. Everyone hourly awaits my arrest. They seem astonished that I am still at liberty. But, my friends, all I can say is: by a miracle, I have achieved the Cadogan.

Moffatt Indeed, sir.

Wilde In spite of everything, I am finally here. And surrounded by friends, I would say, Mr Moffatt . . .

Moffatt I would hope, sir . . .

Wilde And Arthur. Good Arthur. The excellent Arthur as well. Oh Lord . . .

He grips Arthur's hand tightly.

Moffatt Come, you must sit, sir . . .

Wilde No, no, I am steady. I am here but I cannot yet say for how long.

He moves to hide his tears, then animates himself to keep cheerful.

It appears that the whole of London is fleeing. I looked from my coach. Every invert in the metropolitan area is now packing his bags and heading for France.

Ross looks nervously to the staff.

It is a veritable mass migration. I'd never imagined diaspora could be on this scale.

Ross Well . . .

Wilde The takings at certain fashionable restaurants will tonight be counted in pennies. Within twenty-four hours the opera will be stone dead.

Ross (*nervously*) Yes.

He turns and sees his bags on the bed.

Wilde What remain of my worldly possessions. You had them sent over?

Ross Yes. As we agreed, I went to your house.

Wilde Thank you. Thank you, dear Robbie.

He moves over and hugs Ross, then looks into his eyes. Ross speaks quietly.

Ross Please bear in mind, Oscar, you do not have long.

Moffatt Excuse me, do you also want coffee, sir? Have you eaten?

Wilde Have I eaten? Oh Lord, let me think.

Ross Oscar, I'm afraid it's out of the question. You simply do not have time.

Wilde Do I not?

Ross You are here to say your goodbyes to Bosie.

Wilde Yes, of course. But a small drink, please, Robbie, you must not deny me. And then of course I shall get going. I shall go on the instant.

Arthur Do you want to taste, sir?

Wilde Pour away. Hock tastes like hock, and seltzer like seltzer. Taste is not in the bottle. It resides in one's mood. So today no doubt hock will taste like burnt ashes. Today I will drink my own death.

He lights the first of many cigarettes. Ross has turned to Moffatt.

Ross Mr Moffatt, on my orders a cab is waiting downstairs . . .

Moffatt Yes, sir.

Phoebe has appeared at the door by chance, bringing towels.

Ah Phoebe, will you please tell the driver outside that Mr Wilde . . .

Ross His passenger, do not call him Mr Wilde . . .

Moffatt His passenger is here and will be down very soon.

Phoebe Yes, I see, sir.

Ross You have that message?

Phoebe Yes, of course. The passenger who is not Mr Wilde is coming and the message is he will not be long.

She glares at him resentfully, then goes. Arthur hands Wilde the wine.

Wilde Thank you, Arthur.

Bosie looks up, quietly confident.

Bosie I would like to talk to you, Oscar.

Wilde Talk to me? Bosie, truly! You hardly need ask.

Bosie No?

Wilde Of course not. Come talk.

Bosie I had an impression from Robbie . . .

Wilde What impression?

Wilde looks between them.

Bosie Robbie implied that your wish was that I should step back.

Wilde I would never wish that.

Bosie Why, thank you.

Ross is momentarily discomforted by their contact.

Ross I was saying . . . I was saying only that you yourself need to make haste.

Bosie Oscar, even now my cousin is having meetings at the Houses of Parliament to make sure this prosecution need never take place.

Ross Bosie, it's simply impractical. I have no doubt your cousin is doing his best.

Bosie He is.

Ross But there is a train.

Bosie What do you want? That he wakes up tomorrow in some foreign country? And the real possibility he will never get back?

Both of them have begun to raise their voices. Wilde smiles, calm.

Wilde Please, the two of you, I must impose myself. Robbie, what time is it?

Ross It is just past two-thirty.

Wilde And, tell me, what time is the train?

Ross hesitates a second.

Tell me the time the actual train leaves.

Ross The train leaves at four.

Wilde Ah, well then . . .

Ross It connects with the boat.

Wilde The Cadogan to Victoria, let us be realistic. In the name of our common humanity, let us get our priorities straight. Let us pause, let us make the seminal decision: it seems that I still have time for my lunch.

Satisfied, he turns to Moffatt. Ross shifts, furious.

Moffatt Sir.

Wilde Be fair to me, Robbie. I face a long journey. I dread *mal de mer*. I shall need to travel with some ballast inside.

He turns again to Moffatt.

Mr Moffatt, I need something suitable. Perhaps a small lobster. Seafood, certainly. *A l'Americaine*. With some kind of rice.

Moffatt Chef does a rice which is perfumed.

Wilde Or a timbale. Exquisite. Perfect for crossing the Channel.

He turns to Bosie.

Bosie, be quick now. What would you like?

Bosie Nothing. I couldn't. When even now my father is gloating, standing like some mad animal on the steps of the court, screaming that if ever I am seen in your company, then he will have you shot like a dog.

Wilde smiles absently at him and turns back to Moffatt.

Wilde And langoustines I suppose are quite simply unavailable?

Moffatt My regrets. But the season.

Wilde Don't worry. I quite understand.

Ross is still tense.

Ross Very well. It is your decision. I would only remind you the press now know where you are.

Wilde That is clear.

Ross If you stay in this room, I do have to warn you, at any moment the police may appear.

Wilde That will give my lunch an added spice of excitement.

He turns back to Moffatt who is about to leave. Phoebe has returned with towels.

Oh Mr Moffatt, I wonder, with lobster do I really want rice?

Ross Oscar . . .

Moffatt We offer excellent *dauphinoise* potatoes.

Wilde Do you recall if I have eaten those before?

Moffatt Yes, sir.

Wilde And were they not heavy? Are they not more suitably a dinnertime dish?

Ross All right, eat all you like. Just as long as you are quick. But there are things I must tell you. I have to remind you I have been to your house.

The atmosphere is changed at once. Wilde looks thoughtfully at Ross. Moffatt, alert to the mood, bows tactfully.

Moffatt We shall go, sir. I shall bring you both dishes. The rice and the potatoes. Then you can choose.

Wilde Excellent, Mr Moffatt. And thank you, Arthur, as well.

Arthur Not at all, sir.

Wilde Phoebe. Is it Phoebe?

Phoebe It is.

The three find themselves lined up opposite him for an oddly formal moment.

Wilde Throughout this time of trial I've had excellent service. Whenever I've visited, I have been made to feel welcome. It's something which means a great deal to me. No, truly. Thank you. I'm moved by it.

Moffatt Our pleasure, sir.

Wilde is once more on the edge of tears.

Wilde Robbie, a cue for more money.

Ross Oscar, that is not what this money is for!

Wilde You know I can't abide meanness.

Ross Very well. I shall give them some of my own.

Wilde This is in character. Robbie is a true Christian.

Ross Here.

He reaches into his pocket for coins.

Moffatt, Phoebe *and* **Arthur** Thank you. Thank you very much, sir. Greatly appreciated.

Ross Now I'm sorry, but we really do need to be on our own.

Moffatt, Phoebe and Arthur go out. Wilde has gone across to put a glass in Bosie's hand.

Wilde Will you have some wine with me, Bosie? Here. Please. Stay close to me, Bosie. I need you. You and I still have a long way to go.

Wilde kisses him on the cheek. There is a silence. Then Wilde moves away.

Ross I have to report to you. I have seen Constance.

Wilde You saw her?

Ross Yes.

Wilde And what did she say? Tell me, how were the children?

Ross I did not see them. But she assured me the children were well.

Wilde Go on.

Ross She is in the most terrible turmoil. There is only one way to relieve it. She asked me to beg you: she implores you to flee.

There is a moment's silence. Bosie watches from the side.

Look . . .

Wilde You say you caught no sight of the children?

Ross No. My impression was they were playing in the nursery.

Wilde I see. And do they . . . do they yet have any knowledge of what has happened?

Ross Constance says they know nothing at all.

He waits a moment.

For their sake, she says, you must choose exile. If you stay and battle it out at a trial, the prospect of what will be said, what will be repeated in London . . . well, their lives will not be worth living. She is sending them abroad.

Wilde looks up.

Tomorrow.

Wilde She is sending the children?

There is a silence. For the first time Wilde seems deeply hurt.

I see.

Ross Flight is imperative for the whole family. She was relieved when I gave her your news.

Wilde My news?

Ross Yes.

Wilde You said I had already decided?

Ross I described our meeting last night.

Wilde Did you say who was there?

Ross To be truthful, I mentioned the others. But I did not mention Lord Alfred. Understand, I did not think it was fair.

He pauses a second, tactful.

You must realise . . .

Wilde Oh, I do . . .

Ross She has conceived a most passionate resentment. To say at this point that . . . that you still meet with Bosie, that you take account of his views . . .

Bosie interrupts, furious:

Bosie Oh really, I cannot endure this!

Ross Why not?

Bosie This whole thing makes no sense at all!

Ross Why?

Bosie Because we did not decide! We have not decided! My recollection is quite firm on this point. Exile was only one choice among many.

He looks to Wilde, who looks into his glass and takes another draught.

This is what we must all decide upon now.

Ross Oh Bosie, now really . . .

Bosie I mean it. I thought that is what this meeting is for.

Ross Look at the reality! Outside a cab will be waiting. It's waiting! I ordered it.

Bosie So?

Ross It will take him to the station. He can do no other. This is the last boat tonight! Oscar?

Wilde reaches again for the wine.

Wilde Do not distress yourself. The hour is fixed in my memory. I know exactly how soon I must go.

And Bosie is already continuing.

Bosie Oscar cannot leave until he hears from my cousin.

Ross Oh really!

Bosie He will come here by three at the latest, he said. He will bring us firm news from Asquith.

He turns angrily to Ross.

Why are you always so scornful?

Ross Because we all know it is going to be simply too late!

Bosie George Wyndham is a man of considerable influence. He is a Member of Parliament. It is madness for Oscar to run headlong from the country until we know beyond any question that a prosecution cannot be stopped.

Ross It cannot be stopped!

Bosie smiles, confident.

Bosie You know nothing. Robbie, forgive me, but the thinking of better-class people is hardly what one might call a strong point of yours. George is a friend of the Prime Minister.

Ross So?

Bosie Robbie, please trust me. I understand these things rather better than you. My name is good for something, I hope. There is not much point in being born with the name of Queensberry unless there are moments when it can be used.

Wilde is quietly amused.

Wilde I wish I shared your faith in the English. Nation to them is just as important as class. They have united at last in hatred of the foreigner. Yes, because I am Irish.

Bosie That's absurd.

Wilde Is it? Yesterday I looked across the courtroom. It shocked me. I tell you their excitement was more than merely professional. Yes? Did you see that?

Ross nods.

This was a court which ached for a kill.

Ross Yes.

Wilde The whole nation is ready. I have been tolerated for too long a time. No one has rights in this country. One is granted only a temporary licence. And here comes the moment when mine is withdrawn.

But he is already bored with his own theory and has got up to examine the open case on the bed. He takes out some books.

What is this? Did you pack these for me?

Ross Certainly.

Wilde *The Thoughts of St Ignatius.* Robbie . . .

He looks at him reproachfully.

My God. What is this? This only gets worse. Dickens! Robbie, do you not know me?

Ross I was rushed.

Wilde You think I should gorge myself on sentimental morality?

Ross Very well then, tell me, what would you prefer?

Wilde Why, tales of suffering and murder. Injustice. The spilling of blood. Let my reading be only of ravaging, destruction and rape. That is what I want. Nothing else. And for these things the only book worth considering is the Bible. The essential companion to exile. I shall read it continually.

Ross I shall get you a Bible.

But Bosie is quietly furious.

Bosie Oh Oscar, please, you do not convince.

Wilde Not convince?

Bosie You're affecting indifference . . .

Wilde Affecting it?

Bosie You are standing there talking about the books you will take.

Wilde A critical discussion of literature seems to me at all times worth having.

Bosie Oh yes? I am not for one second fooled!

Wilde No?

Bosie Face it: if you flee, it's like admitting you're guilty . . .

Wilde Oh yes . . .

Bosie It's an open confession of guilt. You hand your enemies their victory. What's worse, my father gets everything he wants.

Wilde I fear so.

Bosie What, and that does not disturb you? The thought of it? The shame? Being taken for a coward?

Wilde interrupts, smiling.

Wilde Bosie, you say I'm acting indifference. I promise you, I have no need to simulate. My indifference is real.

Bosie Oscar, please.

Wilde Why? If I flee, as you say, it's disastrous. But if I stay, my prospects are also not good. So why make a choice? What are you asking exactly? Why at this moment do anything at all?

He sits back, confident.

I have always had a low opinion of what is called action. Action is something my mother brought me up to distrust. Why make a decision which does not yet need to be made? What's more, think of this: I am where I wish to be. Consider. I find myself here with you in this room. Yes. With this wine. Where I have been happiest. These past five weeks. The three of us, planning our hopeless campaign.

He smiles affectionately at Bosie. Both Ross and Bosie are silenced.

Outside this room, I will find only suffering. The world is charged. It is poised. My destiny will all too quickly unfold. But while we are here – perhaps you think this short-sighted, but you cannot deny it – the fact is that things are not really too bad.

This is no sooner out than Arthur has knocked on the door, wheeling in a trolley.

Arthur Excuse me . . .

Wilde Ah food, yes, delicious.

Bosie I'm sorry . . .

Wilde Ah yes, please enter . . .

Bosie Oh Oscar, you're not really planning to eat?

Wilde Yes, I am.

Bosie You are a goose. I mean, *why*? At this moment?

Wilde Yes, Arthur, please do set the table down there.

Wilde has faltered getting up. He has almost finished the bottle.

Whoops . . .

Ross Oh God, Oscar, you're stumbling . . .

Wilde No, no. I need a steadying drink. Dear Arthur, some more wine when you're ready . . .

Arthur Yes, sir.

Arthur has pulled out a folding table and is laying it with a white tablecloth.

I'm afraid to have to tell you, sir, there's now quite a crowd in the street.

Wilde A crowd?

Arthur Yes. They look like a lynch mob.

Wilde Indeed?

Arthur They're baying for blood.

Wilde That is quite a coincidence. It has also been wildly exciting in here. The temperature's rising. We live in a veritable cauldron of fear. More wine! And shall we nail up the entrance?

He looks round rather grandly.

This all confirms me in my decision to stay in this room.

Ross shifts, uneasy.

Ross Oscar . . .

Wilde Robbie, please, desist for a second. Allow me this gap. This equipoise. Let me have that. I have perhaps half an hour. Allow me this one sweet moment of peace.

Moffatt appears now at the door.

Moffatt Excuse me, sir. A Mr George Wyndham . . .

Bosie Ah George . . .

Moffatt He asks if he may be allowed to come in.

Bosie Tell him yes.

Wilde If you don't mind, Bosie, I would prefer it if you saw him outside. No, really.

Bosie Why?

Wilde I can tell he'll be breathless.

Bosie Oh Oscar . . .

Wilde It's the breathlessness I cannot face.

Bosie Are you going to be childish?

Wilde He'll rush in, wearing those awful striped trousers and bursting with news which he'll want to blurt out. The very name Wyndham! It exudes self-importance. A person called Wyndham indeed! George Wyndham!

Bosie is nodding as if this confirms a familiar pattern.

Bosie Oh I see, so you're going to be facetious.

Wilde Not at all.

Bosie He may bring you news of your freedom!

Wilde Then please by all means you may see him out there in the corridor. I have said. You are welcome to meet him . . .

Moffatt What shall I say, sir?

Wilde I just don't much fancy the prospect myself.

Wilde is standing, self-consciously capricious, looking for more wine.

Bosie Oscar, George has been working . . .

Wilde I know this . . .

Bosie He has been in Parliament all morning on your behalf.

Wilde Tell him: I appreciate all he has done for me but I do not wish to speak to him now.

Bosie Why not?

Wilde Because it is simple! Open that door and the real world comes into this room.

Wilde has raised his voice. Moffatt retires discreetly.

Bosie You know this has been the whole story . . .

Wilde What story?

Bosie This has been my problem throughout . . .

Wilde (*to Arthur*)The wine! Can you get me the wine?

Arthur Yes, of course, sir.

Arthur goes out.

Bosie It is as if you still can't absorb it. George Wyndham is a powerful man!

Wilde I know that.

Bosie He is my cousin, for God's sake! He has far better things to do with his time.

Wilde I'm sure.

Wilde smiles surreptitiously at Ross.

Bosie For him there is also the danger.

Wilde I see that.

Bosie A man of his standing. The risk he is taking by

speaking on your behalf. And why do you think he is doing it? My cousin George is actually risking his neck! Because by the purest coincidence he happens to hate my father almost as much as I do myself!

Wilde looks at him a moment.

Wilde Why, yes.

Bosie So then why will you not talk to him?

Wilde Oh Bosie . . .

Bosie I mean it! Why won't you? He is waiting outside!

Wilde Oh Bosie, how I envy your spirit!

He stops, the point reached at last.

I do not wish to speak to George Wyndham because the point is George Wyndham cannot succeed!

Wilde seizes on Arthur's return.

Ah, and here comes my wine, thank goodness. Arthur, your timing is excellent, as always, I see.

Arthur Thank you, sir. Do you want me to open it?

Wilde I most certainly do.

Wilde is suddenly fluent, at ease.

Oh yes, by all means, admit your friend in his pinstripes, let him bring us news from the oak-panelled corridors of whispered meetings with all his biscuity, high-minded friends. But Bosie . . . do you believe such meetings can weigh on our fortunes? Even you must see it, it's simply too late.

Bosie Too late?

Wilde Yes. Of course. Ask Robbie.

Bosie Oscar, what makes you so sure that you're not going to win?

Wilde throws up his hands, near tears.

Wilde Oh . . .

Ross Look, Bosie . . .

Bosie No, really. We seem to be glibly assuming that there *will* be a criminal trial. And that should it take place, we are destined to lose it.

Wilde Bosie, do you really imagine I care? Do you think it is the prospect of *losing* which makes me so fearful?

Bosie moves towards him with genuine compassion.

Bosie Oh Oscar, I beg you . . . I beg you, do not give up.

Wilde Give up? Give up? Why should it matter? 'Shall I give up?' 'Shall I carry on?' Either? Neither? Guilty! Not guilty! How can it make a blind bit of difference? The simple fact is: I am cast in a role. My story has already been written. How I choose to play it is a mere matter of taste. The performance of the actor will not determine the action.

Bosie And what is this action?

Wilde The action is: I am being expelled!

He is suddenly savage. Bosie turns away.

Bosie Oh really!

Wilde It's true. I am trapped in the narrative. The narrative now has a life of its own. It travels inexorably towards my disgrace. Towards my final expulsion. And it bears me along on its crest . . .

He seems suddenly almost exhilarated.

Yes, in fact, for me, borne along by this story, there is even an odd kind of freedom. I may wear whatever mask I may choose. Tragic? Defiant? Tearful? Resigned? I may try all these attitudes. I may bring what so-called 'feelings' I like to the role. But they will not have the slightest effect on the outcome. The story has only one possible end.

Bosie is genuinely frightened now.

Bosie Oscar, why do you feel that? For God's sake! After all we have been through! Just see him! What may you lose by it? My cousin is serious. My cousin is desperately concerned.

At this Wilde seems to relax, as if on familiar territory.

Wilde Of course. I do not for one second doubt it. I know that look in the English. They affect a particular furrow-browed earnestness, a desperate considerateness. As they settle one's fate, they arrange their features in a way which is always moral and grave. They speak about law and principle and how much it will hurt them to do the thing they must do. And at the end of the seriousness, the weightiness, the sorrow, the judicious weighing of things in the scales – have you really not noticed? – the decisions they make lead only one way. This is England. There is always a hanging! And this time it's decided: the noose has been fitted and the neck is my own!

Arthur hovers with the bottle.

Arthur Do I pour, sir?

Wilde Pour.

Wilde is so absorbed he has not even turned to Arthur.

Have you never once stopped . . . have you never asked yourself . . . never once wondered why your Wyndhams exist? Why they exhibit all that desperate doggy concern?

Wyndhams exist only to stand in front of the Asquiths. And the Asquiths are the ones who get their own way.

A knock, and the door opens again. It is Mr Moffatt with a second trolley.

Ask Mr Moffatt. Mr Moffatt's not English. The English have been my subject for years. Oh yes, in England the preacher says prayers on the scaffold. Then straight after he dines with the hangman.

He turns as Phoebe joins Moffatt at the door.

And how appropriate! It seems that the lobster is here.

Phoebe has a large tray with a silver dome. Arthur joins Mr Moffatt, who has a trolley with saucepans and a burner.

And it is the lovely Phoebe who brings it . . .

Phoebe Thank you, sir.

Wilde Robbie, please shower her with money at once. Alter my mood! Let us do something noble! Let us try and change Phoebe's life for the good.

Phoebe Sir.

Phoebe is blushing with pleasure. Bosie moves away in despair.

Wilde Since we ourselves cannot be happy . . .

Ross Oh Oscar . . .

Wilde Let another be happy instead. Yes? You agree with me, Phoebe?

Phoebe I'd quite like some money, sir, if that's what you mean.

Moffatt, busying for elaborate meal preparation, looks disapproving.

Moffatt Phoebe . . .

Phoebe I'm sorry, sir. I didn't mean to say that. I hope I gave no offence.

Wilde You did not. You could not.

Phoebe Thank you, sir.

For a second, it seems he might reach out and touch her. They are both moved.

Wilde Robbie, open my pocketbook forthwith.

Ross No, I refuse to.

Wilde What, would you defy me?

Moffatt Sir, would you like us to serve you the lobster at once?

Wilde Lay it forth, by all means. Yes, now is the moment.

Moffatt I'll do it, sir.

Wilde Light up your fire and release some warmth in our hearts!

Moffatt lights the silver spirit lamp, which gives a big pop.

There we are. The flame of Olympia! A little beacon of hope that flickers and flares . . .

Moffatt And shall I ready the sauce, sir?

Wilde Set to, Mr Moffatt. Abduct me down the path of excess!

Moffatt Yes, sir.

The three staff all laugh, busy round the trolley, as Moffatt prepares the sauce for the lobster. Wilde moves over to Bosie and speaks quietly.

Wilde Oh Bosie, I beg you, do not look so sulky. I cannot bear to see you cast low.

Bosie Well, how do you want me to take this?

Wilde In the same way I hope I will take it myself.

An intimacy has returned. Wilde reaches out and touches his hand.

Bosie . . .

Bosie I cannot. Oscar, you know what I feel for you. You have been the luck of my life. But now, you are taking up an attitude that makes no sense to me. You have decided you are foredoomed. It is as if you want your own downfall. You welcome it. You imagine this weakness poetic, it is what you have called embracing your fate . . .

Wilde Is that right?

Bosie How you love that idea! But to me it has no such attraction. It just means that you lack the will to fight back.

Wilde is close to Bosie. Ross watches. The three staff go on with their work.

In your writing, you love to say there is always a destiny. Men are always dragged down by the gods. Do not make this mistake. Do not confuse your life with your art. Such ideas belong only in literature. They do not belong in the world.

He leans further in, assured, not wanting the hotel servants to hear.

These boys . . . these boys who will testify, who will stand up in court and say you took them to bed . . . who are they? They are known to be renters. Blackmailers. The scum of society. Why do you think that the court will believe them? Why are you so sure you cannot then win?

Wilde I have said. I am indifferent to winning. Whatever the verdict, my reputation is gone.

Bosie Ah yes, of course, how convenient. It's all a conspiracy! Everything is out of your hands. Because it's the fault of the English. The English who, as we know, spend the whole day thinking up ways of claiming your scalp . . .

Wilde I didn't say that.

Wilde moves away in despair at this.

Bosie Didn't you? You said something like it. Yesterday, in court, those answers you gave. I watched you. I know you. You have wanted this thing. In some awful part of your being, you love the idea of surrender. You think there's some hideous glamour in letting Fate propel you down from the heights! But I do well to remind you, it happens I am a poet as well. But with a far different outlook. I don't find destruction romantic.

Wilde looks up at his accusation.

Wilde Bosie, oh please, you must not say that.

Bosie Well then, sit in this room until you are groggy. By all means. Until you are musky with drink. Sit here and tell yourself that everything is written in advance in the stars. But I am a different character. I shall confer with my cousin. I shall do what you are too lazy to do. I shall fight. I shall fight for your future and for my own.

Wilde Bosie . . .

Bosie Because I am not cowed. I will not be cowed by what's happened. Unlike you, Oscar, I refuse to give up.

Bosie goes out. Wilde is devastated by his departure.

Moffatt Sir, the meal is now ready.

Wilde Ah . . .

Moffatt The dish is prepared.

Wilde Good.

The table is set out like a vision, but Wilde does not move towards it.

Moffatt The lobster has been softened in butter. Tomatoes have been added, crushed garlic, shallots, tarragon, orange peel, parsley, white wine . . .

Wilde Yes, thank you.

Moffatt We dust with cayenne and then bathe in fresh cream.

Wilde Please.

He still does not move.

In one moment I will be ready to eat it. Robbie, I insist you reward them at once.

But Ross is ready to stand firm.

Now Robbie . . . give me that pocketbook. Give me my cash, I insist. Give it here. You must hand it over. I have to remind you the money is mine.

Ross No, I won't.

Wilde Robbie . . .

Ross I cannot do it in honesty. The money is there to fund you in exile. I cannot allow you to give it away.

The three go very still, sensing the tension as Wilde moves towards Ross.

Wilde Robbie, just pass me the pocketbook. Earlier I asked you to cash me a cheque . . .

Ross I did it.

Wilde Well?

Ross That cheque was intended for one purpose only.

Wilde Its purpose is not your concern.

Ross Oscar, this is what Bosie is saying. You do not protect your own cause. You need this money. With all respect to these people, why would you waste it?

Wilde Give me my money! How dare you? The money is mine!

Wilde has shouted this, and is now swaying slightly. Moffatt is uncomfortable.

Moffatt Excuse me, sir . . .

Wilde No, Mr Moffatt, this does not concern you. Robbie, give me my money.

Ross No, I refuse.

Wilde moves closer. Ross is transfixed.

Wilde Robbie, come close to me. Robbie. Would you wish to upset me? Now, Robbie. Robbie. Look me in the eye. It is my will. Give me the pocketbook.

There is a silence. Ross reaches into his breast pocket and hands the wallet over.

Thank you. Please allow us all to live our own lives.

He moves a little unsteadily towards the group who are standing together.

Mr Moffatt, I have had magnificent service. I have remarked on this already, I know. But the vision of this meal reminds me . . . the standard of service is the highest I've known. For that reason, I would be grateful . . . it would do me honour if I could bestow some reward . . .

Fumblingly, he takes out notes.

For the three of you, say, five pounds for your trouble? Ten, even? Five each?

Wilde has misread Moffatt's reluctance and clumsily taken out more.

Moffatt I'm sorry, Mr Wilde, but we cannot accept.

The group stirs. Wilde is shocked.

Wilde What?

Moffatt No, sir, we cannot. We cannot take this money of yours. If we accepted it would weigh on our conscience. No really. I promise, I speak for us all. Arthur?

Arthur Indeed, sir.

Moffatt Phoebe?

Phoebe Yes, I feel the same way.

It is not true for Phoebe, and they all know it.

Moffatt These last few weeks, Mr Wilde, we have come to know you. No visitor to this hotel has ever been kinder or better regarded than you. And not for what you have given us. Not money, anyway. You have given us kindness. And at this moment your need is greater than ours. Here in this hotel, we see all sorts of people. People of every background and type. But we see very few gentlemen.

He bows very slightly. Wilde, near to tears again, is barely able to speak.

Wilde Thank you. I am very moved.

Moffatt And now we would ask you just one single favour . . .

Wilde Of course. What's that, Mr Moffatt?

Moffatt That you sit down and eat your lunch.

Wilde Yes, of course, Mr Moffatt.

He sits down obediently. They hand him his napkin. They pour wine into his glass. A small ritual. Then:

Moffatt We'll leave you. Goodbye, sir. Call if there's anything you feel you might need.

All Three Goodbye, sir.

Moffatt We will be close, sir.

Wilde Thank you. Thank you indeed.

They go out. Wilde has lifted his fork but then he breaks down, overcome.

I cannot. I cannot eat it.

He drops the fork and gets up, moving blindly towards Ross.

Oh Robbie, Robbie . . .

Ross Oscar . . .

Wilde Robbie, come here please, come here and hold me . . .

Ross Oh Oscar . . .

Wilde Hold me, my dear, my precious, my own . . .

The two men stand in each other's arms.

Ross Oh Oscar . . .

Wilde You think . . . you think I have upset Bosie? What is Bosie thinking, do you know?

Ross I do not.

Wilde had buried his head in Ross's shoulder, but now Ross tenses, and Wilde moves away, the moment past.

Wilde Good God, what's happening? I am awash. I have lost my handkerchief. Oh Lord, are there handkerchiefs here?

He has blundered over to the suitcase, and is now pulling at its contents, clothes going everywhere in his untidy search.

Ross Please Oscar, let me. I packed a bunch of silk handkerchiefs Constance gave me . . .

Wilde Oh Constance, oh Lord . . .

Wilde moves away and lets Ross take over in the suitcase.

Even the sound of her name. Look! Even the lobster reproaches me. Everything reproaches me. Look, just look at its dead eye staring up. To have killed me, it says, and then not even to eat me!

Coldly Ross hands him a handkerchief.

Ross Oscar, I'm afraid the moment has come.

Wilde It's come?

Ross has gone back to put everything into the bag and close it up.

Ross By my watch it's now a quarter past three. Remember, you don't yet have a ticket. If we leave now you will still have a chance.

Wilde Yes.

Wilde is wiping his tears away as he moves across the room.

Now?

Ross Yes.

Wilde You think? How can I leave without Bosie? I can hardly leave without saying goodbye.

Ross Soon enough you may see him.

Wilde I cannot leave if Bosie feels it is wrong.

Ross shifts, containing his temper.

Forgive me, I do not feel fully at ease. It is an instinct, no more. I look. I imagine myself as I pass through that door.

He looks for a moment. Then waves a hand.

No. Not yet. I need to speak once more to Bosie. Yes. Bring me Bosie and then I will go.

He has sat down. Ross is holding the packed bag, ready to go.

Ross Oscar, I am uncertain why you are so keen to delay your departure . . .

Wilde I have given my reasons. I still am not sure.

Ross I can only say if you do not leave quickly – if you do not leave in the next five minutes, in fact – the chances are that tonight you will spend your first night in prison. This is a prospect I do not believe you have faced.

Wilde is silent a moment.

Wilde I have faced it.

Ross puts the bag down, intense, serious.

Ross I have been waiting, I have been standing here desperately, trying not to say this all week. You are locked in a quarrel not of your making! You have done all you have to. Your duty is over and now you must leave!

Wilde sinks deeper into his chair, resentful.

Your friends, yes, your real friends have all tried to tell you . . .

Wilde I have not lacked for the telling!

Ross They have tried to warn you. You have walked open-eyed towards this disaster.

He is nodding, not to be diverted.

If you just stop, if you stop and consider, if you give a moment's thought to how Bosie has actually behaved . . . what he has wanted all along . . . his sole and single intention has always been to make his father respond.

Wilde looks at him, not able to reply.

Yes, and when he had succeeded, when he had goaded his father to a point which he simply could not ignore, then it was not Bosie who was threatened. It was not Bosie who had to risk all in court. Oh no! Instead the boy turns to his dearest friend Oscar and says: 'Could you possibly do this on my behalf?'

Wilde That isn't true.

Ross Oh, isn't it? And that you, Oscar Wilde, so puissant, so brilliant, should be pulled along like a poodle! Where are you? Where is the Oscar we knew?

Ross has hurt Wilde, but goes on regardless.

And now you're delaying because he wants you to stay here! Of course! Stay here in England? Why not? It's your life, not his. You are to stay here and confront this famous list of immoral young men. Yet one thing we're forgetting: how did you meet them? I'm asking. How did you meet them?

Wilde looks sullen, not answering.

You choose not to answer because you know full well you cannot.

Wilde All right!

Ross You choose not to say it but you met them through *him*. Yes! And will *he* face prosecution?

Wilde Now Robbie . . .

Ross Will *his* life be dragged through the courts? No, of course not. He escapes. When he has done these same things and with these same men.

Ross is upset by his own cruelty.

Why does Bosie escape prosecution?

Wilde Robbie . . .

Ross He escapes prosecution because he's a lord! Well, it's true and you know it! When you and I were together, you knew none of these young men. It was Bosie who drew you into this trade. And why? Because Bosie withheld himself.

Wilde turns angrily, having finally lost his temper.

Wilde What is the fatal human passion? What is the source of all sin on this earth? This propensity in all human beings to indulge in the improper rapture, the gratuitous pleasure of giving others advice. Yes, I had rather swim neck-deep in London's arterial sewer, I had rather give up my body to every diseased and indigent tramp in the street, than surrender to this abominable indulgence of telling other people what they should do.

He throws his coat down.

You demand that I make a decision. Here is my decision.
I refuse to go until Bosie returns.

*Ross leaves the room. Wilde gets up and pours himself
another glass of wine. He stands at the table, the meal
cooling in front of him. Then Ross returns.*

Ross He will not be long.

Ross sits on the bed.

Oscar, there are other people who love you. Perhaps you
should remember there are others as well.

Wilde looks at him, then speaks quietly.

Wilde It is not kind. It is not kind of you, Robbie. Is there
not some small part of us which is purely our own? Which
is our soul? Which is our innermost being? And which
we alone should control? You bombard me. It is not fair.
In any civilised war unfortified places are respected. I
knew what you thought. You did not need to tell me.
You know full well: I have done what I did out of love.

Ross looks back at him, saying nothing.

Do not . . . do not seek to destroy me by laying out what
you call the facts. It is cruel of you, Robbie, it is cruel
when you do such a thing. I have acted out of love. I have
defended this love which exists between us, the purest
I have known in my life. More perfect, more vital, more
telling, more various, richer, more vibrant, more sweet.
The redeeming fact of my life.

He turns and looks at Ross.

It is what I have left. It is what remains to me. All else
has now been taken away. So you would now take even
that from me. You would tell me I have been deceived
and used in all this? Consider what you are saying. If

the love between us is not as I think it, then I shall have suffered to no purpose at all.

Bosie appears. His manner has changed completely. The certainty has been replaced by a considerate gentleness.

Bosie Oscar . . .

Wilde Ah, Bosie . . .

Bosie I'm sorry. I have kept you too long.

Wilde Not at all.

Bosie I have been talking to George in the corridor.

Wilde Well?

Bosie I'm afraid his news is not helpful. He has failed. He says that you will be arrested.

There is a slight pause, as Bosie waits for Wilde to take this in.

He says however there is one further thing you should know.

Wilde What is that?

Bosie They are deliberately choosing to delay.

Wilde They're delaying?

Bosie Yes. Till this evening. George says they are employing a sporting metaphor. The fox must be given its chance to escape.

Wilde is taken aback, but he sounds distant when he replies.

Wilde Oh, I see.

Bosie They would prefer it. It would suit them better if you would flee. This brief opening is offered.

Wilde How considerate! And, Bosie, tell me, what do you think I should do?

Bosie shifts and looks round. Wilde takes his cue from Bosie's look.

Ross Excuse me.

Reluctantly Ross goes out of the room.

Wilde No, really. I'm asking. No, truly.

Bosie But surely you must decide.

Wilde Surely. But you must still have an opinion. Well?

Bosie You know I would prefer you to stay here. Nothing George tells me has changed how I think. I still am persuaded that if we pursue it with vigour, there is no question the case can be won.

Wilde Yes.

Bosie But the point is that just at this moment . . . just at this moment itself . . . George is saying that when they come to arrest you, it is in nobody's interest that I myself should be here.

Wilde nods judiciously.

Wilde No.

Bosie If it is known . . . if it is known in the newspapers that you and I were together at the time of arrest . . .

Wilde Yes, of course . . .

Bosie Then that is something which George says will surely further inflame my father and therefore make this whole matter worse.

Wilde I see.

Wilde looks at him, thoughtful.

THE JUDAS KISS

Bosie Now look . . . I have said . . . if you want me to stay with you, there is no question I will. I belong at your side. But in what he's suggesting I confess I do see a sort of brutal wisdom.

Wilde Yes. I discern that brutal wisdom myself.

Bosie takes a step towards him.

Bosie Be clear. I'm not for one second abandoning you.

Wilde No.

Bosie I hope you know me.

Wilde I know you, of course.

Bosie I am leaving for only this interval. I say again. This brief interval, no more and no less.

Bosie looks down before giving more news.

George wants me to go with him to Westminster. He wants me to work with him on your behalf. He thinks he may secure you bail for tonight. Assuming of course that you do not flee.

Wilde looks at him, almost as if not understanding.

Wilde We could meet tonight?

Bosie Yes.

Wilde We could meet this evening?

Bosie If you stay, nothing changes. We meet as we always have done. You may be assured. It is the wish of my heart.

Bosie hesitates before more bad news.

George is saying . . . he is saying my family would like me to travel. They would prefer it if I too went away. But I have told him: no, if Oscar stays, then I shall stay with him.

He has moved closer to Wilde and now looks straight at him.

I shall not leave you.

Wilde No.

Wilde is strangely absent, as if looking at Bosie properly for the first time.

Bosie Have you decided?

Wilde I'm sorry?

Bosie Today. Will you stay or go?

Wilde Oh. I am in the process, Bosie. Kiss me.

Bosie moves across to him and kisses him. The kiss deepens. Then Wilde withdraws a little and hugs him. There is silence.

It is what we fear which happens to us.

Arthur knocks, then opens the door. Ross returns behind him.

Arthur Sir, excuse me, it's Mr Wyndham. He says Lord Alfred must join him now. He says it's urgent. He cannot wait any longer.

Wilde Yes, thank you, Arthur.

Arthur He asked me to insist Lord Alfred must leave here at once.

Arthur stands waiting.

Bosie I'm sorry . . .

Wilde I know. You have no time now. Bosie . . .

Bosie Yes. I must leave.

Wilde spreads his arms in a sudden access of cheerfulness.

Wilde So. We shall meet again but we cannot say when. However. My darling, may it be soon.

Bosie I must go. I must go.

He smiles helplessly, boyish now, laughing at the absurdity of it.

Oh God, what a business! No, truly. Yes, may it be soon. I'm sorry. I'm sorry. As the French say, *à bientôt*.

He goes out, all breathless charm, and Arthur closes the door.

Wilde So. They choose to offer me this opening. The whole world wants me to go.

Ross Yes.

Wilde The world persists in thinking me shallow. They think me feckless. They consider me weak. Flee, and I hand them this ready opinion. Do you know I think I may have decided?

He moves to the wine, resolved.

Open my case, I beg you. I wish to sit here. I wish to read. I shall not run down this hole they have dug for me. I will not stoop to leave on all fours.

Ross puts the cases back on the bed in despair.

Yes. I can run but I choose not to. Die of embarrassment in some hovel abroad? Admit to society they have driven me out? No, I will not give them that pleasure. I am going to do the single thing which will drive them to frenzied distraction: I am going to sit down and get on with my lunch.

He sits rather clumsily down at the table and contemplates the meal in front of him.

My mind is made up. Good. A book. Yes, a book please, Robbie.

*Ross reopens the case to get him a book. Wilde lifts
his knife and fork, but for a moment they are
suspended.*

If I run now, my story is finished. For as long as I stay,
it is not at an end. I prefer my story unfinished.

He turns and looks at Ross.

Robbie, we shall not discuss it. I shall eat and the train
will make its own way. Do you hear? Do you hear that
whistle?

He lifts a hand to his ear and waits.

Do you hear the wheels running away down the track?
What is that? The train is departing. Do you sense the
life that we did not live?

He starts to tuck happily into the lobster.

This lobster's good.

Ross It was better earlier.

Wilde I'm sure. I could not eat it before.

Ross moves across the room, in agony.

Robbie, you know you must leave me also. It is not safe
for you here.

Ross I know that.

Wilde You have done enough. You must not be found
with me.

Ross No. I promised my mother . . .

Wilde You as well . . .

Ross Yes. This morning I promised. If you were arrested,
I promised I would not be there. She said if I am with
you when you are arrested I will be ruined for ever.

Wilde goes on eating contentedly.

Wilde I'm sure your mother knows about these things.

Ross Well, I have always done what my mother said.

Ross has said this with a smile. Now he takes off his topcoat.

But if Bosie cannot be with you. If it seems that Bosie cannot stay . . .

Wilde looks up from his eating. Ross sits down in an armchair.

Ross Then I am not willing to leave you.

Wilde Good. I shall not be alone.

He puts down his knife and fork.

The food is good. The book is excellent. We know the police have been delayed. Once more it seems I have no alternative. I have no other option. It is clear. The moment has come when I must sleep.

Ross You cannot sleep!

Wilde Why not?

Ross They will come to arrest you.

Wilde I am tired.

He has got up from table and lain down on the sofa with only his wine beside him.

Ross They will find you like this.

Wilde It suits me. I do not care for their judgement at all.

He closes his eyes. The room grows dark. Music has started to play quietly again.

Ross I'll sit.

Wilde Let us sleep. Let us hear that metal clacking along the track.

He is about to fall asleep on the sofa. Ross sits, keeping guard over him.

For as long as we sleep we are in safety. The train is going. And I shall sleep.

The music begins to fill out. The room is darkened, but light comes again from the high window and sweeps round in a circle, like the transit of the sun, catching the dust in the air, or the deep yellow beam of a lighthouse, highlighting the room exquisitely as it passes and dies. Then, after a while, light returns to the room itself. They have not yet lit the lamps, so they are silhouetted by the light of a cold London afternoon from the window. Ross does not realise that Wilde has opened his eyes.

SCENE TWO

Wilde You are still here.

Ross Yes.

Wilde Do you remember? Do you remember when we first met?

Ross Yes.

Wilde You seduced me.

Ross Yes.

Wilde You were the first man I slept with.

Ross I was.

Wilde Yet I imagined I knew more than you.

There is a knock and Arthur is again at the door.

Arthur Sir . . .

Ross Yes?

Arthur There's a reporter. He says the police are just about to arrive. They are coming upstairs to take you. He says they are on their way.

Wilde Thank you, Arthur. Will you light the lamps for us?

Arthur goes round and lights the lamps in the room. Wilde has sat up on the sofa and now he gets up. Ross does not move.

I am well ready. Robbie?

Ross Yes.

Wilde You are at my side.

Arthur goes on lighting lamps.

Arthur, when the police arrive, then please admit them.

Arthur Yes sir.

Wilde takes the book Ross gave him earlier.

Wilde Ready?

Ross Yes.

Arthur stands at the door waiting. Wilde sits down, and starts reading the book. It is an image of the solidest Victorian contentment. Wilde turns a page, calm.

Wilde Let them come in.

End of Act One.

Act Two: Deciding to Leave

SCENE ONE

Friday, 3 December 1897. The music is serene as Italian light floods into the Villa Guidice at Posillipo, near Naples. It is late afternoon. The sun is an astonishing wintry gold outside the double doors which lead onto the balcony. The style is seaside vernacular. You can see a white metal rail. There is a sense of sun, sea and the horizon. Inside, modernism. The walls are white. The sparse furniture of the rented house looks forward, in its coolness and pallor, to the twentieth century. The main door gives onto a small hallway, with stairs beyond. The room is uncluttered, with one small table on which there are a pot of coffee, some cups and some sugared buns.

Wilde is sitting in a chair reading. He is dressed like an English gentleman in very formal, dark clothes, which make no concessions to the Mediterranean. His body has grown slack and fat and his face is ravaged by deprivation and alcohol. There is a tension in his movements which is new. Behind him on a pale sofa two men are sleeping under a sheet. They have plainly been there some time. There are clothes on the floor. One of them stirs, and we see that it is Bosie. He is now past his mid-twenties and still good-looking, but no longer radiant with youth. Bosie sits up, taking a moment to wake, but Wilde just carries on reading.

Bosie We never made it upstairs.

Wilde It does not bother me at what level you do it. Please perform at any elevation you choose. To me it's a matter of consummate indifference.

Bosie has sat up. The Young Man stirs beside him.
A mop of thick, curly dark hair, and a body plainly
young and fit.

Your friend looks like the young fisherman.

Bosie He is. That's who he is. That's what he does.

Wilde Can you ask him: is there any chance of a red
mullet?

Wilde lights a cigarette.

It would be nice for the whole household to profit from
the encounter.

Bosie He doesn't fish red mullet.

Wilde Ah. Choosy, is he? A herring, then?

The Young Man has woken, and gets out of bed.
Naked but not fazed, he sees Wilde.

Good afternoon. I am the great Irish poet and dramatist,
Oscar Wilde.

Young Man *Mi scusi. Sono venuto a casa sua senza*
invito.

Wilde *Non fa niente. Lei e il benvenuto a casa mia.*

They have shaken hands. The Young Man goes
unselfconsciously out onto the balcony to stretch.

Ah, all the modesty of an Italian, I see. A generative organ
like a rope that has been dipped in pitch, and, to judge
from the look on your face, also the deep, instinctive
understanding of the needs of English aristocracy necessary
to go with it.

Bosie How you love that word.

Wilde Which word?

Bosie Aristocracy.

Bosie has wrapped the sheet round himself and gone over to the little table.

What time is it?

Wilde Five o'clock. Yes. In the afternoon.

He throws Bosie a quick glance.

It's been another achingly beautiful day. Light dancing on the surface of the sea. A watery sun, and only the slightest cool in the evening to tell you that winter is here. The Bay of Naples jewelled like the scrawny neck of some ageing dowager.

The Young Man has come back into the room and is helping himself to a sugared bun.

All the native dignity of his race, and then that fabulous cock as well . . .

Bosie gets up and goes out.

Bosie The coffee's cold.

Wilde Yes, well, it was hot at ten o'clock this morning.

Wilde calls to him in the kitchen.

What's his name?

Bosie (*off*) Galileo.

Wilde Ah. See stars, did you?

Bosie returns at once and sits, still in a dream. Galileo has gone to sit naked on the floor, with legs crossed, his back against the end of the sofa, looking out of the window. He eats his bun happily.

Oh it's wonderful, it's like a child, isn't it? Who said one can never go back? If only I could go back to that!

If I ever was like that! Like an animal, like a cat. Truly, one should throw him a ball of string. Look at the little fellow.

Bosie You know nothing.

Wilde Sometimes one is hard put to believe in the idea of human progress. Just three hundred years ago the name Galileo was attached to an intelligence that powered the Renaissance and took mankind to an understanding of his own condition to which he had never previously dared to aspire. The heavens opened for Galileo. Today show us a Galileo and we see a kitten on the floor.

Galileo has turned at the repeated mention of his name.

Yes, Galileo, we are talking about you.

Galileo *Che state dicendo?*

Wilde *Sei fortunato di poter' vivere vicino al mare, e poter' camminare ogni giorno sulla spiaggia.*

Galileo *Ah si, si.*

Bosie is eating a bun at the table.

Bosie He's a wonderful man. I met his mother last night. And all his sisters. They live right by the beach. I went drinking with his fellow fishermen.

Wilde Will you meet all of them?

Bosie Eventually.

Wilde I can't wait.

Bosie is undisturbed by Wilde's gentle mockery. It is happy between them.

We can expect a succession of sofa-bound Renaissance geniuses, can we? All waking here tousle-haired and humanist in the afternoons.

Bosie Perhaps.

Wilde One day we play host to a Leonardo, next day a Michelangelo. Will there be a whole gallery of them? A sort of horizontal Uffizi? At the weekend perhaps we are at home to both Piero della Francesca *and* Gugliemo della Porto, maybe – who knows? – even both at once, but all distinguished from their eminent namesakes by the fact they have their bums in the air, and they're offered a sugar bun for their favours.

Bosie Why so superior? You like them as much as I do.

Wilde I do. All I cared for was beauty. I can still see it. From across a gulf. But I see it.

He good-naturedly stubs out his cigarette.

You and I have no friends. Let us have lovers instead.

Galileo *Che cosa dici?*

Wilde Throw him another bun.

Bosie chucks him another.

C'e troppo zucchero?

Galileo *No, o zuccher, me piac assai.*

Bosie What is he saying?

Wilde Why? Does it bother you?

Bosie No.

Wilde You seem to speak to him in his language, one way or another, even if that language in your case is not specifically Italian. My love.

They look at each other a moment.

Bosie What have you been doing?

318

Wilde Reading. My publisher has been kind enough to send me a list of proposed names for the foundation of a British Academy of Letters.

Bosie How ridiculous!

Wilde He keeps me in touch.

He lifts a letter from beside him.

He has enclosed what they call their proposed list of immortals. It is amusing stuff. Personally I cannot make my mind up between the claims of the Duke of Argyll and Jerome K. Jerome. I think probably the former. The unread is always better than the unreadable.

Bosie Are they canvassing your vote?

Wilde Hardly, my dear.

Bosie glances at Wilde, who is lighting another cigarette.

Bosie And writing? Have you done some writing?

Wilde Of course. My play.

Bosie How is your play?

Wilde My play is first class.

He holds up another envelope.

There is a letter for you.

Bosie From whom?

Wilde I'd say from your mother.

Bosie I will look at it later. Thank you.

Wilde puts it down.

Wilde Now as for tonight . . .

Bosie Oh please, not Duse again. We have seen every performance she has given.

Wilde We cannot playgo because we have no money.

Bosie None?

Wilde We have not a penny for tickets. I have been twice to the Post Office while you were practising astronomy . . .

Bosie And?

Wilde Nothing. Nothing has arrived.

Bosie (*frowns*) I thought you were expecting payment for your poem.

Wilde Indeed I am. I am pursuing it. I have written many times. My kneepads are scuffed and scoured by the time I have spent in the supplicant's position. I eat the dirt off the floor. When I visit the Post Office there is a collective Italian groan . . .

He raises his hands above his head.

'There goes Signor Wilde, *lo scrittore irlandese*, who has no money. No money! No money!'

Bosie looks seriously worried at this.

Bosie What do we have? What is left to us?

Wilde A few bottles of brandy. Some coffee. The last servant I have sent away. Beyond that, nothing. Unless there is a chance of your getting a ride on his boat tonight. Perhaps if you went fishing we would at least eat tomorrow. If you became a fisherman.

Bosie No one in my family has ever taken up the professions.

Wilde We can't live on cock.

Bosie nods at the letter again.

Bosie The letter from mother. How thick is it?

Wilde There's no cheque in it. I have held it up to the light.

Bosie Well then.

Galileo has finished his second bun.

Galileo *Che facite po riest d'o giorno?*

Wilde *Non abiamo deciso. Vogliamo andare a teatro.*

Galileo *Teatro? Io, al teatro non ci posso andare. Ho tanto da fare, sono occupatissimo. Al teatro? Io? Come posso andare al teatro?*

Bosie looks to Wilde for a translation.

Wilde He is asking if I will go for a walk so that he can bugger you again.

Bosie And what is your answer?

There is a silence. For the first time the air is cool between them.

Wilde No.

Bosie looks at him. Then goes out to the kitchen. Wilde stubs out his cigarette.

Beauty? Yes. Beauty above everything, and in all things. So much I was right about, you see. Before the catastrophe, before the great disaster, one writes but one does not know. Until one has suffered, until the great suffering, it is all guesswork. One guesses merely. Imagination: a highfalutin word for guesswork.

He smiles. Galileo is content, half listening, not understanding a word.

And by and large, my guesses were right. There is no morality in what is called morality; there is no sense in what is called sense; and least of all is there meaning in what is held to be meaning. I saw this. Before I even suffered. And, suffering, found it to be true. The foolishness of people who say mere beauty. Like mere wit. Or mere being alive.

Wilde nods towards the kitchen.

The man next door, making the coffee, being, as both of us know, exquisitely beautiful and seeming therefore to hold some secret which must be prised from him. But which cannot, I fear, dear friend, be prised in a single night.

He pauses.

Nor even in a single life.

Bosie returns with a full pot of coffee.

Bosie Hot coffee.

Wilde Enjoy it. We are not yet boiling acorns, but in a few days . . .

Bosie You don't seem very worried.

Wilde What do you mean?

Bosie By not having any money.

Wilde Ah. I came at your invitation. If you remember, it was your idea. You promised to look after me. You had money, you said.

Bosie So? Who found the house?

Wilde You did.

Bosie Who paid? At least, who intended to pay? It is not my fault.

Wilde No. The roulette wheel disobliged again.

Bosie Well? We *could* have been rich.

Wilde Ah yes.

Bosie I could have doubled my money!

Wilde If only your success at gambling could equal your grasp of gambling's governing principles.

Bosie has gone back to pour himself hot, thick coffee.

'It can double my money!' Very good! You have understood the potential of the activity perfectly. You understand its lure. You know what it promises. And yet for some reason –

Bosie Very funny . . .

Wilde – you seem not to able to make that little leap –

Bosie All right . . .

Wilde – that some people make: the leap to where it delivers what it promises. Why is that? What is that in you? The promise, but not the fulfilment of the promise.

Bosie looks at him defensively.

Bosie What are you saying?

Wilde I am saying you promised to look after me, Bosie. Yet the tradesmen's bills arrive with my name on the envelope. In restaurants, in bars, waiters turn to me. My pocket's empty, not yours.

Bosie If I had money, I would give it to you. You know that. I have given you everything. Do you doubt my good faith?

Wilde No. Never.

After a moment, Bosie is quiet, serious.

Bosie Everyone left you, remember?

Wilde I do.

Bosie The virtuous Constance –

Wilde Ah yes . . .

Bosie – of whom we all heard so much. The embodiment of virtue, so-called. Faithful, long-suffering Constance . . . where was she? Robbie Ross, the good friend, little Robbie. The trusted adviser, who loved you, who would lay down his life for you . . . where was he? Abroad. All your so-called friends, so-called allies . . . Abroad! Scattered across Europe! Remember?

Wilde smiles slightly.

Wilde You left also.

Bosie Yes. But I was the last to go. Bear that in mind. I was the last.

Wilde I know.

Galileo looks up, catching the seriousness.

Galileo *Ma che sta dicendo?*

Wilde *E arrabiato.*

Bosie is at the table, cradling the hot cup in his hands.

Bosie And yet only *I* am mocked. Everywhere! Your worthless friend! 'Shiftless Bosie.' 'Shallow Bosie.' Oh yes, it is always I who am traduced. But it is I who stayed, who stayed by you until the day of your trial.

He looks at Wilde.

Yes. At least you were tried.

Wilde I was.

Bosie You were fortunate. I have been condemned, and yet I have not even been tried.

Wilde No.

Wilde is quiet, letting Bosie's mood pass.

Bosie I am much misrepresented.

Wilde I know that.

Bosie Even now, in the papers, all across Europe . . . how can I be what they say I am?

Wilde You are not.

Bosie They disregard my poetry. They disregard my status.

Wilde Indeed.

Bosie Your poetical equal, you said. You have said it in print. Your *equal*.

Wilde Just so.

Bosie waits, wanting more.

It is true. I have said it. You are one of the greatest poets in England.

Bosie One of? *One* of?

Wilde Well let us allow that Swinburne is living. Let us allow that Swinburne is alive.

Bosie *Swinburne?*

Wilde I know. But there is a school of thought, plainly backward, plainly misguided, which hands him the palm.

Bosie But you are not of it?

Wilde No. I am of your party.

Bosie Good. And so you should be. I am already the greatest non-narrative poet in England.

Wilde Undoubtedly. Your lyrics are lovely.

Bosie is satisfied and goes on.

Bosie And let it be said, let it be made clear: I am as much the victim of this affair as you. Yes! Quite as much.

Wilde (*quietly*) In your own way.

Bosie Yes – oh yes – everywhere it is said: 'The incomparable tragedy of Oscar Wilde!' How easily said! And how lazily! Because, remember, two have suffered here . . .

Wilde Plainly.

Bosie And in many ways – I am not ashamed to say this – my suffering has been the greater. Oh yes, I know how that sounds, for I have not suffered physically . . .

Wilde No.

Bosie I know that. I would not say that.

Wilde Quite.

Bosie I have not known the deprivations of confinement . . .

Wilde You have not.

Bosie The squalor of the filthy prison cell. Not at all. But you, Oscar, have not known the horror of not being heard, of being disregarded, of being overlooked. The contempt of my peers! My God, is that not equal suffering? There are two people here!

Wilde I know that.

Bosie Two people who suffer and endure! Two human beings!

Bosie's anger is rising dangerously.

But that is not said in the papers.

Wilde No.

Bosie They speak only of the one who stood in the dock. God, how I long to set this whole affair right! God, I long to speak!

Wilde You must not speak.

Bosie Why not?

Wilde When you have spoken it has been a mistake. When you have published . . .

He pauses, uneasy at the memory.

When you have tried to publish certain private things between us . . . references to us, to our friendship, it has not advanced our cause.

Bosie Not advanced it?

Wilde No.

Bosie How is our cause advanced by our forbearance? How is it helped? Is it helpful, do you think, never to say anything . . . never to speak of our lives?

Wilde shrugs slightly in reply.

How will things be changed . . . how will England be changed unless we speak?

Wilde Changing England is low on my list of current priorities.

Bosie What, are we to spend our whole lives shrouded in secrecy, covering our offence in shame?

Wilde So it appears.

Bosie Never daring to speak, never daring to say: 'Yes, we are two men who believe in the highest form of love – the purest, the most poetical, such as that which exists between us'? Love between men? Can we not speak of that?

Wilde Certainly not. Under no circumstances.

Bosie Why are you so sure?

Wilde Trust me. Truly. I understand this better than you. Trust me.

Galileo *Non capisco niente. Di che parlate?*

Wilde Nothing. *Niente.*

Galileo frowns, confused.

No. We have come to Naples to suffer and be silent. Ours is an ethic of silence. Preferably on a substantial private income. Which is, I admit, at this moment, proving the elusive part of the plan.

Bosie Indeed.

Wilde However.

Bosie looks at him moodily.

Bosie You have no courage.

Wilde And you have no strategy. That is why we are perfectly suited. Let this conversation be over.

Bosie You always divert. You always turn away.

Wilde Why not?

Wilde has seen Bosie's bad mood off and now gestures towards the window. The light has begun to change.

The day has started to fade and turn dusky. The sun has begun its nightly cabaret . . .

Galileo *Vado a vestirmi. Nun pozz sta ca' senza fa nient.*

Wilde *Sei benvenuto a utilizzare il bagno.*

Galileo is gathering his clothes.

Let us attend to it. If we can no longer afford the great Duse, we must let nature provide the entertainment.

Bosie reaches out a hand to Galileo which he squeezes before he goes out.

Last evening, the sun passed briefly through ochre, then, in a rare display of good taste, disdained primrose, and settled instead on a colour – oh Lord, I searched fifteen minutes on the balcony until I found the word. The sun was not like topaz. No. Nor was it the colour of saffron. I can only say to you with all the fleeting authority which my literary powers may still command that the sun was like orpiment. Have you heard that word?

Bosie Never.

Wilde is smiling, satisfied. And Bosie is watching fondly, drinking his coffee again.

Wilde So tonight, come, let us not spend the evening indoors in what my fellow Irishmen call begrudgery. Let us go out, let us walk among the youths again and enjoy the gorgeous vulgarity of the night. Yes?

Bosie As you wish.

Wilde It is nearing the hour when I cried every night in prison. I wept every night for a year. For the whole of my first year. At six o'clock.

Bosie watches him, serious now.

This is the hour Christ died.

Bosie I thought Christ died at three.

Wilde Christ died at six. He died at cocktail hour.

Suddenly there is the sound of a bell ringing at the door outside.

Bosie Ah, cocktails!

Wilde Oh Lord, are we expecting visitors?

Bosie No.

Wilde Surely not more fisherfolk? Are they coming to mend their nets in our living room? Will they gut sprats all over our floor?

He shudders in mock-horror. Bosie has moved to collect up all his clothes.

Bosie We're not strong on visitors. Unless it's that woman who comes to deal with the rats.

Wilde More urgently, we have no servants. The social crisis is profound. No, no, no, a lord cannot answer the door. Will our friend answer for us, do you think? Can we ask him? Does he serve by land as well as by sea?

Bosie He serves.

The bell rings again. Bosie has gathered his things up. Wilde calls out.

Wilde *Galileo, per favore, puoi vedere chi c'e alla porta?*

Galileo *(off)* *Certo.*

Bosie smiles as he goes out of the room, passing Galileo on the stairs.

Bosie I suppose there is no question of *your* answering the door.

Wilde As you know, I have always disdained unnecessary motion.

Galileo opens the door, and the visitor takes a step inside. It is Ross. He is paler and thinner than ever, in a light suit and hat. Wilde is taken aback.

(*Quietly.*) It's little Robbie.

Neither man moves. Bosie calls from upstairs.

Bosie *(off)* Who is it?

Wilde *(calls)* Robbie.

There is a second, then Bosie appears on the stairs. He has pulled on trousers and shirt. He is too angry to speak. After a few moments he goes back upstairs.

We did not know you were coming to Naples.

Ross Nor did I.

He looks upstairs, disturbed by Bosie's silent disappearance.

Oscar . . .

Wilde I am temporarily taken aback. We thought you were the witch.

Ross I'm sorry?

Wilde A witch comes to smoke out the rats. We are not much visited.

Ross I see.

Wilde This is a friend of Bosie's. His name is Galileo.

Galileo goes upstairs, saying nothing.

You did not favour us with a telegram.

Ross No. I was not sure you would see me.

Wilde Come, I will always see you.

He gives Ross an icy smile. The light is becoming paler outside.

We have not eaten for days, except stale sugar buns. But we have three bottles of brandy at least, and they are yours to enjoy.

Ross Thank you. Yes. I would like a glass.

Wilde Help yourself.

Ross moves nervously towards the brandy bottle on the side-table.

Bosie was remarking on my reluctance to move. He's right. My whole celebrity, you might say, is now based on that reluctance. I mean not fleeing when you begged me to. Sitting still. Staying still.

Wilde lights another cigarette and settles deeper into the chair.

Ross You look well.

Wilde Do not mock me. My appearance is that of a senior pederastic Anglican bishop who has been locked all night in a distillery. Flatter me by all means, I adore it, but not for my appearance.

Ross busies himself at the table.

Do you bring us news of the arts? Does anyone still paint?

Ross Not in the way you would wish.

Wilde I am sure. The dissemination of photography which ought to release the artist from the drudgery of representation instead panics him into a dreary kind of rivalry.

Ross hands him a glass of brandy in a glass like a toothmug.

Thank you. We are living in dismal times.

Ross Hard times to make a living.

Wilde Please!

Ross For I am scarcely solvent myself.

Wilde You will prosper, Robbie. I predict. You have chosen exactly the right trade for the turn of the century. Art dealing holds snobbery, ignorance and greed in a near-miraculous equilibrium. Capitalism is the coming thing. I have seen enough to know.

Ross You mean, since your punishment?

Wilde Prison was not my punishment. This is my punishment. To your health.

Ross To yours.

They drink.

Wilde Where have you come from?

Ross From seeing Constance. From Nervi.

Wilde Ah yes. Now I understand.

Wilde looks at him, now knowing why he is here. The atmosphere toughens.

You see how we are. You see how we are living.

Ross Yes.

Wilde Simply. The loan of a little money would help me. Duse hopes to stage my play *Salome* but she needs investors.

Ross Again? You asked me before.

Wilde I did?

Ross Some months ago.

Wilde Plainly, my imagination is failing.

He smiles, trying to recover.

A loan is wasted either way, yet for some reason it reassures the giver to believe it is to be used what they call 'constructively'. Nobody lends five pounds for drugs, whereas everyone lends five pounds for an expedition to take young boys up the Zambezi.

Ross Not to you, Oscar. Not to you.

Wilde No. Nor to you, Robbie, when you were less of a prig.

Ross looks down at this overt hostility.

Never mind, I scramble on somehow, and hope to survive the winter. After that, Tunis, rags and hashish!

Ross It is not my fault. Truly.

But Wilde is not impressed by Ross's demeanour and remains aggressive.

Wilde Does it please you, this running between us?

Ross No.

Wilde Why do you do it, then?

Ross, pained, does not answer.

The behaviour of all my friends has begun to mystify me.

Ross When you came out of prison, everyone wanted to welcome you. They wanted to see you. We greeted you. We waited with flowers. We found you a house in France to live in!

Wilde So you are saying your friendship came with conditions?

Ross All friendship comes with conditions.

Wilde is dark, dismissive.

Wilde No. Myself, I gave friendship freely. To anyone. When I had it, I gave money away in the streets.

Ross Oscar, I have tried to help you. I have tried at all times only to help you.

Wilde nods as if this confirmed his suspicions.

Wilde I have had indications. I have had letters. I have had threats. My trips to the Post Office reward me not with cheques but with cheap mottoes. My whole correspondence should be sponsored by the Salvation Army. It is relentlessly elevating.

Ross I have spoken to Constance.

Wilde Yes. Well, I imagined. How is she?

Ross Not well.

Wilde I heard.

Ross Her back is worse.

Wilde I am sorry.

Ross Her spine will not mend. She is confined the whole day and the prognosis is that things will not improve.

Wilde takes this in for a moment.

Wilde And the children?

Ross Yes, she says the children are well.

Wilde Good.

Ross A little bewildered. Cyril is still in Heidelberg, Vyvyan in Monaco. They've learnt to play chess.

Wilde They ask after me?

Ross Often.

Wilde It is the hope of one day seeing them which sustains me. That is what sustains me. It is for that I live.

Wilde looks at him suspiciously.

Ross Constance says she has written.

Wilde She has. Often.

Ross She says you do not answer.

Wilde I have not answered, no.

Ross Why not?

Wilde I have nothing to say!

Ross You do not answer her letters!

Wilde What am I to say? That Duse is fine, but not as fine as Bernhardt? Art chat? Art gossip? The vagaries of the weather in Naples . . .?

Ross She said she feared the worst when she heard you were in Naples. She said nobody goes to Naples at this time of year.

This remark inflames Wilde.

Wilde Plainly, Robbie, you have come to enrage me. You have come to unsettle me.

Ross No.

Wilde You have come to take her part.

Ross Why should I?

Wilde It is not enough to trap me – no, nor to try me – no, nor to send me to prison, to take away my reputation, my position, to take away my London, the London at whose very centre I once stood? This is now not enough. The world, having broken me, now must also come into my house? It will pursue me? It will not let up?

He stares at Ross fiercely, but Ross gives no ground.

Ross The means of it letting up are in your own hands.

Wilde In your view.

Ross No. In Constance's view.

Wilde And these views are not coincident? They are not the same?

Wilde has raised his voice, pressing Ross, but Ross is already shaking his head.

Ross Oscar, you know what you must do. You know what is asked of you.

Wilde Oh yes!

Ross I do not need to speak it. You know already.

Ross moves across the room, containing his anger, and pours a second brandy.

Wilde What is this sense that I have let you all down in some way?

Ross I have not said that.

Wilde I would like to understand this. Explain to me. No, truly. You feel that somehow I have *failed* you? Is my offence that I am free? What would you wish? You would prefer me back in prison?

He laughs at the absurdity of it.

I am not just to live, but I must also live in a way of which you approve?

Ross Not I. Constance. I speak *to* Constance. I do not speak *for* her.

Wilde No? You mean you do not sit with her in Nervi, consoling her? You do not sit together in darkened rooms, under rococo cornices, drinking mean glasses of sweet wine, your heads bowed together, adopting the same low, regretful tone? Speaking together of 'Oscar, poor foolish Oscar . . .'

Ross You made her promises. In prison you made her certain promises.

Wilde Well?

Ross These promises you have not fulfilled!

Wilde shakes his head, disbelieving.

Wilde What is this? Am I to be tried again? In my own living room? Is the universe now become a court of law? Were my three trials not enough? Were proceedings only temporarily suspended during my imprisonment? Are we now to put up the dark wood panelling and pull on our wigs again? What are we saying? Did rain stop play? Are we now to resume?

Ross Oscar, you made an agreement. You signed it.

Wilde So?

Ross She has the right to enforce it.

Wilde The right. What right? The same right she has to rebuke me?

He stubs out his cigarette, furious.

She writes. She charges me that I have not written to her. She sends me pictures of the children. I look at them. I cry. All evening I weep. What am I to say? How am I to write? She writes again. 'You have said nothing about the photographs. What a brute you are! It is clear you do not love your children.' She wants me to answer. How can I? It is too cruel. I, who have spent my life holding language up to the light. Making words shimmer in the light. How am I to say to her, 'I love my children so much I cannot write'?

338

He is overwhelmed, on the verge of tears.

It is all a bribe. It is all bribery. 'Behave as I would wish and one day you will see your children . . .' I sat with them, I played with them in the nursery. For years – yes, regardless – before the theatre, after the theatre – hurrying home to see my children – yes, even though I left to travel down the darkest East End street, to smear my mouth against men whose names I never knew, men whom I never saw, pressed against walls, in the dark, in the rough dark – yet every night I came home and told my children stories of ghosts, of fairies, of monsters and of enchanted lands . . . These are my children, Robbie. The nursery was my home, not the bedroom.

He lifts one hand, helpless.

And now she holds my boys like pieces in a game. She will move them forward or she will hold them back. It is not right. I have never seen them from the day I was sent to prison. What are we? Animals? Lower than animals. The animal holds its cub close, lets its cub come near . . . No, I cannot speak of it.

Wilde is too distraught to go on.

Ross Oscar, it is a war. You know that. She must use what she has. You must lay aside your feelings against her. They lead nowhere. They lead to your exclusion. They will lead to your extinction.

There is silence. The light has changed again, losing colour and warmth, chilly and very clear outside. It is dusk.

I am here today to tell you she will divorce you if you do not leave Bosie.

Wilde Leave him?

There is a pause.

Leave him? And go where?

Ross You promised not to take up with him. You signed
a contract.

Wilde No.

Ross You did!

Wilde I have re-read the contract.

Ross Well, it is clear.

Wilde The contract which I signed while I was in prison
specifies that I was not, on my release, to take up with
a disreputable person.

Ross So? Well?

Wilde So. Lord Alfred Douglas is not a disreputable
person.

Ross Oh please!

Wilde He is not. Not legally. Not by legal definition.
Because his reputation has not been tried. It has not been
tried in a court of law.

Ross Are you serious? Are you seriously proposing this?

Wilde I am legally disreputable. But he is not. Oh yes,
Bosie may not be liked. I have sensed sometimes that
some of my friends do not like him. You yourself, Robbie,
do not '*like*' him, am I right? I admit that I myself have
used him to good effect in society. He serves as a repellant.
He drives all kinds of unwelcome people away. It may
be – I admit this also – that he is known throughout
Europe as a gilded pillar of infamy. By rumour alone,
he is a universal by-word for sin and depravity. However.
I have learnt something in my time in the courts. The
fact is this: until he is tried he is not disreputable.

Ross You think this will help you? You think this argument will weigh?

Wilde Well, I am hoping it may.

Wilde smiles, skittish, but Ross is angry.

Ross Oscar, you know who he is. You know why people are angry.

Wilde No, tell me. Why are 'people' angry?

Ross Because you have returned to the very man who precipitated your downfall!

Wilde Of course. How could I do otherwise? He alone understands. He alone has suffered a comparable disaster to my own.

Ross In prison, you promised . . .

Wilde Oh . . .

Ross When you realised what he had done to you, you promised. But now, now you have resumed with this creature . . .

Wilde Be quieter. He is above. He is in the room above.

Ross No. I have always wanted to know. Since the day you met him, I have wanted to ask: what does this man have?

Wilde Robbie . . .

Ross What quality does he have? What is it that compels you?

Wilde I have no duty to explain. Even for that. Even for that reason I have returned to him. For the very reason that it is my right. I choose to exercise that right. What is the use of a right you cannot exercise?

341

Ross And what is the purpose of a love which gives you nothing in return?

Wilde You know nothing of what passes between us.

Wilde is suddenly emphatic.

For this very reason: that no human being on earth may ask of another: what do you see in him?

Then he relents, quieter.

He adored me. In the first days, in the early days, he adored me.

Ross I adored you.

Wilde It was not the same.

There is a pause.

I have the right. It is my right. If I choose to do it, I do.

Ross Even after he has destroyed you!

Wilde just looks at him, not answering.

Constance wrote to you. She asked you to visit her.

Wilde I could not visit her.

Ross Why not?

Wilde I was just out of prison. Be fair, Robbie. It was difficult. I was confused. I was not myself.

Ross Bosie asks, and you are back –

Wilde All right . . .

Ross – what? Within one week? Within ten days . . .?

Wilde All right!

Ross Constance asks and you ignore her.

Wilde He offered me a place. Here we are. We would work together. We would write. It is a future.

Ross Do you wonder she is angry? The one thing she asks you not to do!

Wilde She? Not just she! The whole world!

Wilde laughs, bitterly.

You are all spited. You are all rebuked. Every one of you. The world put me in prison in order to prove they could destroy my relationship with Lord Alfred Douglas.

Ross The world?

Wilde Yes. Now you discover you cannot. So the world seeks its revenge.

He nods, sure of himself.

I am shunned by you all, and my work goes unperformed, not because of the sin – never because of the sin – but because I refuse to accept the lesson *of* the sin. To alter my life now would be to admit I was wrong. A patriot put in prison for loving his country goes on loving his country. A poet in prison for loving boys loves boys.

Wilde looks at Ross unforgivingly.

I have taken my punishment. Was that not enough? Was that not what was asked of me? Have I not suffered? Have I not endured? But no, the rules are now to be changed. I have done my term, but now new obligations are to be imposed. No longer is punishment enough. The moral *of* my punishment must be stuffed down my throat. I must choke on it.

He is so savage that Ross is stopped, hesitant to ask the next question.

Ross Do you really see no difference . . . Oscar, do you see no difference between those who put you in prison and those who now seek to help you?

Wilde Oh yes. There is a difference. Once I was punished from simple malice. Now I am punished in the interests of moral example.

Ross That is not fair.

Wilde Is it not? How do you see it then?

Ross is deeply shaken by Wilde's answer.

Please. Tell me. What, in fact, is my allowance? What am I paid? What does she pay me?

Ross Well . . .

Wilde Three pounds a week? Less. One hundred and fifty pounds a year.

Ross Yes.

Wilde By a signed agreement. Signed by both parties.

Ross Exactly.

Wilde Negotiated by you. My only source of income. By divorcing me she discontinues that allowance. I am left with nothing.

Ross looks down.

Ross Yes.

Wilde The scheme now is that I shall have no food at all. It is proposed to leave me to die of starvation or to blow my brains out in a Naples urinal! And what's more, the scheme is put forward on moral grounds! What perfection of hypocrisy!

He turns away, definitive now.

344

Please, kill me because you hate me. But do not kill me because you wish to change me.

Ross Constance does not seek to kill you. You are doing it yourself.

Wilde waves a hand at him. Then, shaking, lights another cigarette.

Wilde Well, so be it. The public loves poets to die in this way. It seems to them poetically right.

Ross That may be the effect. Oscar, that is not the intention. Myself, I owe Constance nothing. She is not my friend. You are my friend. I have sought nothing but to go between you. Only to be the go-between.

Wilde Then get me some brandy.

The remark is brutal. The room is darkening. Wilde has not moved from his chair. Ross goes to pour from the bottle into Wilde's glass.

I have never come across anyone in whom the moral sense was dominant who was not heartless, cruel, vindictive, log-stupid and entirely lacking in the smallest sense of humanity. Moral people are simple beasts.

He looks at the measure Ross is pouring.

Leave the bottle.

Upstairs Galileo is heard, calling in Italian to Bosie. Ross looks up as he pours himself another drink.

Ross It is your business. It is your decision.

Wilde Yes. As you say.

Ross He is a repellant. Use him by all means. But repellants are indiscriminate. They also drive away those whom you will need as your friends.

Bosie appears, dressed like an Englishman in pale trousers and jacket, Galileo behind him. They are both laughing, the picture of careless youth. Bosie has clearly resolved to be easygoing to Ross.

Bosie Ah, Robbie, greetings.

Ross Thank you.

Bosie You have made a long journey.

Ross Yes.

Bosie We have not seen you here before.

Ross No.

Bosie My friend Galileo is taking me out dancing. Do you wish to accompany us?

Ross I cannot. I am leaving tonight. By the night train.

Bosie Already?

Bosie smiles affectionately at Wilde.

Oscar?

Wilde Forgive me. My dancing days are over.

Wilde reaches out to the table and holds up the letter between his fingers.

Your mother's letter.

Bosie Thank you.

Bosie goes across the room to take it, perfectly at ease.

Well, it was good to see you,. Robbie. However briefly. Don't wait up. I'll be late.

Wilde You have your key?

Bosie I do. Goodbye, everyone. Enjoy yourselves.

Wilde Oh yes.

Galileo *Arrivederci. E stato un piacere. Alla prossima.*

Wilde Dance for me, Bosie. Dance one for me.

Bosie laughs and goes out with Galileo. Wilde reaches out and takes Ross's hand.

And will you not stay with me Robbie? Will you not stay here tonight?

Ross I cannot.

Wilde No?

Ross Truly, I cannot. I must return to England.

Wilde Ah.

It is darkening now outside the window.

In prison, I tell you, after several months – I was ill, my stomach wrecked, attended by dysentery, working on a treadmill, then thrown in my cell, gasping for breath, for air . . . the governor of the prison visited. He said, 'Wilde, you must learn patience . . .' I replied, 'Patience I would happily learn but what you are teaching me is apathy . . .'

Suddenly his eyes are filled with tears at the hopelessness of his situation. Ross, kneeling before him, is also overwhelmed.

I have enjoyed our talk. I see no one. I shall miss you, Robbie. I shall miss the chance to talk.

Ross I am sorry. It hurts me to say . . . I do not know how to say this. But I must dispatch a message to Constance . . .

347

Wilde looks away, letting go of Ross's hand, not
willing to dignify this with a reply. Ross knows the
answer and gets up.

So. Well, it is so. Good to see you, Oscar. I have very
little. I can leave you two pounds only. Even two pounds
is not easy. My mother bought my ticket. I myself am at
some considerable inconvenience. Yes, art is a thriving
racket as you say, but not when you are known to be
Oscar Wilde's oldest friend.

He has the money in his hand.

Ross So? Shall I leave it here?

Wilde Leave it.

Wilde waves a finger like a cardinal. Ross puts the
coins down on the table beside him. He wants to
move close, but Wilde speaks to stop him.

I shall one day see you again.

Ross knows this is final. He goes, closing the door
behind him. Wilde does not move. Music begins to
play, swelling and filling the room. The light fades to
near-dark. The lighthouse beam sweeps round again,
from outside the window, catching Wilde briefly in
the light.
  There is a passage of time. It is night. Wilde is still
sitting in the same chair. Most of the brandy has gone.
Only his burning cigarette indicates his presence. Then
light comes from a gas lamp held by Bosie as he
comes downstairs, still dressed. The music fades as
Bosie is surprised to see Wilde.

SCENE TWO

Bosie Oscar . . .

Wilde turns slightly.

You're here.

Wilde Yes.

Bosie Were you here all along? Have you been sleeping?

Wilde No.

Bosie You did not hear me come in? Why did you not say anything? You did not speak to me.

Wilde I was struck dumb by the fact that you came back alone.

Bosie Very funny.

Wilde Thank you.

Bosie puts down his lamp and picks Wilde's notebook up from the table.

Bosie Ah, I see. Have you been writing?

Wilde Yes. I have been writing my play.

Bosie In the dark?

Bosie holds the book a moment, but Wilde takes it and puts it back down.

You are extraordinary.

Wilde You think so?

Bosie You sit here. When did you last move?

Wilde Oh, quite recently. I have occupied this chair for only one single transit of the sun.

349

Bosie lights another lamp and the room begins to brighten.

Do you know, when I lived at Tite Street I once took a cab to a dinner party just three houses away?

Bosie Nothing surprises me.

Wilde It was my own individual protest against the mindless cult of athleticism.

Bosie smiles affectionately.

Buddhism, similarly, has always been a closed book to me. A whole religion devoted to the cause of breathing. To what purpose? We breathe anyway, will we, nill we. My own endeavour in breathing, as in all things, is to expend as little energy as possible.

Bosie Are you planning to move?

Wilde No.

Bosie Have you slept at all?

Wilde No.

It is the first time we have seen the two of them alone, and the tone is relaxed.

Ideally, I like to drink anise. My favourite anise is the second. I drink it not because it makes me sleep – nothing makes me sleep – but because at the moment I drink it I *believe* that I shall sleep. An illustration of the perfect usefulness of science. The potion necessary to make me sleep does not exist. But the potion that provides the illusion that I shall does.

Bosie Yes.

Wilde Indeed.

He stubs out his cigarette.

I drink the second anise. I am filled with the conviction:
'I shall sleep tonight.' Belief is everything. Faith is
everything.

He is thoughtful a moment.

It is the same with love.

Bosie With love?

Wilde Yes.

Bosie In what way?

Wilde The vulgar error is to think that love is a kind of
illusion.

Bosie Is it not?

Wilde No. It is the fault of bad poets who encourage
this mistake. 'I am completely enraptured,' lovers say, as
if somehow they were being deceived. When the affair
ends they say, 'I have been stripped of my illusions.'
When they cease to love they say, 'Oh. I see him clearly
now.'

Bosie Are they not right?

Wilde No, Bosie. The reverse is the truth.

The two men look at each other.

The everyday world is shrouded. We see it dimly. Only
when we love do we see the true person. The truth of
a person is only visible through love. Love is not the
illusion. Life is.

There is a silence. Bosie shifts.

Bosie You heard me come in?

Wilde Yes, of course. Hours ago.

Bosie I was early.

Wilde I heard you moving about.

Bosie I have been thinking.

Wilde I can tell.

Bosie After all, we have been here three months.

Wilde Yes.

Bosie We cannot just go on.

Wilde No.

Bosie I mean, without money.

Wilde Plainly. As you say. You are right. *The Ballad of Reading Gaol* is to be published next year.

Bosie What did Robbie say of it?

Wilde He did not mention it. My feeling is, he did not like it. Silence is always the most potent form of literary criticism.

Bosie watches Wilde, wary now.

Bosie How was Robbie?

Wilde Robbie? Oh. Himself.

Bosie Yes. Robbie is always himself.

Wilde He is always quiet. People who speak quietly are always held to be modest. Why? It seems to me the height of arrogance not to make the effort to make yourself heard. Always I lean towards him. My ears are bad, but not that bad . . .

Bosie Yes.

Wilde Lord deliver us from the conceit of quiet speakers.

Bosie Did he bring you good news?

Wilde Good news?

352

Bosie A long way to come . . .

Wilde Indeed.

Bosie Can you tell me what he said?

Wilde affects indifference.

Wilde He told me that Whistler is still at his daubs.

Bosie Oh . . .

Wilde The Café Royal is still full. Men sit taking care not to cross their legs. The wink is outlawed as an acceptable form of social intercourse. Gentlemen seeking advancement in society cover their arses with three layers of tailored material. Frankly, I should be carried shoulder-high by the cutters down Savile Row, for now a whole generation of respectable people must conceal their nether parts behind high-priced, redundant fabric. My arrest, thank God, has had some commercial benefits.

Bosie But not for you.

Wilde No. Surely.

Wilde knows he has not succeeded in sidetracking Bosie.

Bosie Oscar, I have come to a conclusion.

Wilde Ah.

Bosie I have come to believe that we are in some way at fault.

Wilde At fault?

Bosie Has that not occurred to you?

Wilde frowns, not wanting to speak.

Do you think that human beings just live? The lot they are handed, the ordeals they undergo . . . do you think these depend purely on the workings of chance?

Wilde I am sorry. I am not following you.

Bosie looks at him, preparing himself.

Bosie Oscar, it is not my wish to hurt you . . .

Wilde Surely . . .

Bosie But do you not feel that the way we are living here in Naples – the place we find ourselves in – do you not find in this some sort of judgement?

Wilde Judgement?

Bosie Yes.

Wilde is frowning, bewildered.

Come. Look. Look around you. The empty rooms, the appalling lack of servants, the rats – please! The absence of money, the hunger even, the futility! You! I! Our ceaseless disputes! The sometimes barren evenings – has it not occurred to you, have you not thought? The nights, the nights you sit alone in that chair, the loss of your friends, the collapse of your reputation . . .

Wilde Ah, that.

Bosie starts to backtrack.

Bosie No . . .

Wilde Go on. Please. Build your case.

Bosie Oscar . . .

Wilde It is beginning to sound positively monumental.

Bosie smiles, apparently conceding.

Bosie I sound too harsh, it is not my wish to be unkind to you . . .

Wilde Never.

Bosie But have you never thought that perhaps we live like this because this is what we deserve?

Wilde Deserve?

Bosie Yes.

Wilde Goodness. A big word, 'deserve'. I have never been sure I understand it. Please. Explain to me gently. Possibly I am obtuse.

Bosie Oscar . . .

Wilde There is some justice, is that your contention?

Bosie Perhaps.

Wilde There is *justice*, is there? At work here we find our old friend, *Fate*?

Bosie Well . . .

Wilde Fate is at work, is it? Doing its worst?

Bosie I fear so.

Wilde What you are suggesting is – let me be clear – you think that Fate is not blind? What is this, Bosie? A late conversion?

Bosie No. An early conversion.

Wilde Fate has dealt us this hand, but only because what? We have lived in the wrong way?

Bosie Not we, Oscar. You.

Wilde nods, understanding at last.

Wilde Ah, I see. Yes of course. Now I have your drift. The old cause . . .

Bosie Yes. The decision to lie.

Wilde Oh, of course.

355

Bosie And the decision to persist in the lie. From this all else stems!

Bosie has suddenly raised his voice. Wilde reacts, reaching for the brandy.

Wilde We have discussed this, Bosie. We do not need to discuss it again. I think I preferred it when you spent the night fishing.

Bosie I cannot forgive you! I cannot forgive you this . . .

Wilde No, you have said.

Bosie Lying in public! Isn't that your principal achievement? Isn't that the thing for which you will be chiefly known?

Wilde It may be.

Bosie You were given your theatre! You were given your chance! The Old Bailey! You could have defended Greek love!

Bosie is passionate, indignant.

How will history judge you? History will forget you . . .

Wilde No doubt.

Bosie You will be known for ever as the man who was ashamed to admit his own nature! When a better time comes, when this kind of love is accepted and understood, then you will be condemned because you took the coward's way.

Bosie suddenly shouts out again.

Did you ever consider the simple expedient of *telling the truth*?

Wilde In public?

Bosie Of course.

Wilde appears to think for a moment.

Wilde I think I can safely say never.

Bosie From this . . . from this central evasion, all else follows! With you, everything is compromise! Everything is dishonesty! I cannot live like this!

Wilde No, plainly. I know how important honesty is to you.

Bosie is calmer, wanting to get to his real point.

Bosie Oscar, I have wanted to say for some time: it is worse, truly – I know this is difficult to hear – but, from my point of view, our situation is far worse for me.

Wilde Ah yes.

He pauses a second.

How so?

Bosie I am young.

Wilde Ah.

Bosie My life lies ahead of me.

Wilde Of course.

Bosie You are old. Your best days lie behind you.

Wilde I suppose.

Wilde looks mildly surprised.

I mean, if you want to put it that way.

Bosie To be destroyed when you are in your forties, yes it is sad, yes it is tragic, of course. I do not deny it.

Wilde No . . .

Bosie I have never denied it. But for me! The prospect of being destroyed when my life is still before me!

Wilde Yes, I see.

He flicks some ash, but Bosie is not listening.

Plainly it's inconvenient.

Bosie I cannot allow it!

Bosie pauses, reaching the real subject.

Also. Remember: we have not spoken much of this lately, but since I first met you, I have always told you, I have always made clear: it is not in my nature finally to be with men, to love men only . . .

Wilde No.

Bosie I am not disposed, as you are, to love my own sex . . .

Wilde is impassive, not responding.

For me, as you know, it has been only a phase . . .

Wilde Of course . . .

Bosie Since adolescence it is only a phase I have been passing through.

Wilde That's right. Though occasionally with an appetite which the imperceptive might mistake for positive relish.

Bosie nods as if this is just the kind of remark he had been expecting.

Bosie Oh yes, very good . . .

Wilde I'm sorry . . .

Bosie You may make your jokes . . .

Wilde Thank you.

Bosie You have always made cheap jokes.

Wilde No. Not always. Once people paid for them. And paid handsomely.

Bosie I am not an invert!

Wilde No.

Wilde pauses, then speaks quietly, but Bosie does not hear him.

Just a brilliant mimic.

Bosie Oh yes, certainly, as you say, I have indulged myself . . .

Wilde Yes. Once or twice . . .

Bosie I have had particular experiences. I have slept with men . . .

Wilde Now steady on, Bosie, don't get carried away . . .

Bosie I admit I have let events overtake me . . .

Wilde Indeed. That night in Capri.

Bosie Please! You have joked enough!

Bosie is momentarily threatening.

I have indulged myself, yes, but always, *always* knowing that I could stop at any time.

Wilde That is fortunate.

Bosie At any time!

Bosie is relieved to have established his point.

God knows, since I came down from Oxford, I have seen enough of your friends, I have known enough old queens . . .

Wilde Indeed.

Bosie My God! The horror of it. Ending up like that. No thank you! To find myself at forty or fifty, painted, rouged, sitting in bars . . . no, not for me, that life. This

is not the destiny of my family. That is not my future.
I have always known that I would move on.

Wilde And will you? Is that what you are saying? Will
you now move on?

*There is the silence of a crucial point reached. Bosie is
still, sincere.*

Bosie Oscar, you know that I will not leave you. I will
not leave you against your will. It would be wrong. I
asked you here.

Wilde You did.

Bosie It was at my request. I shall not dishonour that
request. Too many people have left you, too many
people have betrayed you. You have not been good at
choosing your friends.

Wilde On the contrary. I have the gift of choosing them.
Holding on to them has proved to be my *faiblesse*.

Bosie Yes. You know what I mean.

Wilde I do.

*There is a silence, each of them knowing what is
coming. At the window light is beginning to break,
the first grey outline of morning on the horizon.*

Dawn is coming. I know it. I shall not need to turn.
Already I feel it like a hand. I feel the light at my back.

Bosie takes a step towards him.

Bosie Oscar . . .

Wilde You must forgive me, but I have heard you.

Bosie Heard me?

Wilde Yes.

Bosie What do you mean, you have heard me?

Wilde I have sat here. I have been listening. All night I have been listening. I have heard you moving overhead.

Bosie I see.

Wilde Every step, every movement you have made. I have heard your intent. I thought: a winter trip. Can it be? A return to Capri? But I reasoned that the season had ended. Even Europe's damned souls . . . even we do not go to Capri in December.

Bosie shifts uneasily.

Bosie Oscar, it is just . . . for you, yes, to be in Naples, to write every day . . . there is a project here for you which is virtuous, which makes sense. But for me there is nothing. Truly.

Wilde waits, saying nothing.

And I have a family to return to.

Wilde I see.

Sensing the quiet of Wilde's response, Bosie begins to gain in confidence.

Bosie My mother has written.

Wilde Yes. I had noticed that as well. I should request gainful employment as a concierge. I miss nothing. You have read the letter?

Bosie nods.

When did you read it?

Bosie Oh, at the café . . .

Wilde Ah . . .

Bosie With Galileo. That is when I decided to come back.

Wilde You were pleased with its contents, plainly?

Bosie She has offered me money.

Wilde Ah, good. Well then . . .

Bosie She has offered me an allowance. She is willing to forgive.

Bosie looks down, moved.

You must understand. For me, this is important.

Wilde Of course . . .

Bosie There are times – yes – when I have despaired even of my mother's love. I have not been certain she would love me again. But now she is prepared to overlook the past.

He pauses before the crucial information.

She is offering me three hundred pounds a year.

The two men look at one another.

Wilde Ah well . . .

Bosie Yes . . .

Wilde Three hundred is something. No one can deny it. But tell me: this money, does it come with conditions?

Bosie Oscar . . .

Wilde What makes me ask this? Do I have gifts of the paranormal? Are there conditions attached?

Bosie looks at him, not answering.

After all, not one minute ago you promised to stay with me.

Bosie I did.

Wilde So, then. I have sat here. I have listened. I have heard you upstairs. Are you the only man on earth who *packs his bags to stay where he is?*

Wilde has given these words sudden bite. In reply, Bosie becomes formal, as if summarising a legal position.

Bosie You have heard me. Oscar, you have heard my intention. I have said I will not leave you without your consent. That is what I said. I await your consent.

Wilde says nothing. Bosie shakes his head slightly, as if injured by his silence.

I have wanted nothing but your happiness. I have wanted only to make you happy. But in this as in everything our relationship has been a failure.

Bosie is frowning, at an apparent impasse.

So what will you do? Will you live . . . will you go on living here alone?

Wilde I plan to live with you.

Bosie Oscar, I have said. It cannot be. I cannot live with you.

Wilde is smiling, infuriatingly calm.

Wilde Last night Robbie was sent here by my blackmailing wife. I refused to disown you. In return she has cut me off.

Bosie No!

Wilde Yes. Now I have nothing. It amuses me. I admit I am amused. How often have I said the words, 'I cannot live without you'? Up till now, I have spoken them from the heart. Now I speak them from the pocketbook. Look in my eyes, Bosie.

Wilde looks up into Bosie's eyes.

'I cannot live without you.'

There is something so ridiculous in this that both men smile.

363

Bosie It is funny . . .

Wilde Yes.

Bosie In some way it is funny.

He moves away, nodding.

As it happens, I may be able to help you.

Wilde How?

Bosie You dislike my family, you think them inconsiderate. But you do not realise: they have long accepted some blame. They know that in bringing your prosecution you acted in some sense on my behalf.

Wilde In some sense?

Bosie Indeed. My family has known . . . the Queensberrys have known that they do have obligations towards you. There is a debt of honour. My mother says in her letter that she wishes to make that debt concrete.

Wilde Concrete?

Bosie In her letter she says this.

Both men are now tense, Wilde poker-faced, knowing the end is near.

Wilde Ah well.

Bosie Yes . . .

Wilde To the heart of things.

Bosie Yes.

Wilde Just how much concrete is she offering?

Bosie is ready, precise.

Bosie She will pay you two hundred.

Wilde Two?

Bosie In two instalments.

Wilde When?

Bosie The first at once.

Wilde A hundred at once?

Bosie Yes.

Wilde The second?

Bosie Within a month.

Wilde Two? Is that all?

Bosie No.

He pauses slightly.

Three hundred more as soon as she has it.

Wilde Five? Five in all? Five hundred?

Bosie nods. Wilde is impassive.

Bosie She attaches one condition. To your money, as to my own.

Wilde Of course. The whole world wants that condition. Here we are, hurting no one. And yet.

The light is growing behind Wilde. He tries to stir. His limbs are stiff.

I have sat here too long. I need to move. Help me.

Bosie goes over and takes both Wilde's hands. Agonisingly, he pulls Wilde's bent figure to his feet. Wilde pulls himself upright. He looks around and then takes a few shaky, wheezing steps.

Thus it is. It is done.

Bosie You agree?

Wilde How can I not agree? More conventionally it is you who should receive the pieces of silver, but in this case it is me.

Wilde waves a hand.

You are free. You have always been free. Go.

Wilde goes out. Bosie looks at the room for the last time. Wilde comes back surprisingly soon, and surprisingly quickly, carrying a glass of water.

No speeches, please, Bosie. No reproaches. I have a horror of sentimentality. The lump in my throat is not from the release of my emotions but from the tightening of the noose.

He looks casually at Bosie.

When is your train?

Bosie Soon.

Wilde The first train?

Bosie Yes. It leaves very soon.

Wilde And the first hundred? When will I see that?

He has moved to another chair from which he can watch the dawn. The speed of his acceptance has made Bosie uncomfortable.

Bosie Oscar, I was never born to be a rebel . . .

Wilde No.

Bosie I met you purely by accident. And yet I often consider how because of that accident I have become an outcast.

Wilde Indeed.

Bosie To me this is a paradox. All I have ever wanted is reconciliation with my family. This way I have it. In my mother's offer I see some way back.

Wilde Good. In your layer of society, ties of blood always triumph over ties of sentiment. I will be happy to be the agent of the Queensberry family reunion. Plainly if the Queensberrys are reunited, then my passage of suffering has not been in vain.

Bosie can hardly miss his tone.

Bosie Oscar, I would not wish you bitter.

Wilde No? Not bitter, then. How would you wish me?

Bosie I am fond of you. At the end, I would wish you at peace.

Wilde smiles, amused by this remark.

Wilde At peace? Oh, surely. Do not fear for me. I have understood my actions, as you have not yet understood your own.

Bosie What do you mean?

Wilde The governing principle of my life has been love. But of yours, it has been power.

Bosie looks at him, horrified.

It is the family failing. I am sorry for you, Bosie. A love of power confers a whole bouquet of rewards, but peace is not among them.

Bosie is silent.

You called me back, you led me to Naples, not as an expression of your feelings, but in a demonstration of your will.

Bosie That is not true.

Wilde Do not distress yourself. I promise you, I shall be at my peace long before you are.

He says this oddly. Bosie is disturbed.

Bosie What are you saying?

Wilde You have taken from me the thing you most envied.

Bosie What is it?

Wilde What you have wanted all along.

Wilde puts his glass down, and goes back to his old seat. He picks up his notebook. and holds its blank pages up in the air. Bosie looks across at the empty book above Wilde's head.

There is nothing. The pages are empty. What do I write? Shopping lists for things I have no money to buy. You have achieved your aim. You have achieved my silence.

Bosie is outraged at the accusation.

Bosie How can you say that? How can you say such a thing? I respect your talent. I revere it. I am a poet myself!

Wilde smiles to himself but Bosie moves round the room in genuine shock.

What, you would leave me thus? With this accusation? You would accuse me – what? – of wanting to silence the greatest dramatist of the modern stage?

Wilde Are you the excuse for my silence? Or the cause of it? Whichever, that is the effect. That is the result. To lose my life will be as nothing. But to lose my art . . .

He is overwhelmed, the reality of Bosie's departure finally seeming to be real to him.

Come towards me. Walk. Take some steps. Our business is not complete.

Bosie moves slowly towards him.

I have known you six years. I will know you no longer.
Come closer.

They are now unnaturally close, just short of touching.

You will never be free until you ask my forgiveness. Kiss
me.

*And Bosie leans in for the Judas kiss. It is quite short,
and when it is over Wilde smiles almost contentedly,
a rite enacted. He puts a hand kindly on Bosie's arm.*

And now I imagine you must go on your way.

*Bosie turns and goes out. The sun is coming up,
beginning to give warmth to the room. Wilde turns
out the lamps, then drinks the remains of his water.
On the stairs Bosie reappears, carrying his luggage.
He puts it down by the door.*

In prison I had the chance to read the Christ story. Over
and over. It seemed to me the greatest story I ever read.
But it has one flaw. Christ is betrayed by Judas, who is
almost a stranger. Judas is a man he doesn't know well.
It would be artistically truer if he were betrayed by John.
Because John is the man he loves most.

*This has been said without bitterness or accusation.
And Bosie does not seem offended, just at the end of
a chapter. He nods slightly.*

Bosie Well, I should be going then.

Wilde Yes.

Bosie It's time I was leaving. If there are any letters, will
you send them on?

Wilde I shall.

Bosie So.

There is a moment's pause.

Goodbye then, Oscar.

Wilde Goodbye.

Bosie goes out. Wilde opens the balcony doors to catch the warmth of the morning sun. The music plays. Wilde turns to us, his voice filling the theatre.

All trials are trials for one's life, just as all sentences are sentences of death, and three times I have been tried. The first time I left the box to be arrested, the second time to be led back to the House of Detention, the third time to pass into a prison for two years. Society, as we have constituted it, will have no place for me, has none to offer; but Nature, whose sweet rains fall on unjust and just alike, will have clefts in the rocks where I may hide, and secret valleys in whose silence I may weep undisturbed. She will hang the night with stars so that I may walk abroad in the darkness without stumbling, and send the wind over my footprints so that none may track me to my hurt: she will cleanse me in great waters, and with bitter herbs make me whole . . .

Wilde goes back to his chair where he picks up his book and starts to read. The sun rises, brilliant now over the sea.

End of Act Two.

MY ZINC BED

For Nicole
my love

My Zinc Bed was first presented at the Royal Court Theatre, London, on 14 September 2000. The cast was as follows:

Paul Peplow Steven Mackintosh
Victor Quinn Tom Wilkinson
Elsa Quinn Julia Ormond

Director David Hare
Designer Vicki Mortimer
Lighting Designer Rick Fisher

A Rainmark Films production of the play, produced in association with Robert Fox Ltd and presented by HBO Films, was transmitted by BBC-2 Television on 25 August 2008. The cast was as follows:

Paul Peplow Paddy Considine
Victor Quinn Jonathan Pryce
Elsa Quinn Uma Thurman

Director Anthony Page
Production Designer Luciana Arrighi
Costume Designer Jane Robinson
Director of Photography Brian Tufano
Film Editors Peter Boyle, John Scott
Music by Simon Boswell

Characters

Paul Peplow
Elsa Quinn
Victor Quinn

There is no Shakespeare; there is no
Beethoven; certainly and emphatically
there is no God; we are the words;
we are the music; we are the thing itself.

Virginia Woolf

ONE

The stage is a black void. Paul Peplow stands before us, alone. He's an attractive man, in his early thirties, thin, saturnine, tousled, as if he has just woken up. He wears an untidy linen suit and a tie, and his manner is self-deprecating.

Paul Joseph Conrad says that inside every heart there burns a desire to set down once and for all a true record of what has happened. For myself, nothing that has happened, nothing that can happen, compares with the passage of a single summer, from May to September, the trickiest summer of my life, the cyber-summer when I first met Victor Quinn.

TWO

Victor Quinn has appeared along a corridor of light and is advancing towards Paul, already talking. He is in his early fifties, anonymous, thickly built. His background is hard to place, for he has lost his native northern accent. He wears an expensive suit, but no tie.

Victor 'Many are the stories with interesting beginnings, but harder to find are the stories which end well.'

He stops short of Paul, not yet shaking his hand.

Paul I'm sorry?

Victor Surely you can't have forgotten.

Paul Oh I see.

Victor Your own words.

Paul Yes.

Victor Though maybe you write so many you lose track.

He smiles and shakes Paul's hand.

Victor Quinn.

Paul Paul Peplow.

Victor Of course.

Victor gestures towards a chair, leaving Paul free to sit or stand as he chooses.

'End well' in which sense? A story which ends well, meaning 'well', meaning happily for its subject, or 'well', meaning in a way which satisfies the reader? Or did you intend both? Is the ambiguity deliberate?

Paul Both, I think. It was just a book review.

Paul waits, not willing to show his discomfiture.

Victor Drink?

Paul No thank you.

Victor Of course. Wrong of me to ask.

Victor flashes a smile at him.

Well. As you know, I don't often agree to be interviewed.

Paul It's kind of you.

Victor Not at all.

Paul Why are you normally so reclusive?

Victor Have we started?

Paul has got out a notebook.

Ah. The book's coming out.

Paul Please.

Victor How can you call me a recluse? I live in the centre of London.

Paul But you don't give interviews.

Victor I'm not an exhibitionist, no. I'm a simple man. My question is always 'To what end?' To what end would I tell people, say, my favourite restaurant? My favourite tailor? That the world should beat a path to the restaurant? That I should have to wait longer for my suit?

Paul Do you have a tailor?

Victor No. I buy off-the-peg.

Paul makes a note.

If you'd like something to eat.

Paul No thank you. And how did you know I would refuse a drink?

Victor Ah.

Victor smiles, pleased with this question.

I believe you belong to what cooks on television call the vulnerable groups. 'Remember: don't put brandy in this pudding, it endangers the vulnerable groups.' You don't need to say more. I know about these things. 'Hello, my name is Victor. I'm an alcoholic.' You see. I've followed the course myself.

Paul It's not really a course.

Victor No. A course implies an end . . .

Paul Yes.

Victor And in this case there is no end.

He looks at Paul thoughtfully.

379

I've studied the meetings. At the time I was trying to understand the techniques.

Paul What techniques exactly?

Victor Well, Paul, we can talk about anything you like. But for this particular subject, you first have to concede the accuracy of my intelligence.

Paul hesitates a moment.

Paul I go to the meetings, yes.

Victor Yes, that's what I thought.

Paul I have no idea how you know. To be honest, I'm surprised you've heard of me at all.

Victor England is a series of clubs. No club more celebrated, no club more socially advantageous than yours. Under the guise of admitting their fallibility, people meet in fact to advance their own cause.

Paul You obviously didn't go very often.

Victor No.

Victor gestures to encourage Paul to speak.

You say. You say what you think these meetings are.

Paul A means . . . one means of people helping one another.

Victor looks at Paul for a moment in a way which makes it clear that Victor thinks him naive.

I suppose we should start by discussing Flotilla.

Victor Go ahead.

Paul Its recent move to the stock market.

Victor A transparent success. What's your question?

Paul Whether you did it for the money.

Victor Now perhaps you understand my distrust. What do I answer? 'I did it for the money.' People will think I'm greedy. 'I didn't do it for the money.' Then they'll say I'm unworldly. More likely, I'm lying. I'm a hypocrite. Paul, you of all people understand: the modern newspaper interview is a form as rigid and contrived as the eighteenth-century gavotte.

Paul Shall I just put: he refused to answer?

Victor Meaning: he's a prick.

They both smile.

He consented to an interview, then he wouldn't answer the questions!

Paul Why 'of all people'? Why did you say 'me of all people'?

Victor A poet.

Paul Ah.

Victor I read poetry. I read yours.

'Love was the search, the wheel, the line,
The open road and the steep incline;
Things speeding by, the final turn in view,
Next: something disastrous, overwhelming, new.'

I hardly believe you would now be paddling in journalism if it weren't purely for the money.

Paul No.

Victor You'll drink to that.

Paul Yes. So to speak.

Paul smiles, amused by Victor's manner.

Victor I liked the idea, I promise you.

Paul Of this interview?

Victor No. Of the meetings. I thought the meetings amusing.

Paul Amusing? Obviously you aren't alcoholic.

Victor I'm not.

Paul The meetings are a discipline.

Victor Of course. They wouldn't be addictive if they weren't.

Paul Oh, I see . . .

Victor All cults make similar demands.

Paul I think it's childish, people calling AA a cult. It's ignorant. I tell you what: I actually believe it's quite dangerous.

Victor Do you? I'd have thought it's a classic cult.

Paul Why?

Victor The chairs, the coffee, the soul-searching . . .

Victor hastens to explain.

Believe me, I'm not denying its usefulness.

Paul You couldn't.

Victor It is the means by which many people survive. Or they believe it is.

Paul It saved my life. I was found on the M4, dodging the traffic. And naked, in the middle of the night.

Victor Huh.

Paul I don't need to question the value of AA.

Victor is completely still.

Victor What brought you there? What brought you to the motorway so late at night?

Paul does not answer.

It's none of my business. You're right. Presumably you believe that one drink will take you on the road to hell?

Paul I do believe that, yes.

Victor It's what they teach you.

Paul It's also what I believe.

Victor It isn't true, you know.

Paul Isn't it?

Victor Of course not. The cult makes rules. It demands obedience. The cult has invented the slogan: 'One Drink, One Drunk.' But it isn't actually true. If you had cured your own addiction, in the privacy of your own home, then you could perfectly well drink socially again.

Paul I can't take that risk.

Victor You won't take that risk, you mean?

Paul looks a moment.

Paul I think I'm missing something here. I'm here to do an interview. That's what I'm here for. No doubt you think you're being clever, you're being provocative. Wind up the monkeys! It's dinner-party stuff. 'Oh my God, you don't go to that ridiculous AA, do you?' Only, tell you what, one thing I've noticed –

Victor What thing?

Paul Most of the people who attack AA are ten times more fucked up than the people they're attacking.

Victor smiles, not fazed.

Victor But you must have views. You must have theories . . .

Paul No. I have no theories. I have one aim in life . . .

Victor Just one?

Paul My aim is to get to bed sober tonight. That is my aim. And I have found pragmatically that the only means of achieving it is through AA. It's the only method which works. And you have no fucking right to talk about it.

Paul has raised his voice but Victor does not seem perturbed.

Victor Have you thought . . . have you considered what it would mean to be cured?

Paul Of course. Naturally. I think of little else.

Victor But that's my point. If you can't drink at all – ever – then by definition you're not cured.

Paul What's your idea of cured?

Victor 'Thank you. I'll just have the one. Just the one for me. Thank you.'

Victor smiles, pleased with his own answer.

You should think about it, Paul. Consider. It's only groups which demand total abstinence. Why? Because their intention is not to stop you drinking. That is only a side aim. Their principal aim is to retain you as a member of the group.

Paul It's a familiar argument. It's also nonsense.

Victor Really? I'm interested. Tell me why.

There is a moment's pause before Paul decides to take the plunge.

Paul Look, if you really want to know: of course I went into AA kicking and screaming. Everyone does. Believe me, I had a thousand reservations . . .

Victor But presumably you'd bottomed . . .

Paul Yes.

Victor That's the phrase they use.

Paul I bottomed.

Victor The M4.

Paul Not just the M4. Not just that one night, believe me.

Victor Other nights?

Paul looks at him a moment.

Paul You wake up in the morning and you've fallen down three flights of stairs. But even so. Even then. I was still reluctant. I clung to the thought: I'm not the sort of person who sits in a circle stripping himself bare.

Victor I'm sure. A poet.

Paul Even when I was young, at college, in the student common room, come that dreaded moment, come eleven, come twelve, people have been drinking and they begin to spill. How unhappy they are. You can imagine. I was out of that room like a shot.

Victor Somehow I see you alone with a girl come midnight.

Paul Whatever. I was not in the common room, telling all and sundry my innermost thoughts. However. You go to the meetings because you have to. Because it's your last chance. Your only chance. If we were alone on this earth, then what would it matter? Oh sure, everyone has the right to destroy their own life. But to destroy the lives of others?

Victor Ah yes. 'Others.'

Victor has stopped, thoughtful.

Paul You're right. I was frightened of AA. Yes. Why do you think I was frightened? I was frightened because in my heart I knew it would work.

Victor I see.

Paul Yes.

Victor Because it works?

Paul That's why. I no sooner walked into the room than I intuited: oh my God, this is going to work.

Paul shakes his head.

'I'm not the sort of person who does this,' you say. But what sort of person are you by that stage? What have you become? A worthless drunk.

Victor Yes. It's that word 'worthless' I have trouble with.

The two men look at each other.

Paul I'll be honest. I'm broke. Yeah. I'm completely broke. I don't have a fucking penny in the world. I can't get a bank account. The editor pays me in cash.

Victor Where do you live?

Paul Camberwell. Stretching the charity of a last remaining friend. You?

Victor Regents Park.

Paul Good. Well that's something solid for the article.

Paul's sudden unsteadiness has brought them close.
Victor speaks quietly, opening up for the first time.

Victor I was a communist.

Paul Yes.

Victor waits. Paul starts writing.

What are you saying? Is that how your interest in cults
came about?

Victor Sort of. Apparently the newspapers have taken
to calling me a one-time Marxist. They can't bring
themselves to use the proper word. I'm most insistent.
I wasn't a Marxist. I was a communist. I use the full
shocker.

Paul All or nothing, eh?

Victor That sort of thing.

Paul And you mean it was a cult? There were rules?

Victor Conditions of membership, yes. All clubs have
membership rules or they aren't clubs.

Paul England, you were saying . . .

Victor Yes. A series of clubs. The English love clubs. Not
of course for the pleasure of allowing people in . . .

Paul No.

Victor Oh no! The far headier delight of keeping people
out! They love that! English communists, we were a
select little band. A snotty little group we were.

Paul It's a familiar progress, isn't it, from student
politics? Communist to entrepreneur?

Victor I still believe in history. A way of looking at things.
For years computers were just whopping great dinner

plates spinning in glass-panelled rooms. Then suddenly –
whoosh. Of themselves uninteresting. But you spot the
moment.

Victor shrugs.

Not that I claim any credit.

Paul You could equally well have been wrong.

Victor Exactly. It was luck. I stumbled across an idea.
Analyse the market, make informed predictions based
on available financial data. Pretty soon – this was the
1990s – there was scarcely an investor who wasn't using
Flotilla software.

Paul What were you doing before?

Victor Importing virgin olive oil. Stupid, I agree. I
mistook changes in life-style for historical shifts. That's
what I mean. I'm as vulnerable to bullshit as everyone
else.

Victor smiles, pleased at the thought.

Capitalists make me laugh because they understand
nothing. They talk about strategy and markets as if they
were in control. They use soothing devices like big cars
and hotels and servants. They use luxury as a sort of
massage to persuade themselves they've acted brilliantly,
that their actions have been brilliant . . .

Paul Whereas in fact?

Victor They've worked hard and had a bit of luck.

Paul Don't you use big cars?

Victor Never. Or only for the children, anyway.

Paul How many children do you have?

Victor pauses, wanting to lay down a principle.

Victor Communism is night class. It's where you learn. Who is doing what to whom? If you don't believe that the rich spend their time on this earth effectively fucking over the poor, then I don't see how you make any sense of what goes on in the world at all.

Paul smiles, risking his neck a little.

Paul But, forgive me, nobody could mistake your wealth.

Victor No?

Paul I don't think so. To look at you, it's clear.

Victor Is it? I'm rather insulted.

Paul You make certain assumptions. I've noticed you use certain techniques. Which, rightly or wrongly, I associate with the rich. Or at least with the powerful. What I mean is: you'd read my poetry.

Victor Well?

Paul Is it a manner? Is it a game? You read my poetry before the meeting. You put yourself instantly at an advantage. 'I know who you are. I've read *This Too Shall Pass*.'

Victor Yes. I see. You think that's specifically a technique of the rich?

Paul And, what's more, learning a whole verse.

Victor 'Love was the search, the wheel, the line . . .'

Paul A line maybe, but a whole verse!

Victor Too much?

Paul If the purpose was to unsettle me, then I'm afraid you've succeeded. I've been uncomfortable ever since you arrived.

Victor Forgive me, but I think you would have been uncomfortable however I approached you.

Paul blushes, off guard. He reaches for his notebook in confusion.

Paul We'd better go on. When did you leave the Party?

Victor 1975.

Paul And do you miss it?

Victor Let's say, it's like New Zealand. I'm glad it's there but I have no wish to visit.

Paul Put it another way: do you regret its decline?

Victor looks at him, a little wistful.

Victor It's the world that's changed, not me. Or changed more than me.

Paul In what way?

Victor Politicians now boast of being plumbers, not architects. The word 'ideological' is never now mentioned.

Paul Except with the word 'baggage'.

Victor That's right. Now we solve problems. Everything is a problem, and we solve it. Nothing is decided in advance, because nothing is believed in advance. It's as simple as that. That's how we proceed. That's how we get things done. The containable life.

Victor stares at Paul a moment.

You could say the whole world's in AA.

Paul is quiet, speaking after a moment.

Paul Can I ask you something else?

Victor Please.

Paul What's your interest in the meetings?

Victor I had a friend who quit.

Paul Quit alcohol?

Victor No. Quit AA. Much harder. My friend came home one evening . . .

Paul Came home? To your home, you mean?

Victor My friend came back from a meeting. She had become convinced that the purpose of the cult was to reinforce her feelings of worthlessness, not to try and assuage them. She never went back.

Victor sits back, as if having said the final word.

Paul Surely she knew she would have to confront her illness?

Victor Confront it by all means, but then move on.

Paul Do you think an addict can ever move on?

Victor Ah well.

Paul Truly?

Victor You're right. This was at the heart of the issue.

Paul It is. It is at the heart.

Victor My friend felt they were replacing her dependency on drugs with a dependency on coffee and confession, on what you would call the dreaded circle of chairs. They were sustaining her – how do I put this? – in a sort of suspended anxiety. They were instilling what would become a permanent fear of the great crash round the corner. She came to feel no crash could be as terrible as the fear of that crash. In order to preserve that fear and to magnify it, they were forbidding her self-respect.

Paul In that case I don't believe she was alcoholic.

Victor No?

Paul An alcoholic has no self-respect.

Victor looks at Paul. Then he speaks, silvery.

Victor I gave her a gin and tonic. She drank it. And we then played Scrabble all evening.

Victor looks deeply pleased at this, but Paul is not buying it.

Paul I don't believe she was addictive in the first place.

Victor Believe what you like.

Paul I don't believe it.

Victor is now looking at him very hard.

Victor Paul, it seems to me you have a problem of self-esteem.

Paul How so? In what way, specifically?

Victor You accuse me of mugging up your poetry with the purpose of flattering you. Does it not occur to you – does it really not occur to you? – that you insult yourself with this suggestion more than you insult me?

Paul I don't understand.

Victor Do I have to spell it out?

He waits, looking at Paul who still doesn't get it.

Your poetry is the reason I have long wanted to meet you.

Paul Oh. Oh, I see.

Paul is taken aback. He searches for a reply, but Victor is ahead of him.

Victor What did you like to drink?

Paul I'm sorry?

Victor What was your favourite drink?

Paul Mine?

Victor Yes.

Paul A fatal weakness for Manhattans.

Victor I would never have guessed. Fiddling about with cherries, you think that's time well spent?

Paul And you?

Victor Oh. I like a Martini.

Paul As well spent as fiddling about with olives.

Victor And if I offered you one now . . .

Paul just looks at him.

That's it, isn't it? If you were cured, you would be cured of the desire. And who wants to be cured of desire?

Victor decides suddenly to wind up the meeting.

It's been a great pleasure to meet you. I have given up reading the newspapers, but my impression is that the modern practice is for the journalist to write the story before the encounter. What I am saying is: write what you like. Your poetry has a flair for the dramatic. I trust that flair. Invent my character, by all means. I shall stand by whatever opinions you ascribe to me. I shall be your invention.

Paul Thank you.

Victor Consider yourself liberated from the facts.

He shakes Paul's hand.

I'd very much like it if we could meet again.

Paul Yes. I'd like that too.

Victor turns and goes.

You didn't tell me. How's your friend doing?

Victor Oh. She's doing fine.

Victor has gone. Paul turns from the scene and speaks directly towards us. Behind him, the feeling of the stage changes to suggest the new location.

Paul As job interviews go, it was one of the more peculiar. No piece ever appeared. I told the editor that my subject had been a no-show. He said it was typical of the man's notorious arrogance not even to turn up. Someone was needed to write copy for his website, turning the prose of the internet into something like poetry. I started working for Victor the following week. I was beginning to think I was going to be happy, doodling around, manufacturing sentences. I'd taken to staying on in the evening, long after everyone else, because I felt more secure than at home. Looking back, I think that may have been a mistake.

THREE

Elsa Quinn is sitting on top of Paul's desk, her feet on a chair below her. It is evening, in a large place of work. There is a feeling of modern technology. Overhead lights stretch away into the distance. Elsa is in her early thirties. She is wearing a short dark skirt and a white shirt. She is Danish by birth, but next to nothing of her accent remains. At this moment, she has a pleasant air of amusement, as if someone has just told her a joke.

Elsa And so what was she like?

Paul Who?

Elsa This woman. This woman who drove you nuts.

Paul You'd have to meet her for yourself to decide.

Elsa Why?

Paul *Why?* Because why do you think? Why do you think, for goodness' sake? Because from me you will get a partial account.

Elsa Why?

Paul Because . . . Oh, just *because*! Why do you think?

Elsa She really got to you?

Paul has no need to answer. They smile together.

Paul And also she wanted to be an actress, which was also not easy. Because I had to watch television – and . . .

Elsa That's not such a hardship.

Paul I don't know . . . look at her in helmets and things.

Elsa Viking helmets?

Paul No. Police helmets. Obviously.

Elsa It's not obvious.

Paul It's what actors have to do. Or the ones she knew. They play police all the time. Or doctors. They play very few Vikings. She was a doctor for a bit in a series where they went to the cupboards at the ends of the wards and made love.

Elsa frowns.

Young doctors, you know, working thirty-five-hour shifts and fucking each other in the middle of the night. We're So Tired All We Can Do Is. Underfunding as eroticism, that sort of thing.

395

Elsa You had to watch your girlfriend with other people?

Paul Simulating, yes.

Elsa How was that?

Paul Not bad, actually. Quite fun, actually, in a kind of way.

Paul laughs.

I always think I should have minded it more.

There is a silence. Elsa recrosses her legs. Paul just sits, thinking.

I minded it more when she did it in real life.

Elsa looks at him a moment. It's a decisive confidence on his part.

Elsa Is that why it ended?

Paul Oh.

Elsa It is over?

Paul Oh yes. Long over.

Paul thinks, then casually springs back to life.

And apart from anything there's the ridiculous incongruity.

Elsa Like?

Paul Explaining to a friend, 'Oh I'm crazy about this woman, she's so extraordinary, I'm going out of my mind.' They say, 'Do you mean the dark one?' I say, 'No, the dark one plays the radiotherapist.' 'Oh the pathologist,' they say. 'It's the pathologist you want to kill yourself for.' It seems so arbitrary. Because she was this face on television so everyone thought they knew her. But in fact only I knew her.

Elsa Only you?

Paul Well, me and the dozen others. The dirty dozen, as I came to think of them.

Elsa watches, not moving.

Elsa Why did you say, 'She wanted to be an actress'?

Paul Did I?

Elsa You said, 'She wanted to be an actress.'

Paul Oh yes.

Elsa But she was an actress.

Paul That's what I'm saying. In the world's eyes. To me, she was something else.

Elsa What was her name?

Paul ignores the question. He turns to Elsa.

Paul What about you?

Elsa Oh . . .

Paul Any such figure in your life? Why are we talking about this?

Elsa It's often more interesting . . . don't you think . . .?

Paul In what way?

Elsa Talking to people you don't know?

Paul Maybe. I don't live that kind of life any more.

Elsa What? What life?

Paul Oh you know. Girls. Bars. Girls go with bars in my mind and bars are long since forbidden.

Elsa Bars frighten you?

Paul No. Everything frightens me.

They share the absurdity and the moment unlocks him.

Oh look, well what happens is . . . for goodness' sake you know about this . . .

Elsa Do I?

Paul You're focused on one thing, aren't you?

Elsa You tell me.

Paul Your recovery. Isn't that right? You want to recover. That's all you want. And the other person . . . well, the other person has got tired of clearing up . . . You can't blame them, it's fair enough, they're just tired of tidying up after . . .

Elsa Well, yes . . .

Paul You know about this?

Elsa gives nothing away.

Elsa Go on.

Paul Every night you're sick. You're reeling. Whatever. You're in agony.

Elsa The guilt!

Paul Exactly.

Elsa You're drinking again.

Paul And the other person says, she says, 'I don't want to play nurse. I refuse to play nurse. I won't do it.'

Elsa Especially when they play nurse on the television already.

Paul nods, gaining momentum.

Paul So then after a while you start to think, OK, this isn't too bad, I'm beginning to clean up, I'm sober – hey, this is really much better.

Elsa One day at a time.

Paul Precisely. As you say. You think: at last. I deserve a fucking break.

Elsa You do deserve a break. It's true.

Paul I've been to fifty thousand fucking meetings. And I deserve a break.

Elsa And? Instead?

Paul looks at her, deciding once more how far to go.

Paul Instead – like the trick of an actress to be – I don't know – not to play roles exactly, no she doesn't do that, Clem didn't do that – but to slither about, to slide all the time. And you long for someone who is constant . . .

Elsa Yes.

Paul You have no right to ask, God knows you have no rights – you're a snake, you know that, you're lower than a snake – but you do long for someone who does not slither about.

Elsa Yes.

Paul Then one day she turns to you, she informs you that she is an honest person, she is an unusual human being, because she cannot live in an atmosphere of lies, she cannot bear dishonesty. 'Sorry,' she says, 'but that's my character' – so she must tell you she's been meeting other people, other people who are, as it were, *not you*, the reason being, Clem says, that you were a drunk and so what was she meant to do?

Elsa Do you believe her?

Paul Believe her how? What, believe she slept with them?

Elsa No, believe her reasons.

Paul She slept with a dozen other men. A dozen. Finally, what the hell do her reasons matter?

For the first time Paul lets his feelings show. Elsa watches from the desktop, still giving nothing away.

Elsa They matter.

Paul And then, well then, when you've been clean for a week or two she turns round – you are struggling to hold on, you are struggling to maintain the relationship – she looks at you and she says: you know what she says?

Elsa I think I can guess.

Paul You're warming up the dinner from Marks and Spencer's. You've turned on the television. You're pouring the Coca-Cola. She says 'Do you know something, Paul? Since you've tried to clean up you've got kind of *boring*. Have you noticed? You were so much more interesting when you were drunk.'

Elsa Yes. And were you?

Paul Early on she said, 'No commitments.' Later I said, 'I agreed, no commitments. But somehow when you said no commitments, forgive me, I did not foresee the number twelve.'

Paul shakes his head.

Anyway, then the plan is, the project is: you are to return to the meetings . . . 'Hello. My name is Paul. I'm an alcoholic.'

Elsa And go through the scene . . .

Paul Yes . . .

Elsa Discuss the *details* of the scene . . .

Paul Exactly.

Elsa Her duodecimal behaviour . . .

Paul looks despairingly at her.

Paul Whoa, mind you, I'm not saying – let's be clear – AA is my sole hope, my sole source of hope . . .

Elsa Is it?

Paul For sure. I should be there now.

Elsa 'Should'?

Paul But you'll understand if occasionally I say, 'I can't get to the meeting, I couldn't get to the meeting, I was held up at Flotilla, I ran into the boss's wife . . .'

Elsa I'm glad you did. I'm really glad.

There is a moment suspended between them.

People don't want to know me. They want to know my husband. Or rather they want to know me because that way they get to meet my husband.

Paul Does that upset you?

Elsa Not at all. It amuses me.

Paul Why?

Elsa I've a life of my own. And let's face it, he's a fascinating man. Why should people not want to meet him?

Elsa looks away.

When he met me, I was a drunk.

There is a silence. They look at each other, straight in the eye, a deep bond between them. In the distance,

401

the bell of a City church chimes. Silently, overhead squares of light begin to go out around them in irregular rhythm, as if whole areas of the building were being evacuated. Neither of them moves.

What time is it?

Paul Eight.

Elsa Wow.

Paul I know.

Elsa I must get going.

Paul Yes.

Elsa It's silly. We must be the last people here.

Elsa doesn't move, just stays, sitting on the desktop. Paul waits to see what will happen.

Paul What about you?

Elsa What?

Paul Victor said you used to go to the meetings.

Elsa I did.

Paul You stopped?

Elsa I did.

Paul You don't . . .

Elsa What?

Paul I'm asking if you're clean.

Elsa Well . . . I have two children, remember?

Paul Does that make it easier?

Elsa Not at all. No, on the contrary.

Paul Then why do you mention it?

Elsa Because whatever feelings of guilt you suffer from, I suffered much worse.

Paul Ah.

Elsa Paul, I'm not a stranger to self-hatred.

Elsa is looking at him very directly.

Why do you imagine Victor employed you?

Paul You say. You tell me. Why do you think Victor employed me?

Elsa I imagine in some way you remind him of me.

Paul looks her straight in the eye, not responding, giving nothing away.

Paul Tell me what we're doing. Tell me what's going on.

Elsa slips down off the desk, moving for the first time. She smiles, apparently at ease.

Elsa What are we doing? We're talking.

Paul Thank God.

Elsa That's all.

Elsa sits in a nearby chair. She crosses her legs.

I've no right to talk about this. As you say, I hardly know you. I came in here by chance. I was looking for Victor, actually . . .

Paul He'll be back soon, he said.

Elsa Well, good.

They look at each other, neither shifting their gaze.

Paul You see, it's the bit . . . forgive me, it's the moment when you rustle your legs . . .

Elsa I'm sorry.

Paul No. The sound of your stockings.

Elsa I'll try to sit more discreetly.

Paul It's fine.

Elsa barely moves.

Elsa Are you going to hold on and wait?

Paul I've nothing else to do. My flat's empty as usual. And there's nothing in the larder.

Elsa You should stock up. What do you live on?

Paul Pulses, they're called. And cheap nourishing stews.

Elsa is gazing at him, unwavering.

They tell you at the meetings not to get hungry – hunger's the enemy, they say –

Elsa Or angry –

Paul Hungry. Angry. Lonely. Tired.

Elsa Oh no. You mustn't be any of those.

Paul looks down, embarrassed.

Paul The point is, you see, it's not just Clem.

Elsa No . . .

Paul I don't mean just Clem I have to avoid. Ridiculous. All women I have to avoid. I'm happier with blokes. Or in groups. Five's a good number. Or four. Two makes me jumpy. Forgive me, speaking generally . . .

Elsa Of course.

Paul In general.

Elsa Of course.

Paul Talking is fine. This is fine. Talking to you is fine. But all contact, any real closeness, I have to avoid. I'm a recovering alcoholic.

Paul checks with her, but she does not react.

What's good is, I've had to face the question: what makes me drink?

Elsa What was the answer?

Paul Finally? Anger. It's anger. Anger makes me drink. Therefore I have to avoid anger. Another way of putting it. Emotion makes me drink.

Elsa So what do you do about that? Avoid emotion?

Paul Yes.

Elsa Avoid life.

Elsa goes onto the attack, ignoring his protest.

Paul No.

Elsa You think it's that simple? H-A-L-T! Hungry! Angry! Lonely! Tired! You think it's that easy? You really sit there and buy that stuff, do you?

Paul It's quite convenient, actually. Anyone you don't like you can tell them to fuck off. You're licensed. Anyone gets on my nerves I have the perfect reply. 'I'm sorry. You're endangering my recovery.' That's the advantage of it being a disease.

Elsa Is it a disease?

Paul Of course it is.

Elsa There's no medical proof.

Paul It is. It's an illness.

Elsa That's what they tell you. That's what they want you to believe. They love saying that. 'It's a disease and it's incurable.'

Paul So it is.

Elsa It's for life. For the rest of your life you're an unexploded bomb.

Paul looks at her warily.

Is that what Clem thought?

Paul Clem?

Elsa Yes.

Paul I don't know. I don't know what Clem thought.

Elsa She blamed the drink.

Paul Yes, of course.

Elsa That's what I hate. Clem sleeps with twelve men and she blames the drink. She doesn't blame herself.

Paul Well . . .

Elsa You see, that's what gets me. Paul, I'm telling you, you have to break out.

Elsa impulsively gets up, animated now, excited as if a problem were solved.

Look at you for goodness' sake, you're thirty, you write like a god . . .

Paul Don't say you read poetry as well.

Elsa We read it together.

Paul My God! In bed?

Elsa Inevitably. Sometimes to the children.

Paul Stop.

Elsa *This Too Shall Pass.*

Paul I'm a poet. One reader's an epiphany. Find two and you hang out the flags.

But Elsa is not deflected.

Elsa Paul, look at yourself objectively. See yourself from the outside. You're young, you're talented, you're good-looking. Analyse. What exactly is this problem of yours?

Paul 'Analyse'! You sound like him.

Elsa Socio-economically, you, Paul, belong to the world's most privileged group.

Paul I don't have a fucking penny!

Elsa Paul, you're an elective intellectual who doesn't have to work in the fields.

Paul Now you sound even more like him.

Elsa You enjoy the company of rich women.

Paul Do I?

Elsa You get to listen to rich women rustling their stockings. Paul, please tell me, just what exactly is your problem meant to be?

Paul picks moodily at the arm of his chair.

Paul You don't know. You know nothing of what went on in my life.

Elsa You lost a girl. That's all.

Paul I lost the 'girl', as you call her, because of a habit I had, which was that I could not walk past a glass of whisky at fifty yards without wanting to drink it. No.

Correction. Without drinking it. And then the rest of the bottle. Drink humiliates you and then it kills you!

Elsa Do you really believe that was the problem?

Paul Believe it? I know it. I was drunk for ten years!

Elsa just looks at him, unrelenting.

Elsa Paul, not everything that happens is always your fault.

Paul I didn't say it was!

Elsa No, you didn't. But I look at you and I know you. I *was* you, remember? I was twenty-five, an idiot, and coked out of my head. 'I'm not a stranger to self-hatred.' Remember?

Paul I don't know what you're saying!

Elsa Yes you do. That's what's interesting. In your heart you do.

Elsa is clear, as if she has just understood something.

Elsa Why do you think Clem slept around?

Paul No. You tell me. Why do you think she did?

Elsa Do you really want to know?

Paul Yes.

Elsa It'll come as bad news.

Paul Break the news.

Elsa Really?

Paul I can take it. I promise. Please. I can take it.

Elsa pauses a moment to take aim.

Elsa Clem slept with other men because that was her choice.

Paul No!

Elsa Yes! That's what she chooses to do. That's who she is. That's her identity. She's twelve-man Clem. Grant her the dignity of her own actions. Because when you blame them on your drinking, then insidiously you begin to insult her.

Paul No.

Elsa Yes! She's an adult. She's a grown-up. It's her life. She chooses to sleep with twelve men! That is her magnificent choice.

Elsa turns back with the definitive diagnosis.

Paul, you are not addicted to alcohol. You are addicted to blame.

Paul is shaking his head in protest.

Paul I can't believe this. I can't believe what I'm hearing.

Elsa Why not?

Paul Because I know what I did: I drove this woman from my bed by my behaviour. By serial dishonesty. I lied. I told lies consistently for the eighteen months we were together. I barely let out a single word that was true. I deceived her.

Elsa Yes, but why?

Paul Why do you think? Like all drinkers. To hide my drinking, of course.

Elsa Was that all?

Paul No.

Elsa What else did you lie about?

Paul Oh, things.

DAVID HARE

Elsa What things?

Paul What does it matter? It becomes an attitude.

Elsa Say.

Paul looks at her, reluctant to go on.

Say.

Paul If I'm honest . . . also to hide my contempt.

Elsa Your contempt?

Paul Yes.

Elsa That's a strong word. Contempt for what, Paul? Hide your contempt for what?

Paul Well, if you want to know, I hid my contempt for her acting.

Elsa Why?

Paul Because it was fucking awful.

Elsa I see.

Paul Yes!

Elsa Bad, was it?

Paul It was embarrassing. It was the pits.

Elsa Ah, now . . .

Paul Yes!

Elsa Well now . . .

Paul That's what I really thought. She tried to be alluring but she came across as vulgar. And she couldn't say the lines.

Elsa is nodding, at last at the heart of things.

Elsa So. Now we progress. Now we understand. You were in a long-term relationship with what is known technically as a 'bad actress'.

Paul Very funny.

Elsa Seems to me clear what drove you to drink.

Paul You know nothing. You insult me. You know nothing at all.

Elsa just looks at him.

Elsa And one more thing. Was she clever? Was Clem clever? Was Clem as clever as you are?

Paul looks at her, not answering.

You fell in love with an idea, didn't you, Paul? You had an idea of her.

Paul Yes.

Elsa Oh yes. And one more thing. One more thing, Paul. About her acting. Was its awfulness your fault as well?

There is a silence. Then Paul suddenly gets up and moves a distance away, further than we knew the area reached. Elsa stays where she is.

Paul I can't do this. I can't. I can't do this.

Elsa Do what?

Paul Argue. Relate. Honestly, I got out of this. I stopped this. I put it all behind me. I've been dry for over a year. I have one hope. I have one thread of hope. I go to the meetings. I go home. I listen to music. I can't . . .

Paul stops dead, unable to speak.

Elsa You can't what, Paul? You can't what?

Paul I can't . . .

Elsa gets up and moves quickly across the room to him. She takes him in her arms, cradling his head. He is crying. Elsa holds him, then she looks into his eyes.

Elsa You can't what?

Paul begins to kiss her. He pushes her down against the top of a desk. They stay in each other's arms, passionate. Paul begins to pull at her shirt, loosening it from her skirt. It looks as if they might go on, but after a few moments they separate. They move to different parts of the area. After a while Paul speaks.

Paul For you it was easy. It was easy for you. You had Victor. Isn't that right? 'Oh no problem! I kicked alcohol. I didn't need AA.' But you had Victor to help. Who do I have?

Elsa Me. You have me.

The sound of Victor outside.

Victor Elsa! Elsa! Are you there?

FOUR

Paul moves out of the scene to talk to us. Behind him, the feeling of the stage lightens and changes. Victor and Elsa disappear.

Paul On the whole, all things considered, I think I can say now with some certainty that Elsa was not what I needed. I was a recovering alcoholic. I needed stability. An awful lot of fascinating things happen when you fall in love with Elsa Quinn. But I don't number stability among them.

Jung says that when we love another person what we are really doing is trying to compensate for a lack in ourselves. But Jung also says that the search to complete yourself with another person can never succeed.

FIVE

Summer. Sunshine. A feeling of outdoors. Victor is heading towards Paul. He is more casually dressed than we have seen him before – without a jacket – and he is wearing sunglasses. He is carrying a silver tray with two beautiful glasses on it. He proceeds to set them out with elaborate care on a garden table. Beside them, he lays out nuts and olives.

Victor I'm making margaritas but there's no way I'm going to offer you one.

Paul There's no way I'm going to drink one.

Victor Quite right.

He sets down the tray. Paul stands looking out at the evening. Victor is skittish, in wonderful spirits.

And suddenly it's summer at last.

Paul Mmm.

Victor Beautiful, isn't it? The park stretching away . . .

Paul You're very lucky.

Victor smiles at him from the table.

Victor Do you remember how to make them?

Paul Not clearly.

Victor You put the glasses in the fridge. You put the salt round the glasses.

Paul You put the tequila in the freezer.

Victor Yes, and the Cointreau in the shaker.

Paul That's right.

Victor Your aim is something lip-puckeringly cold. It should have the kick of a donkey. Cold as hell in the mouth, then hot as hell as it goes down. Is there anything better?

Paul It depends.

Victor flashes a smile at Paul.

Victor I'm sure Elsa's coming out. She's somewhere around.

Paul With the children?

Victor ignores this, gesturing expansively at the surroundings.

Victor So what do you think?

Paul What?

Victor Of the place?

Paul Oh, it's wonderful.

Victor It is, isn't it? We've only been here six months. I don't know if Elsa told you . . .

Victor stops.

Paul What?

Victor I don't know what Elsa's told you. In general.

Paul Oh. In general, she's told me . . . just this and that, really. I've only met her a couple of times, I think.

Victor About what?

Paul About?

Victor Yes, what's she told you about?

Paul About the house.

Victor I see.

Paul Setting her heart on it and how there's room for the children.

Victor I don't want to bore you with what you already know.

Paul Please.

Victor Bore you?

Paul No. I mean . . .

Victor seems disturbed by the loop.

Victor Elsa – what? – Elsa – what? – told you, for her it's great because it's so near work. She can walk to work. Excuse me.

With no warning, he suddenly goes out. Paul speaks to himself.

Paul Jesus Christ.

Paul takes his jacket off. Victor appears at once bearing a triumphant jug of margaritas.

Victor And how *is* work? How are you getting on?

Paul Oh . . .

Victor I'll be frank. I'm surprised.

Paul Why?

Victor I had you down as a Luddite.

Paul I can't think why.

Victor The stereotype of a poet, I'm afraid. Poets always long to go back. Childhood. Lost love. How would poets get by without them?

Paul But why else did you appoint me? Unless you thought I could handle it?

Victor Some people can't.

Paul And if I'd failed, would you have sacked me?

Victor Paul. With relish.

Elsa comes into the garden. She is wearing jeans and no shoes, caught very much off her guard at home. She clearly doesn't know Paul is going to be there.

Paul Ah . . .

Elsa Paul, goodness. How are you?

Victor I'm sorry. I invited Paul here back for a drink. He was at a loose end. I thought it would be nice.

Elsa It is.

Paul Elsa.

Elsa Paul.

They shake hands, a little stiffly. Victor is pouring two glistening margaritas. Elsa turns back to him.

Are you going to say hello to the children?

Paul Oh God, should *I* have said hello to them?

Elsa You don't have to.

Paul I'm not good with . . .

Paul gestures to indicate imaginary dwarfs.

Elsa Nobody's good with . . .

Elsa makes the same gesture.

Except other . . .

Elsa makes it again.

And sometimes not even them.

Victor I'd rather drink margaritas. How was your day?

Elsa Did you get Paul a Coke?

Paul I'm fine. I'm . . .

Elsa What?

Paul . . . enjoying the evening.

Victor takes a first draft of margarita.

Victor Perfection.

Victor takes one across to Elsa, who has sat down.

Paul Victor was just telling me what a pleasure he would take in sacking me.

Elsa I've no doubt. 'You have to be ruthless.' Victor always says, 'Oh you have to be so ruthless in life.'

Victor It's true. You do.

Elsa He always manages to imply somehow that it's a terrific effort. You don't like to say, 'Victor, for you it seems to come quite easily.'

They smile together. Paul is watching, trying to interpret their behaviour.

Paul I don't think I could look someone in the eye and sack them.

Victor Couldn't you? Why not? What would stop you? If you needed to do it, what would stop you?

Paul Scruples.

417

Victor Scruples? Scruples about what? Losing their good opinion? Is that what matters to you? That everyone should think you're a nice person?

Paul No.

Victor What then?

Paul That I should *be* a nice person.

They all three smile.

Victor Ah, very good . . .

Elsa Yes.

Victor . . . but can one be nice in this world?

Paul That's a different question.

Victor Is there such a thing as nice?

Paul There's such a thing as good.

Victor There's a noun, yes. Elsa does good. It's clear. She administers a charity. So by definition my wife does good. The homeless acquire homes. The roofless roofs. But *is* she good?

Elsa I don't claim to be good.

Elsa has become very quiet.

This drink is very strong.

Victor Is it?

Elsa Yes. It's very strong. It's almost pure alcohol.

Victor looks at her a moment, then he goes on as if he hasn't heard her, moving to pour himself another.

Victor Of course, there was one time something called good. When I was young, there was something called 'the common good'. It's rather gone out of fashion, don't you think? Of course, if I'd been cleverer I'd have spotted that earlier. I wouldn't have wasted all those years selling newspapers at the factory gates.

Elsa Were they wasted?

Victor I would have entered this business earlier. Hence: I'd be richer. I'd be freer. I'd have an even bigger house.

Elsa You don't think you're being just a little imperial, my darling?

Victor Just a little, yes. Something in the mood of the evening, perhaps.

Victor turns to Paul.

Did Elsa tell you how we met?

Paul No.

Victor I met her in a bar, it's true. In Copenhagen. She was smashed.

Paul Had you been married before?

Victor Never.

Elsa Victor doesn't believe the young should marry.

Victor It's so.

Elsa This is one of his favourite theories.

Paul Try me.

Victor I'd have thought it was obvious. It's a problem of evolution. Ask a Darwinist. Fidelity's effectively impossible when you're young. In my experience, you leave the young alone for five minutes, at once they fuck each other.

Victor turns casually to Paul.

You'd know about this.

Paul Would I?

Victor I'm speculating. I look at the young men in my office – I miss nothing, I love office romance, I adore it – I look at them all with their stiff little cocks, and the women wet, wet with longing, longing for adventure and I think: no chance.

Victor shrugs at the inevitability of it all.

Paul You think to get married you have to be older?

Victor Plainly, it's a plus.

Elsa Say Victor's age.

Paul But Elsa was young.

Victor Yes. She was also exceptional. And she had two children.

Paul I didn't realise. I thought they were yours.

Victor No. Not mine.

Elsa I arrived with the children.

Paul frowns, trying to get back on track.

Paul So – what? – you just walked into a bar and saw her?

Victor She was irresistible.

Elsa Tell Paul what you said.

Victor Oh. I told her she was fruit which had fallen to the ground.

Victor colours. At once it's intimate between them.

Elsa A long time ago.

Victor Not for me.

Elsa Soft fruit.

Paul watches as Victor stands behind her, taking her proffered hand.

Victor hates philanderers.

Victor It's true. I do.

Elsa He hates them.

Victor You say to a girl you can't live without her. You say to her, you're my whole world. Then a few weeks later you say the same thing, with just the same conviction, only this time you're saying it to someone else. So what's your excuse? Were you lying the first time? 'No, no,' people say, 'I believed it at the time.' But that's not good enough.

Victor looks at Paul a moment. Then he puts his hand on Elsa's shoulder.

Things are true, or they aren't.

Elsa is quite still. Then Victor lets go of her and heads out.

Victor I'm getting you a Coke.

He's gone. At once Paul moves away.

Paul I'm not going to survive. I can't survive this.

Elsa Why not? It's Victor. He's just being Victor, that's all.

Paul Jesus, they tell you at meetings. It's the golden rule. At all costs, avoid stress. Never get yourself into stressful situations.

Elsa Do you want a margarita?

Paul No thank you.

Elsa It might get you through.

Paul No thank you!

Elsa It's getting me through.

Elsa smiles to herself.

Paul What is this? *Faust?*

Elsa I don't think so.

Paul Is he Mephistopheles? Am I playing Faust? I'm to make a contract, am I? To lure me to my doom?

Elsa I don't think so.

Paul What's the idea? I'm to raise a glass to my lips and be magically transformed into a human being again?

Paul turns back to her.

Was it just chance he asked me back here?

Elsa Of course. Chance. That's Victor. It's whim.

Paul 'Stiff little cocks!' What is going on? 'The young men with their stiff little cocks . . .'

Elsa Paul, there is no conspiracy. It's a summer evening. We're having a drink and enjoying the evening.

Paul shakes his head.

Paul Elsa, you're married, for Christ's sake. You have two children.

Elsa So?

Paul What the hell did we do? I've been thinking ever since, what the hell were we doing?

Elsa We kissed.

Paul Yes.

Elsa We kissed in the office.

Paul Yes. It was great. But we're not doing it again.

Elsa How was it? How did you say it was? 'Great', did you say?

Paul No.

Elsa Did you say 'great'?

Paul No.

Elsa What's 'great'? What does 'great' mean?

There is a silence. Then Paul moves away again, trapped. It is very quiet and intimate between them.

Paul All right, I know what you're going to say, but I'm not going to listen.

Elsa 'Great' meaning you were touched?

Paul All right . . .

Elsa 'Great' meaning I reached you? Something reached you? Something made you feel you were alive?

Paul Yes.

Elsa 'Great' meaning you're not sitting alone in a room in Camberwell? 'Great' meaning for ninety minutes in my company you weren't actually scared?

Paul I'm scared now.

Elsa Why?

Paul I can't love you without alcohol. If I'm to love you I have to have alcohol.

Elsa It isn't true.

Paul Elsa, I can love you and drink. Or I can not love you and not drink. That's the choice.

Elsa Nothing in between?

423

Paul No.

Elsa Nothing? For the rest of your life? That's the choice for the rest of your life?

Paul I don't have a life. I left my life behind me on the motorway.

Elsa Why?

Paul Because I had no faith.

Elsa In what?

Paul In myself. In the future. I drank because I had no faith.

Elsa And now?

Paul Stick with Victor. Victor has faith. And I don't.

Victor comes back in, carrying a Diet Coke. He is in even more cheerful spirits.

Victor Diet Coke, so it is.

Paul addresses us directly.

Paul (*to us*) Victor came back . . .

Paul continues the scene.

Well, that's been worth waiting for.

Victor Good.

Paul I could murder a Coke.

Victor hands him the Coke. Paul speaks to us meanwhile.

(*To us.*) The sun went down over Regents Park and the three of us sat on the terrace just watching the lovers. The young lovers paraded before us in the sun . . .

Victor Perhaps you'll have dinner with us.

Elsa Yes.

Paul Thank you. I'm not sure I can.

Victor There's a restaurant round the corner. I was there the other evening. Their menu is delightfully Greek. It offers 'steak cooked on your desire'.

Paul Goodness.

Victor I told them: I'd love my steak to be cooked on my desire. In fact when it comes to it, I'd like a whole Mongolian barbecue cooked on my desire. And everyone could feast. Know what I mean?

He beams triumphantly.

The whole world could feast on my desire.

Elsa Are you drunk, Victor?

Victor I am going to enjoy the benefits of another margarita, if that's what you're asking. My third.

He leers a little as he pours himself another.

I am free to drink, so I shall.

Victor lifts his glass, beaming, expansive.

Paul (*to us*) We watched the young people moving round the park, lying on the grass, kissing, easy, the girls resting on the young men's shoulders, the young men resting in the young women's laps. How real their happiness seemed and how simple . . .

Victor has moved behind Elsa's chair and put his hand again on her shoulder, the two of them making a picture of happiness. Paul smiles at them, at ease. Evening is coming down. We have jumped time.

(*To us.*) How simple it would be to be happy.

425

Victor Did you know I was a tour guide for a while –
on top of a double-decker? I never told you, did I? After
I left the Party.

Paul (*to us*) Victor began to talk.

Victor I specialised in misleading information. I used to
love pointing out the place where General Eisenhower, to
thank the British people for their heroic war effort, had
built a life-size statue of Micky Mouse. The whole bus
craned their necks to see. I always said 'life-size'. I loved
saying 'life-size'. 'We are now passing the spot where
Lord Nelson first made love to Lady Hamilton.' I usually
chose the Elephant and Castle.

Elsa What are you saying?

Victor They saw it, you see. They saw the statue.

Elsa People are gullible?

Victor No. They're romantic. They see the statue when
it isn't there.

Paul turns again to us.

Paul (*to us*) Victor talked. He talked, it seemed, to fill
the air, to fill the space between us, so that none of us
need be lonely, so that none of us need stop, none of us
need ask ourselves what we were feeling . . .

Victor I read in the paper: apparently they did a survey.
Bus conductors, on average, live five years longer than
bus drivers.

Elsa What does that prove?

Victor Up and down the stairs. Up and down, up and
down. The activity may be meaningless but the very fact
of it keeps you alive.

Victor mimics the movement on the stairs with his hand.

Paul (*to us*) I had no idea what he knew, if he knew, but I knew the safest thing was to keep quiet, the safest thing was to let him talk . . .

Victor The personal computer, I would have to admit, is the only significant human invention which is exactly half the size of the instruction manual you need to understand it.

Victor laughs, as if the idea satisfied him.

Paul (*to us*) Nothing had passed between us save a kiss, one kiss grabbed one evening in an empty office . . .

Victor I often say it's like buying a book where the footnotes are ten times longer than the text.

Elsa Yet people go on buying them.

Victor People!

Paul (*to us*) Why had she given it? What had it meant?

Elsa stretches in her chair, like a cat extending itself.

Victor Another margarita?

Elsa Thank you. I will.

Paul (*to us*) The mystery of it seemed to deepen as the evening went on. And its promise.

There is a long silence. Time has jumped. It is nearly dark. The last of the sun's rays gleams across the park. The torrent of talk has come to a halt. The evening turns purple. Elsa speaks very quietly.

Elsa Victor always says we can't know.

Paul I'm sorry. I'm sorry, I wasn't listening. I was miles away.

Elsa Victor says we shall know nothing until we are laid out on our zinc beds.

There is a long silence. The light is unearthly. Victor and Elsa are both looking at him as if he has been asleep. Paul is lost for a reaction.

Paul Goodness. What a macabre thought.

Victor Not really. I'm hoping that afterwards they're planning to tell me what everything meant, because there seems very little chance of finding out at the time.

He looks a moment into his glass, then turns and speaks directly to Paul.

She won't give me children.

Paul What?

Victor She refuses to give me children. On the grounds she has children already. It's true. It's the point of difference between us.

Paul I see.

Elsa I had my children accidentally when I was young and stupid. I've never felt quite ready to have any more.

There's a pause.

There it is.

Paul nods slightly, acknowledging the gift of the confidence. Victor shifts, uneasy.

Victor The boys, believe me, are wonderful.

Paul How old are they?

Victor Oh . . .

Elsa Fourteen and twelve. By different fathers.

Elsa looks straight at Paul a moment.

Yes, I made a real mess. Thinking in that awful young way that I could do anything. I could cope with anything.

Victor Well? And you have.

Victor reaches down to kiss her. There is a moment of suspended gentleness. Paul watches, then he turns to us.

Paul (*to us*) Something in the way he kissed her, and in the sadness between them. Something in the passion, in the passion between them which was everything and which was nothing. A feeling rose in me, so overwhelming, so strong, that I sat, powerless, handing my life over, no longer caring where it went . . .

Paul turns back. Victor is standing quite still, lost.

I'd like a drink.

Victor I'm sorry?

Paul I wonder, could I have a drink?

Victor Are you sure? Do you think . . .

He looks a moment to Elsa.

I mean, I'm not saying . . .

Paul I'll just have the one.

Victor looks again to Elsa.

Elsa He only wants one.

Victor takes one last, uncertain look to Elsa who is sitting quite still, watching from her chair.

Victor Well . . .

He pours the last of the jug into a glass and hands it to Paul, who stands up to take it. Then Victor smiles. A small onset of energy.

I need to say goodnight to the children. Then we should eat.

Elsa Yes.

Victor Eat with us, Paul.

Paul smiles in assent. Victor picks up the tray and takes it out. The night is purple. Elsa has not moved. Nor has Paul. The feeling is extraordinarily intimate between them.

Elsa I'm glad you're here, Paul.

Paul I'm glad, too.

Paul lifts the glass and begins to drink. The stage darkens.

SIX

The stage is void again. Paul stands before us. He is now dressed in a light mackintosh.

Paul There are always a thousand reasons to drink, and not many reasons not to. I told myself it was because I was being dicked around, and it wasn't my fault. People were behaving in bewildering ways, and what was I meant to do? That's one of things about being an alcoholic. It's always easy to play the victim. But looking back on the summer you might well ask: which one of us was the victim? And which one was doing the dicking around?

SEVEN

*An opening of light. Elsa has opened what appears to
be a door and is standing inside. She is wearing a light
dressing gown. She looks peaceful and warm. Paul is
standing outside, soaked from light summer rain. He
grins, a little foolishly. He carries an exhausted bunch of
wet flowers, still in their paper. He speaks with elaborate
care, never slopping or slurring, making a careful effort
to be coherent.*

Elsa Oh God!

Paul I know. Can I come in?

Elsa stands aside to let him by.

Elsa You're drunk.

Paul Well, I wouldn't say I was drunk. I'd say I'd been
drinking.

Elsa I'm going to get you coffee. How long have you
been drinking for?

Paul Not much.

Elsa No, that's not the question. How long?

Paul How long? Very short. Maybe two days.

Elsa Paul, for fuck's sake have some coffee and shut up
because I don't know what you're doing here anyway.

Paul Victor's abroad. He's gone for business.

Elsa I know. I know. You don't need to tell me.

*Paul stands, not taking his coat off. Elsa goes to get
cups and saucers.*

Paul Do I find you just little bit ratty?

431

Elsa No. More a little bit guilty.

Paul Why?

Elsa Because we thought you could handle it. Victor and I thought you could handle it.

Paul I'm in AA for Christ's sake – of course I can't handle it! Of course I can't handle it! I have a physio-fucking-whatsit-chemical relationship to alcohol. I'm an alchie! What on earth made you think I could handle it?

Elsa Coffee.

Paul Look at your skin.

Elsa hands him coffee.

Elsa Me, I'm going to have a drink. And you're not allowed.

Paul is digging in his pocket, getting out pages from his notebook. Elsa pours whisky.

Paul And apart from anything, I didn't tell you, I'm writing again. It's true. Poetry pouring out of me . . .

Elsa So is that what this was about? You really can't write when you're dry? Is that what you're frightened of?

Elsa is staring at him. Paul picks a couple of fallen pages off the floor, not wanting to admit it.

Paul Poets are stubborn fuckers. Have to be. There's no danger of dying of encouragement. I wrote a poem about you. It's here somewhere.

Paul puts his notebook back and pats his pocket.

I mean, they don't tell you, do they? That night with the margaritas, I took one sip and I thought, 'Oh yes. I remember. Drink makes you happy.'

Elsa Briefly.

Paul Oh, what, and we look down on 'briefly', do we?

Elsa We distrust 'briefly'.

Elsa is pouring an immediate second scotch.

Paul Are you having another one?

Elsa Why, are you counting?

Elsa surprises Paul with her savagery. She softens.

Did someone give you flowers?

Paul No. They're for you.

Elsa Poetry. Flowers.

Paul I'd kiss you but I suspect I smell like a pet shop.

Elsa takes the flowers out to put them in a vase. She speaks from the next room.

Elsa I was expecting you.

Paul Really?

Elsa As soon as Victor left the country. I thought you'd come dog-trotting across the park.

Paul Where are the boys?

Elsa With friends.

Elsa comes back with a vase.

It was clever of you to find flowers with only twenty-four hours to live. I can throw them out before Victor gets back. I won't have to answer his questions.

Paul Has he been asking questions? What did he say?

Elsa When?

Paul That evening. The evening we all had dinner. What's that about? What does he want?

Elsa 'What does he want?' It's a marriage. However wonderful. Finally, it's a marriage, like any other. Don't you write about these things?

Paul Do I?

Elsa Aren't you a writer? Or does Peter Pan not get mixed up in this kind of stuff?

Paul is taken aback at this sudden aggression.

Paul Don't you think we have to discuss this?

Elsa Why?

Paul He said you had no friends . . .

Elsa We have a few.

Paul And he seemed to be – I don't know – asking me to help.

Elsa He was.

Paul Well?

Elsa Isn't it clear? We've reached a deadlock, that's all.

Paul How?

Elsa Isn't it obvious? He's restless. You can see. Victor is restless. He wants children. So that's why, yes, Victor's beginning to get desperate. We've reached a point where neither of us knows what happens next.

Paul waits. For the first time, Elsa lets go, the feeling pouring out of her.

Paul, I go to work every day, for God's sake, I go to the Foundation, I spend the day in practical ways. A hard day's practical work, raising money – being practical,

434

giving people help. What do you call it? 'Putting something back'. That's what I do. I put something back. Then I walk home, I walk back through the Park . . .

Elsa looks him in the eye again, firm.

Elsa I've done it for six years, Paul. I've put in six years.

Paul So?

Elsa I keep my eyes down. I work every day. I'm calm. I come home, I talk to the boys.

Paul What are you saying?

Elsa I'm saying, yes, it's only because of Victor that the Foundation exists. But it's only because of Victor that I exist.

Paul I see.

Elsa Yes. I feel real. Because of Victor.

There is a silence.

If you'd asked me ten years ago with my daffy head full of coke and my twat in the air, if you'd met me and asked me, 'Will you make it to the age of thirty-three . . .?'

Paul What were you?

Elsa What was I?

Paul Someone said you were an air hostess.

Elsa I was. I was an air hostess, I was a model, I was a shop assistant. What was I really? An international junkie –

Paul OK . . .

Elsa – of epic proportions. And if you'd said to me . . . yes, one day, one day you'll marry your father – it's true, you'll marry your very own father – or at least someone just like your father, except fifty times nicer, fifty times kinder – then I would not have believed you.

Paul I see.

Elsa Yes. I married the man my father should have been.

Paul How was your father?

Elsa A pig. A drunk. Yours?

Paul Pig-ish.

Elsa Yes.

Again, Elsa is unforgiving.

Paul, I made myself a promise, I made a decision.

Paul When?

Elsa Some weeks ago. You threw me. It was your fault. You threw me off course.

Paul I did?

Elsa Yes.

Paul That night? When we kissed?

Elsa Then. And I made a decision not to discuss Victor with you. Never to discuss our relationship with you. Whatever happens.

Paul I'm not asking you to diss him.

Elsa It's not a question of dissing him. It's a question of privacy. It's a question of respect.

Paul is frowning, having trouble getting this.

Paul OK. I'm just asking.

Elsa I know what you're asking.

Paul And?

Elsa And I won't tell you.

Paul What?

Elsa Anything. Least of all about whether we're happy or not. There's a line there and I promise you, I'm not going to cross it.

Paul Right.

There's a slight pause.

Are you?

Elsa What?

Paul Happy?

Elsa Well, what do you think?

Elsa has gone to pour a third drink.

Paul Are you sure you need the glass? Isn't the glass a bit . . .

Elsa What?

Paul Intermediate? Why not just jam the bottle to your lips?

Elsa looks at him a moment, not rising to the joke.

Elsa Tell me, I'd be interested, come on, tell me why are you here?

Paul Why am I here? Why do you think?

Paul looks at her in disbelief.

I was out of work. I'm broke. I'm trying to dry out. I'm sent by the worst newspaper in England to go interview the Marxist maniac of Regents Park.

Elsa So?

Paul I don't *like* being a drunk. Believe me. I don't *want* to be a drunk. Nobody *wants* to be a drunk.

Elsa Of course not.

Paul I've studied a thousand methods of how not to be a drunk. And I promise you the method least recommended by experts – the one thing experts all really agree on – is: don't use the falling-in-love-with-a rich-man's-wife aversion therapy method.

Paul turns round and raises his arms to the skies.

Fuck! That's what's wrong! I'm hopelessly in love!

There is a sudden silence. Elsa smiles, but Paul persists, desperate to define what he wants to say.

Elsa You don't make it sound very pleasant. What am I meant to do?

Paul And if one more therapist tells me that I only fall in love with what I can't have and it's because I can't have it, that's why I fall in love with it, then I'll punch the fucking bastard on the nose.

Elsa You loved Clem.

Paul I was fly-half to a rugby team that loved Clem. The therapist's point, exactly. Whereas you, you have a husband, who's real, who's solid, who radiates solidness. Computers! Opinions! Suits!

Paul is overwhelmed. At last he yells out what he has plainly wanted to say all along.

Why don't you give him children, for fuck's sake?

Elsa What?

Paul Well, that's what he's saying, for God's sake.

Elsa I know that's what he's saying.

Elsa is so surprised at this attack that she stands lost for a response.

I know that's what he's saying!

Paul Well?

Elsa Is that what you came to ask? Is that what you're doing here?

Paul shrugs, as if it were easy.

Paul It's all he wants. Be fair. Give the guy a break.

Elsa Give him a *break*?

Paul Why the hell don't you give him children?

Elsa Have you understood nothing? Do you think I don't want to give this man children?

Paul How do I know?

Elsa Do you think I wouldn't if I could?

Elsa gestures to the world outside.

What do you think it's like, walking across the park, day after day, walking back across the park, keeping my eyes on the ground? Another day, doing my duty at work? Who do you think I am?

Elsa waits, but Paul says nothing.

I was human trash.

Paul I know.

Elsa I was on the floor of a bar.

Paul I know. Do you think I don't know?

Elsa My knickers ripped in half, my breath stinking of vomit and waiting to be thrown out with the empties.

Elsa looks at him, her eyes welling up with tears.

'Take my hand,' he said. 'Take my hand.'

Elsa turns away, overwhelmed.

And since that day he has been steadfast.

Paul I'm sure.

Elsa Not one day has gone by in which he has not been resolute. In which he has not been loyal.

Paul looks down.

Paul I'm sure.

Elsa He gives me confidence when I have no confidence myself. When, like you, I know I could within seconds be back in that bar, like you, back in that gutter again . . .

There is a silence.

He's strong. We're not. We're alike, you and I. We're the same.

Elsa is suddenly on the verge of tears.

That's why I don't give him children. I don't have the confidence.

Paul Elsa.

Elsa I don't have the belief.

Paul is watching her now, taken aback at her sudden vulnerability.

Why do you think I sat on your desk? Ridiculous.

Paul No.

Elsa What am I? Absurd?

Paul No.

Elsa Why do you think I laughed with you? Kissed you? And the reason I was drawn to you . . . the reason I long for you . . .

Paul What?

Elsa can't speak.

What?

Elsa When I see us together . . .

Elsa shakes her head, overwhelmed.

I see us.

Paul How?

Elsa We go off to bars and go down together, go down laughing together, spiralling together . . .

Paul No!

Elsa Yes! That's what I see.

Impulsively, Elsa moves towards him.

Tell me I'm wrong.

Paul Elsa . . .

Violently Elsa digs into his pocket. She finds his notebook which she throws away onto the floor.

That's my notebook, for God's sake.

It's a messy struggle as Elsa reaches again into the pocket of his mackintosh. There's a half-emptied half-bottle of scotch in it. She takes it out and holds it out.

Elsa We're the same. Where do we find life that isn't in a bottle?

Paul moves towards her.

Paul Give it to me.

Elsa No.

Paul Give it back.

Elsa No.

Paul Elsa . . .

Elsa I won't.

Paul I won't drink it. I'll pour it away.

Elsa No.

Paul I won't drink. Elsa, if I'm with you, I won't drink.

Elsa looks at him, not sure. He has his arm extended out towards her.

Paul I promise. I make you that promise.

Paul looks at a pot plant beside him.

Paul What's this?

Elsa It's a ficus.

Paul I'll pour it in the ficus.

Elsa The ficus will die.

Paul I'll take that chance.

Elsa stands a moment, wavering now.

Paul I'll pour it in the ficus and I won't drink again.

Elsa hands him the bottle. Paul tosses it unopened aside into the pot-plant. She moves quickly and throws herself into his arms. They kiss, passionately, pulling at each other's clothes. Paul takes her head in his hands and looks into her eyes.

He said you were cured.

Elsa Did he?

Paul Yes. He said, one gin and tonic. You drank one gin and tonic, he said. You played Scrabble, he said.

Elsa looks into his eyes a moment.

Elsa Do I look cured?

Now it is her turn to take Paul's head in her hands and to look into his eyes.

Do I feel cured?

EIGHT

Paul moves out of the scene to talk to us. Behind him, the feeling of the stage changes again, Elsa disappearing into the dark.

Paul What did I think? What did I think at that moment? That I could be solid in the way Victor was solid? Never. I knew I could never replace him. But I felt the power of her and her warmth. The alcohol drained out of me and her warmth filled me. I vanished into her warmth and was consumed.

Victor appears a long way away, reading a file. He stands, quite still.

The hour that followed was the happiest of my life.

NINE

And now Victor, wearing a new, shinier suit, is advancing towards Paul. His manner is louring, aggressive, as he heads towards Paul at his desk. The evening sun slants across the offices.

443

Victor Ah, Paul, there you are. I'd begun to think you were avoiding me. I must have drawn the wrong conclusion.

Paul I think you did.

Victor Everyone dies after their last meal but that doesn't mean they were poisoned.

Paul Quite.

Victor gives him a chilly smile.

Victor You've heard of our problems?

Paul I think everyone has. I'm afraid they're pretty common knowledge.

Victor There you are. Capitalism at its most infuriating and obtuse. Re-financing. Private equity. Private equity insisting on a change of management. Making it a condition. What are we? Ping-pong balls? I've spent the whole day in the City trying to raise a rival bid. A bid for what? To take over my own business!

Victor has sat down, shaking his head, putting down the Financial Times *in disgust.*

Victor And everyone says it's normal. It's accepted as normal. An economy used to make things. Now? A world in which ten people do something and the other ninety speculate. Normal?

Paul No.

Victor It's a game, nothing else. Everything becomes a question of confidence. We don't say confidence trick. We say confidence creation. Because we lack any wisdom ourselves, we all pretend that the market is wise. It's a form of camp.

Paul waits, not knowing what Victor wants.

Paul Is there something you wanted?

Victor Why? Should there be?

Paul No.

Victor No hierarchy in the cyber-business. A cat may look at a king.

Paul waits, lost for the purpose of the visit.

Of course the market gets to me. Of course it does. Why would it not? The humiliation of being judged by people who know nothing. Not for myself. Believe me, I'm not upset for myself.

Paul No?

Victor The money I lose is immaterial. If the business goes belly-up I'm still a rich man.

Paul Can it go belly-up?

Victor I have my creature comforts. My house, my wife . . .

Paul Yes.

Victor As you know. As you well know.

This time Victor looks straight into Paul's eyes. Paul is becoming more nervous.

I apologise if we led you astray the other night.

Paul It's fine.

Victor Back on the taste, isn't that what they say?

Paul Yes.

Victor Back on the brew. You tied one on. No, really. I felt guilty.

Paul No need.

Victor Have you drunk since?

Paul Have I . . .?

Victor Since that evening? Have you drunk again?

Paul No. Not a drop.

Paul is firm. Victor watches.

Victor Tell me, this is academic, I'm just asking, there's not a hint of reproach, but do you lie about your drinking?

Paul Compulsively.

Victor I see.

Paul Like all drinkers.

Victor smiles.

Victor All the time or just occasionally?

Paul It's . . .

Victor Though it doesn't really matter, does it?

Paul Not much.

Victor That's the beauty of lying. You need only do it once to spread infinite distrust.

Paul says nothing.

Good for you. You're right. It's nobody's business but your own. Drink yourself to death if you so please.

Paul Thank you.

Victor Men fought and died in two world wars for the right of people like us to destroy ourselves.

Paul I wouldn't put it quite like that.

Victor Wouldn't you?

Paul No.

Victor How would you put it? How do you explain the current passion for addiction? Tell me, Paul, why does it have such allure?

There is a sharp edge to Victor's question which makes Paul hesitate, frightened to answer.

People say lack of faith, don't they?

Paul They do.

Victor But do they know what they mean?

Paul I'm not sure what it means.

Victor Me, neither.

Victor looks at him a moment.

People say to me, 'Oh, you're so lucky because you had faith.' As if having faith were such a wonderful thing. But Stalin had faith. Hitler had faith.

Paul That's right.

Victor Faith in itself isn't so wonderful.

Paul No.

Victor Regardless.

Paul Quite.

Victor Would it be wonderful to believe in the virgin birth? I don't think so. Or that the trees speak to you? Wouldn't that just mean you were mad? You'd call it faith, but so what? Faith's not valuable. Not in itself. It's what you have faith in that matters.

Paul Of course.

Paul looks nervous, not knowing what Victor will say next. Victor is bitter now.

Victor I had faith. But then it was stolen from me. I was the victim of a robbery. Like millions of others. History came along and clobbered us on the head. No victim-support scheme for us.

Paul No.

Victor Just thrown out into the world and told to get on with it. Given a sharp lesson and told we could have no effect. Do I seem ridiculous to you?

Paul Not at all.

Victor I have felt ridiculous.

Victor shrugs slightly.

What does it mean to say that I was angry? For years. 'I was angry.' Why? Because the world was not as I wished it to be. Yes.

Paul Is it for anyone?

Victor Of course, it now seems peculiar. What was it? Arrogance? I used to say to myself even then, as I sat stuffing leaflets into envelopes, denouncing iniquity, 'What is this? What are you doing?'

Paul Yes.

Victor I used to ask myself . . .

Paul I'm sure.

Victor Even at the time. Giving my young life. I used to wonder: 'Things are not as they should be, you say? So the purpose of the world is what? That Victor Quinn should be pleased with how it is arranged?'

Paul It's a good question.

Victor 'Who is Victor Quinn? God?'

Paul Hardly.

Victor 'All this rage, all this indignation, what does it mean? What, you feel the world is somehow not meeting your expectation? The obligation of the world being to please Victor Quinn?'

Victor shakes his head.

Did I waste those years? Or they did waste me? Or were those the only years I ever lived?

Victor suddenly lets go.

What bloody right do these people have to value us?

Paul None.

Victor None!

Paul However.

Victor looks at Paul.

Victor I took a shine to you, Paul.

Paul Yes.

Victor I took you on because I liked you. But you think that I must live with it, is that what you think?

Victor holds his gaze, not relenting. Paul doesn't answer.

The poet! The philosopher! Bringing the message the philosopher always brings.

Elsa has appeared at the back of the area. She is windblown, distraught, as if she has not slept.

Elsa Victor, you're here.

Victor Yes.

Paul Elsa . . .

Elsa I was worried. You haven't been home. I've been trying to call you.

Victor Have you?

Elsa I've been trying to find you.

Victor What, and you were concerned? Why were you concerned, my darling?

Paul has got up awkwardly to greet her, alarmed by her appearance. Victor turns back to Paul.

As you can tell, we had a row. Last night.

Elsa Yes.

Victor We had a splendid row. It's rare. We never row. I stormed into the night. I did a runner.

Elsa Victor, we're meant to be going to a concert.

Victor Of course. When?

Elsa Now.

Victor Would Mozart match your mood right now? I'm not sure he would match mine. All that life-affirming can seem awfully jangly when it hits you at the wrong angle.

Elsa What are you saying? You don't want to go?

Victor Go with Paul. Take Paul. Affirm life with Paul.

Paul hesitates a moment.

Paul I can't. I have to go to a meeting.

Victor stands looking out the window, as if he had known this would be Paul's answer. The light outside is lemony and fading.

Victor Summer's end, you see. Always a moment of calm. The slight change in the air. Oh it's still August. The sun beats down. But touched with the knowledge of what is to come.

Elsa shifts, impatient with his mood.

Elsa This is all to do with work.

Victor You think so?

Elsa Of course. You may lose your business. You may be about to lose your business. Of course you're depressed.

Victor turns, his face blank. Then impulsively he heads for the door.

Victor . . .

Victor I'm going to have a drink. Come and join me, please.

Paul I've made a new vow.

Victor Have you? And will this one last? Aren't we patterned? Aren't we programmed? Don't we always promise, 'Tomorrow I'll stop. Tomorrow I'll be good'?

Paul looks at him, not answering.

It's the disease of more, isn't that what they say?

Victor looks at him a moment, then gets up and goes out abruptly, in silence. Paul goes to his desk and starts quickly gathering his stuff together. Elsa watches, panicked.

Elsa What are you doing?

Paul I'm going. I'm leaving my job and I'm going.

Elsa Paul . . .

Paul I have to. I have to get out.

451

Elsa Why?

Paul stops for a moment and looks at Elsa, as if the answer were obvious. Then resumes packing.

Paul It's not hard to say, is it? It's not hard to see why.

Paul gestures in Victor's direction.

Look at him, for God's sake. Just look at him. Look at his mood. What do you think it's about?

Elsa I know what it's about. It's not to do with you.

Paul Last night you quarrelled. You think that's coincidence? You think that's just chance?

Paul resumes throwing his possessions together. Elsa is serious now.

Elsa What are you saying?

Paul It's not love.

Elsa Isn't it?

Paul No.

Elsa I thought it was love.

Paul No. It's addiction. We're addicted to trouble. We both love trouble.

Elsa moves towards him, lowering her voice for fear of Victor's return.

Elsa Paul, I was happy with you.

Paul I know.

Elsa For those hours, I was happy with you.

Paul Elsa. I'm happy drinking. So?

Elsa No!

Paul Yes! I'm happy with a drink in my hand. Tell me: what's the difference?

Elsa is shaking her head.

Elsa You think I live that kind of life?

Paul No.

Elsa What do you think? You think I want affairs?

Paul No.

Elsa Is that how you see me?

Paul looks at her, the answer self-evident.

Then don't run out on me.

Paul Elsa . . .

Paul shakes his head, helpless now, as if he could do nothing.

Elsa You haven't thought. You haven't thought what you're doing. This is who you are. This is you, Paul. You're the person who runs. You think it's to do with alcohol? It's not. Don't you see? It's to do with who you are. Given the slightest reason. Given the slightest excuse.

Elsa looks at him, pleading.

You have a friend in trouble. His business is in trouble. You're the first friend he's made in years.

Paul Am I?

Elsa Don't run.

Paul You barely know me, Elsa. You barely had time to know me.

Elsa You're scared. You're just scared. You're scared because you're in love. You're more in love than ever.

There is a silence, and an admission in the silence.

Paul Yes.

Elsa And?

Paul looks tempted for a moment.

So?

Paul You're married, Elsa. You'll never leave him.

Elsa What makes you so stubborn? What makes you so sure?

Paul I am sure.

Elsa Oh it's easy to be you. It's so easy.

Paul Is it?

Elsa Oh yes. The heartbreaker. When anyone needs you, you run. When anyone loves you, you go.

Paul I love you. It's true. Explain. How does it help if I stay?

They stand, looking at each other. Victor comes in, whisky bottle in hand. His mood has darkened.

Victor Not even dusk and there's no one to be seen. My modernist corridors deserted. Glass reflecting only glass. It's a business for obsessives they say. But where are they? On their August beaches, or in their back gardens. Fled. All fled.

Victor turns with a note of drama.

And not a soul remains. Whisky?

Elsa No thank you.

Paul shifts, uncomfortable.

Paul has something to tell you.

Victor Tell me?

Paul It isn't good news. I admit I'm feeling an idiot.

Elsa He wants to leave.

Victor I see.

Elsa Paul's insisting he leaves.

Paul Victor, can we be honest? The fact is, I'm actually hopeless at the job.

Victor Really?

Paul 'The unsinkable Flotilla.'

Victor Huh.

Paul 'Float into the future with Flotilla.' 'Hey there, killer, try Flotilla.' I can't do it. I can't write to order.

Victor Too much the poet? Too much your own man?

There is a silence. Then Victor smiles, accepting.

It's not easy, is it? It's never easy, is it, when you try to help?

Elsa shifts, knowing where he's heading.

Victor I tell you, I was sleeping last night in Regents Park . . .

Paul I'm sorry?

Victor Didn't I say? I slept the night in Regents Park.

Paul You didn't say, no.

Victor Beneath the stars.

Paul Is that legal?

Victor It's not illegal.

Elsa I didn't know.

Elsa is standing some way away, shocked.

I didn't know where you were.

Victor After all, I had to sleep somewhere. Isn't that what men do? When they quarrel with their wives?

Elsa I had no idea.

Victor Didn't you?

Paul What about? What was the subject of the quarrel?

There is a brief silence. Victor looks across to Elsa.

Victor I lay last night beneath the stars, the stars bright above me, felt the earth moving below me, the planet hurtling through space. I lay in the night, listening to the random noises of the night, thinking of Elsa in her bed two hundred yards away. I thought of the many nights we had passed, she shaking from the agony of addiction, the passage from high to low, from frenzy and finally to calm . . .

Victor thinks a moment.

What was the subject of the quarrel? We quarrelled about love. I'd had an idea. For years I'd had an idea. An idea of what love might accomplish. Foolish. No good.

Victor turns a moment and looks at Elsa.

Victor Don't we most of all resent the person who helps?

Elsa That's not what I said. That's not what I was saying.

Paul looks between them, unable to fathom the depth of their feeling.

Victor Yes, last night we quarrelled.

Elsa Yes.

Victor Yes, we quarrelled as we have never done in our lives.

Elsa It's true.

Victor As if a whole life's anger rose up and seized us by the throat.

Elsa He told me I was weak.

Victor That's it.

Elsa He accused me of being weak. I defended myself.

Victor She did. She defended herself well.

Elsa That's why we fought. That was the beginning of the fight.

Victor Absolutely. The fight spread, as it were, from there.

Paul Fight?

Victor Argument, Paul. Dispute.

Paul And was it resolved?

There is a silence. The stage is darkening. Victor turns to look out onto the weather. Then Elsa speaks, clear, compassionate.

Elsa Are we ever cured?

Victor That's the question.

Elsa How do we know? Yes, I can sometimes go without drinking. Months go by. And, yes, at another time, I taste just one drink. 'Just the one,' I say. Paul is right. It's for life.

Victor is sitting quite still, listening.

I asked Victor to accept that. I want him to accept that.

457

It is almost dark now, the dark before rain. The three of them are still.

I was lucky to meet a man. I met a good man. But I met him nonetheless, loved him nonetheless, or rather, have tried to love him. I still do. I still will.

Elsa stands behind him, and now leans down to kiss him. Victor is moved. It comes on to rain outside the windows.

Victor My love.

Victor moves and takes her in his arms. The two of them are reconciled. Paul stands at the side, useless, irrelevant. Then Victor unfurls himself and turns to Paul.

I'm sorry. I apologise. Private. Private stuff.

Paul Of course.

Victor Forgive us.

Victor looks him straight in the eye. Then he reaches out and touches Paul's arm. Then he recovers and cheers up.

So. You're determined to go?

Paul I am.

Victor You submit your resignation?

Paul I do.

Victor It's done. It's accepted. Why not? Collect your cards. Elsa, I think we're moving on.

Elsa has been wiping her eyes behind them.

Fair enough. After all, it's a freelance culture, that's what they tell me.

Paul That's what I've heard.

Victor The idea of long-term employment is a thing of the past. A job is no longer for life.

Paul Well, I've only been here three months.

Victor Excellent. You've grasped the principle exactly.

Paul Thank you.

Victor Paul, you are the modern man. Experience becomes a ceaseless search for experience. Slap! It goes on your CV. 'I worked for Victor Quinn.'

Victor turns.

It's been a summer, eh? What a summer.

Paul Yes.

Victor It's what a summer should be.

Paul You think?

Victor In the cold months we have to work, we have to live, we have to get on with living. So let us use the warm months for stopping to think. What do you say, Paul?

Paul I agree.

It has stopped raining. The evening is lightening outside. Victor is standing opposite Paul. He reaches out and embraces him.

Victor Is perfect friendship always brief?

Victor releases Paul and now steps back.

Hmm. 'Moderation in all things,' said my mum. And died at the age of forty. I miss her. I still miss her. Don't fear for me.

Paul I shan't.

Victor History threw me up. It may now cast me down.

Paul I hope not.

Victor It worries me not at all. I have written my epitaph. 'He may have buckled but he did not break.'

The two men smile, uncertain how to part.

And it's time to say goodbye. Not the last time we shall see you, I hope.

Paul No.

Victor And you must say goodbye to Elsa as well. I insist. I insist.

He turns to Elsa.

Elsa. If we hurry . . . At least the second half of the concert.

Victor walks quickly away. He becomes a small figure as his back disappears down the long corridor. Elsa has got up.

Elsa You won't forget me?

Paul No.

Elsa Promise you won't forget me.

Elsa moves towards him and kisses him on the cheek.

It's rare, isn't it? It's rare to find love.

Paul looks at her a moment. Elsa turns and goes quickly out. Paul puts his things down, and stands. Then Paul turns also.

TEN

The stage clears, and becomes a void again. Paul moves forward and begins to speak directly to us.

Paul Joseph Conrad says that inside every heart there burns a desire to set down once and for all a true record of what happened.

As everyone knows, Victor Quinn died soon after in a car crash, driving himself not on the M4, but in Leytonstone, an East London suburb. His blood was three times over the permitted alcohol level. Elsa went to identify the body. At last, she said, Victor lay on his zinc bed.

The Flotilla software was bought out by Microsoft. After a while Microsoft said the software was unreliable and replaced it with products of their own. One day – like the Roman Empire – Microsoft will itself be replaced. This too shall pass.

ELEVEN

Now from the distance, Victor approaches, in characteristic good spirits, full of life, talking as he comes.

Victor 'Many are the stories with interesting beginnings, but harder to find are the stories which end well.'

Paul is waiting as if they were meeting for the very first time. Victor smiles and shakes hands with Paul, as he once did, introducing himself.

Victor Quinn.

Paul Paul Peplow.

Victor Of course.

Victor stands, impressed at meeting Paul.

That's why personally I prefer to read thrillers. For years I read only thrillers. In a thriller the writer is obligated at least to make an effort at an ending.

Paul That's right.

Victor The novel, to the contrary, remains unresolved.

Seemingly in response to his words, a City church bell at once tolls, deep. The stage changes shape to find Elsa sitting, as she once sat, on Paul's desk.

Paul Elsa crossed and uncrossed her legs, and the bell of a City church rang as she looked at me, not speaking. Just looked at me, looked deep into me.

Elsa looks tenderly at Paul.

Elsa Paul, you are not addicted to alcohol. You are addicted to blame.

There is a silence. Then the lighting changes once more.

Victor When the party is over, I pride myself I will know when to leave. Why hang on? I don't want the host yawning all over and longing to go to bed. I read the other day: most people die in the small hours, when their resistance is lowest.

There is a silence. Then Paul speaks directly to us.

Paul When I think of Victor now it is as a helpless giant, lolling, struggling, tied down with little strings, flailing, now he is dead, in something like innocence . . .

Paul stays facing us at the front of the stage while Victor speaks behind him with his usual crispness.

Victor I prefer jazz to the classics and always will. What about you?

Paul Oh . . .

Victor A jazz musician is someone who never plays the same thing twice. The classics mystify me. Why listen again when they're always the same?

Elsa appears at the back of the stage, miles, miles away from us in a little pool of light.

Elsa They deepen.

Victor Do they?

Victor turns and begins to walk away from us towards her.

Elsa They deepen each time.

Victor reaches Elsa and in a gesture of instinctive love she reaches out and takes him in her arms, embracing him. They are tiny figures in the distance.

Paul For myself, well, it's embarrassing to admit, but I drank again for a while. The result was a book of poetry which to my amazement did even better than the first. For a brief while, I became somewhat well known.

I did see Elsa. Of course I did. I saw her a number of times. But there comes a moment – doesn't there? You tell me, doesn't there come a moment? – when you have to decide between what you can handle and what you can't.

Let's say, another way of putting it: I'm sorry. I have to go to a meeting.